MAKIN[illegible] [illegible]MALL

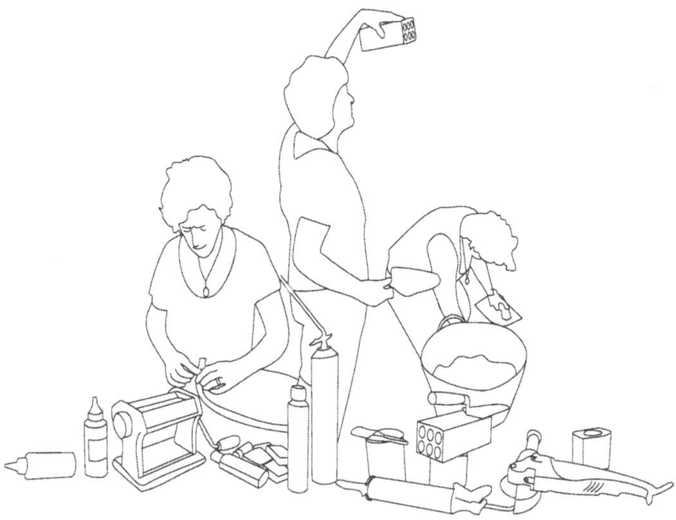

Angie Scarr

Publishing Data

First published 2018 Sliding Scale Books (SSPB08)

Plaza De Andalucía 1, Campofrío, 21668, Huelva, Spain.

Design by Angie Scarr & Frank Fisher

ISBN 978-1727092998

Dedicated to my family, and virtual family -
because family matters.

Contents

Introduction

I remember when I was about fifteen, meeting my friend's Grandma. My friend described her to me (the grandma would have been around 70 at the time). She said "I love her. She's amazing. She tells such tall stories. And the best thing is they're all true!" I decided then and there that that was the point of life. To fill it as full as possible and end your days telling barely believable stories.

I don't know what happened to my friends grandma. She won't be alive now of course but I knew at least I was on the right track when around a quarter of a century later I met my now-husband Frank. He told me he enjoyed my tall stories even though he didn't believe them at first.

I have the problem that my butterfly mind too soon leaves one project for another and I couldn't imagine actually planning and having the 'stick-ability' to complete a project like this book, even if I didn't have to worry about making a living in the meantime. However a recent couple of ignorant comments on an Expat forum have made me decide that although I'm heading for little old lady-hood fast, when I hear people dismiss my or other peoples intelligent opinions as "old peoples mentality" it really annoys me. My dad's words now ring in my ears. "I'd rather be an old has been than a young never wozzer". I never understood the "never wozzer" bit because I felt that it left the possibility that the person referred to had any chance of achieving anything in their lives and maybe the type who commented like that didn't. But I guess that it's kinder, less arrogant and just slightly more encouraging than saying "a young never will be".

Throughout the years I've always written. Quite apart from the anecdotes that went along with my articles in magazines, I wrote when I found something funny or frustrating or unjust. I wrote when I was sad or confused or when I woke in the night with some family argument still unresolved. This was often my way of emptying my head, my way of documenting the things that happened in my life and sometimes I just needed a rant. I'm not a very social person. In fact you could say that I'm a bit of an introvert, under the surface, so there weren't many other ways of venting my rants and any sparks of inspiration.

When I found out I had a serious and life threatening cancer, I realised it was time to finish some unfinished jobs. The first job I finished was my dad's memoirs which I titled with one of his regular sayings. When I finished I was really excited at finally getting it done. For my dad, for myself and for my family. And possibly for a few people around the world who might be interested in his car bodgeing and house bodgeing exploits.

A couple of days after finishing that book I hit a very bad patch where my upbeat became downbeat and thoughts of my illness came crowding in. It was definitely time to start again and this time with my own scrappy stack of stories. This book is the result. Those stories now glued together with a narrative of my life of trying to make a living as a craftswoman and my love affair with house renovations and latterly with self-building in the beautiful Sierra de Aracena in inland Andalucía. I might be an old has-been but I'm happy to say I "woz". And, in fact, I still am because I've given cancer the small c it deserves. As I write this, thanks to the medical team at Riotinto Hospital I'm hopefully beginning my new life without it. Lets see how many more stories I can make … Or make up.

I

Parents And Childhood

How can I go back on what made me what I am without mentioning my parents. Because we're all a result of our parents right? Good or bad. Present or not present. Both nature and nurture ... or lack of it.

I was pretty lucky. I had a balance between parenting and healthy ignoring in favour of much more interesting things than children. My parents were a little odd. Just a little. Not weird or anything like that, but they didn't really fit into the place where I woke up to my first memories. My first sentence at the age of 2 was "I can see Patterton Tsurts". I can still remember struggling to vocalise the words "Patrington Church".

We had moved from Gateshead where my little sister was born a couple of months previously (though I don't remember that part), to the little village of Patrington, into what seemed to me to be an enormous country house my parents had bought for a song and started to renovate. My next memories were of watching and helping (or hindering) the stripping of wallpaper to reveal the green and red painted plasterwork of "Beggars Roost". My parents thought this an appropriate name since a former owner had given alms to the poor. The name of course was often changed by comical relatives and friends. The smell of cement, plaster and wallpaper paste and the old coke boiler were very formative and are still evocative, as is the smell of hot ironing. I've always appreciated to this day the smell of construction materials, which is a very good job, because for the last two decades I've never been very long away from them.

Seeing my parents transform a dilapidated old building into a palace and bringing 4 children up in a very 'Darling Buds of May' fashion was what gave me the real belief that anything was possible.

It was a charmed childhood. My dad always seemed to me an uneasy balance of tortured poet, engineering genius and down to earth slightly miserly family man. My mum, slightly over the top, extremely creative, motherly but with a bit of a "Mrs Bouquet" chip on her shoulder and a telephone voice to match.

No, we didn't fit in. How strange in a 1950s and 60s village, was a woman who rebuilt a vintage motorbike, and rode it around in a boiler suit, while her husband rebuilt his own vintage Bugatti from boxes of bits. This was not the only crazy mechanical thing my mum did. At one time they got right into VWs, both the cars and the caravans. I remember one day my mum had the engine out of one dilapidated but running car into another good chassis with a duff engine, while my dad was away at work. dad came back to a fully functioning car and a pile of rust.

They had a brief affair with VW campers as well and I remember them converting a non-camper version into a camper using caravan windows a rivet gun and plenty of fibreglass and resin.

This was not the only creativity I witnessed. One year in the early 1960s when it snowed particularly heavily, mum and dad knocked up not one toboggan, but one each. Mum got into making kayaks another year. Dad made shrimping nets. We lived a "River Cottage" lifestyle, driving home from long days on the Spurn peninsula with several buckets of shrimps which dad had poached from the sea, wedged between our knees with the bare minimum of water to keep the wriggling masses of grey crustaceans alive. In another bucket or two an equal number of brambles, the picking of which was strictly prohibited by the warden whose distinctive glasses and canvas bag we had to keep a watchful eye out for. In season there would be samphire from the river bank at Sunk Island, to be eaten freshly boiled and buttered or pickled in large Kilner jars. The life Hugh Fearnley-Whittingstall and lately Kevin McCloud are rediscovering … we had.

We picked and topped and tailed green beans and packed them into stoneware jars. Any excess of soft fruit, and there was excess, was made into fruit juice and bottled. My favourites were raspberry and blackcurrant. Sometimes they would start to ferment and we had to drink them a bit more quickly. So I would have a party with my dolls. We knew what alcohol was, though it was almost a 'dry' family, and I know the dolls especially enjoyed our minor alcoholic treat.

My mum had a series of monogamous relationships with different arts and crafts. Throwing herself fully into this or that hobby until she mastered it and then doing a complete change to the next big thing. I'm sure this affected us and I remember we were always creative.

On the TV programme "Would I Lie To You", Greg Davis' assertion was that he made up a secret language with his sister and the opposite team didn't believe it was true. I thought everybody did that. I'm not sure everybody designed 3 dimensional mazes on paper like my brother and I did though. That complex 3 dimensional thinking speaks of what we've both done since.

My dad came over as having middle class pretensions because of his family's former shipbuilding business, But secretly I fantasise that his mum Daisy, who died tragically young, was not only a violinist, which we knew … but perhaps a wanton Gypsy violinist, and that's where his passion and his occasional depression and maybe his, and my dark eyes and sallow skin came from!

Pluviophile and dancer down lanes.

I was a dreamer; the type whose teachers would sigh deeply and say, "if only she would concentrate". But no,

I'd be distracted by anything, especially whatever was going on outside the window. I just loved weather. Hot weather, cold weather windy weather. I loved what we used to call the 'cloudburst' when the sky seemed to dump everything all at once. When I was about eight whenever it rained I would go to my bedroom to look out over the back garden, the cricket pitch and the street, resting my chin on my arms as the rain hammered down. It was exciting and energising. Then as the rain slowed I'd return to my drawing or cutting out or whatever it was that I was doing that day. Maybe painting water over the little grey dots in a magic painting book, or reading a Beano or Bunty comic.

I was a kicker of leaves, a skipper over mud and a splasher in puddles. I used to dance and sing in the country lane on the way home from school. A journey I used to do on my own because my big brothers were already at senior school and my sister was still in primary and perhaps picked up by our mum. Though I remember picking her up myself from time to time as well. I was happiest when I was totally alone though and given to fantasies. I may have been a ballerina or a fairy one day, another a grumpy old woman wrapped up in the folds of the cloak mum had made for me.

Another time I might be a bird. Flying was often on my mind and if I couldn't fly for real sometimes I would imagine I could. I'd throw myself at the banks of the side of the road zig-zagging; powering up the slope to do a jumping take off. Then spinning with my arms outstretched until I was just a little dizzy and had to challenge myself to carry on in a straight line. I have the same feeling now when I see 'free runners' on TV. That was what I was doing then. And what I wistfully wish I were able to do now.

The first time I had any inkling I might have some artistic ability was in my third year of primary school when, having had two teachers I really didn't like much, and to be honest I'm not sure they liked me, I finally got a teacher who I could look up to. I don't remember her name which is a real shame because she really did have an influence on me. Every week she would bring in one of her childhood toys and give it to the student who had behaved well that week or who had done something else to merit it. I don't remember any of the other toys but one week she brought in a big black Reeves paint box full of little white porcelain palettes of colour. I was totally smitten. I think the teacher could see it in my eyes but I like to think that I was very well behaved that week and that my painting of a cat was the most extraordinary thing my teacher had ever seen. The painting went up on the wall and I went home with the coveted paint box.

My creativity was a little more 2 dimensional than it is now, but even then I was drawing fruits and vegetables and cutting them out and making my mum pretend to buy them using cut out money and taped up miniature paper bags ... I haven't changed much.

Adulthood

I always had the desire to master whatever I got into, so I too have been a serial creative and a serial monogamist. My employed life has been short enough to be irrelevant because I never learned to be deferential enough to fit into any situation where my boss wasn't more able than I. The same with my relationships. This is why I'm both self employed and finally, happily married to a man who is more able and grounded emotionally than me, and who has skills I couldn't possibly master! As I'm writing this Frank is trying to tell me the difference between "Coding" and "Scripting". It still doesn't mean a thing to me but the fact that it's second nature to him means that work I throw at him and questions I ask all come back with positive results.

When I am asked about my past by my Catholic neighbours and friends I often simply use the word "complicated". And so it is, but sometimes I will tell the whole story, because, as I get older I start to realise that being 'an old has been' and having tall stories to tell, and most of them actually being true is way better than the alternative. Even being judged for the relationships and the ensuing children means less to me than it ever did because I took my experiences into my own parenting.

Sometimes got it wrong but must have got something right because all my three children from three different relationships have grown up interesting and articulate and more than anything have become independent and fairly grounded people, taking responsibility for their own lives and their own decisions in a way that the children of friends with an ostensibly more stable and comfortable background often aren't equipped to do. So, I have to say, mistakes aside, that the best of my work and my life has to be my children.

But along the bumpy ride I've had some really interesting self employment. When I was a teenager I used to go along with my parents to auto-jumbles. At first my dad went as a buyer, later starting to buy and sell bits and pieces of old cars. I loved the hustle and bustle of the auto-jumbles and antique fairs to which they were often attached. Pretty soon I started buying bits and bobs especially old fans and belt buckles, that I thought were beautiful and under-priced and then selling them again on dad's stand, having cleaned and repaired them. I also went to auctions with him and picked up bits and pieces. Sometimes not the pieces I originally wanted but I just had an eye for the cool and unusual. I remember once going to Baitsons Auction Rooms with my dad and buying an old Wrights Soft Soap advertising chair, probably originally from a chemist or grocery shop. Someone had painted it black but I could see the enamelled sign under the paint. I bought it for fifty pence when nobody else seemed interested. Dad was impressed when I stripped off the old paint and gave me a fiver for it. A fair profit in those days. He sold it on for £25 and one day I saw it back in my local art gallery as part of a big exhibition of advertising memorabilia. Dad was impressed. And with a loan of that same £25 from my dad, I put an ad in our local paper for button boxes and antique clothing. And people cleared out their attics and told wonderful stories into the bargain. I started having an antique clothing and accessories stand side-by side with my dad.

I'm not ashamed to say I used my age and my (then) slight figure to my advantage and got noticed by being the little girl who would dress in a different period costume for each fair. Sometimes a Victorian wedding dress, not white, but navy blue and black. Another time a full 'flapper' outfit or a 1930s Crepe de Chine day dress. The other stallholders and customers were the same sort of people as the miniaturists that I hang around with now. In fact I'm fairly sure I met Tony Knott in those days and believe I also sold a set of ceramic dolls to Pat Kay before I knew her properly. We met again years later on trips to Arnhem on the Hull to Rotterdam ferries. I knew that I'd met her somewhere before but it took me ages to realise where. Of course neither of them would have recognised the skinny little girl in a Victorian dress from the woman you could later draw just using circles. I earned myself enough pocket money to take myself off to Italy with a friend and her family for my 18th birthday, but later sold my business to my cousin. I was 19 and I had other plans and my first proper boyfriend.

I was a late starter in my age group but rapidly made up for it by having my first child Dominic at 20. Bucking the trend by being a single parent rather than the other two choices of marrying the father or having the termination which was almost forced on me by an arrogant doctor who didn't much take to me making up my own mind, and shouted at me - what sort of a life would my mixed race illegitimate child have? Not for the first, or the last time I went against accepted wisdom. And although my life changed onto a track that meant I was never going to marry a rich man and live out my days in leisure. I've never regretted that decision.

My dad had had a Victorian upbringing and for him what I had decided to do was outrageous. I'm told, (somewhat too regularly) by my elder brother, that my dad considered disowning me and had to be talked out of it. I think this is something of an overstatement because my dad was married to a woman who had had a child 'out of wedlock'; my own mum having given birth to daughter, who was adopted from an 'unwed mothers home', when she was only 19 herself. But chips on family shoulders run deep so I was told I would be adding to the stress on my mother's heart. I knew that there would be family 'gossip' and I felt sure, from my mum's own long carried shame and fear of being judged, that her brothers would most likely have been using the silly and judgemental phrases of the day "The apple doesn't fall far from the tree" and "She's no better than she ought to be".

So I moved to York to lessen the embarrassment families still felt back in the 1970s, where I boarded with a divorcee and started my first proper business. I was hand painting fabrics, making up clothing and selling on a York market stall as part of a co-operative. However when my landlady got a new boyfriend I moved out and, in a failed attempt to get a council house in that area, I moved into a freezing cold caravan with my tiny new baby.

Soon, with the help of my mum who became my landlady, I moved back to Hull and started life as a single parent there. I was still making hand painted clothing but this time with a side order of superhero costumes and work for small theatre companies making hand painted costumes for a handicapped theatre group and masks for an Egyptian play at a local college. I even made a full set of cloaks for a Freemasons group called the Rosicrucians. Exactly as you would imagine from films. Long hooded robes with insignia and crosses on. More than a little weird at the time but since I've moved to Spain and regularly see the Easter parades … well no, it still seems weird.

When my son was just a little boy I met with the older brother of a school friend, and he moved in. I adored him … but he had demons which were to grow over the next few years. We married and quickly decided that another child would be a good idea. So at 24 we had Alan, and my new husband went out to work while I spent some time as a full time mother. But this suited neither me nor my husband, who decided he'd be happier at home with a guitar and a bottle of cider … so I went back to work. This time working on one of those 1980s job creation schemes as a playschemes leader where I learned about non-competitive play.

I probably learned my teaching skills from this. But this job was only for a year and during this time I reignited my interest in buying and selling and started to go to auctions again, bidding and getting hold of 'stuff' including fabrics, for a song. As luck would have it I came across a huge haul of nylon fabric just when the children's play world got interested in parachute games. So when my year as a play schemes leader came to an end I started Gasworks. Why Gasworks? Because working for yourself was in old hippy-speak "a gas". And because my factory unit was inner city funded. I was making parachutes with "no strings attached".

I could have written out in full the next stage of my life story. But, being an habitual crier whether happy sad or simply frustrated, instead I think I'd rather leave it under the simple heading; "Emotionally abusive relationship, alcohol, jealousy and panic attacks" The only thing I really benefited from during this time was picking up a guitar and writing poetry and songs. Songs my husband dismissed as "self-indulgent". One of them about that marriage called "Bad Luck Man" actually won me the best Acoustic blues song of the year at Burnley Blues festival a couple of years later, proving that revenge really is a dish best served cold.

All this was naturally followed on my prompt sheet by the simple word "Divorce", and almost equally obviously by "New Relationship" which in turn almost inevitably resulted in another child. I say almost, since luckily, my lovely daughter just managed to nip in before my turn came up on the waiting list that I was on for sterilisation.

Gasworks was successful enough for a few years in spite of the fact I had to re-finance it partly from the sale of my little house. We moved into a bigger unit in the Innovation Centre in Queens Gardens. I say we, because by that time I had a couple of part time employees and one self employed helper. I had "fast Sal" who was a new-romantic with her hair piled a foot high onto her head. I'm not sure how many bottles of hairspray she used or how her lungs are now, but that hair was impressive. And so was her speed at running down the ten or twelve seams it took to make up our circular parachutes. I couldn't have employees in every day because some days were devoted entirely to cutting up to 15 ft sections. Our biggest circle was thirty foot diameter. I was getting through acres of rip stop nylon from a company called "Perseverance Mill Company" What a lovely historic name.

I had noticed that we had one competitor but their product was only listed in a catalogue as "special needs equipment". I got in touch with one of the suppliers catalogue companies and our product was featured in the main large play equipment section of their catalogue. This was a great partnership. They sent their orders directly to us and we posted on to the customer and billed the catalogue. What we lost in mark-up we gained dramatically in exposure. Our customers were largely local authorities who all wanted to get into non-competitive play. Plus a smattering of local community groups and schools. I then made a business mistake trying to introduce a second product line which were one and two metre diameter globes known as 'Earth balls'. I asked a local business to help me by making screen prints, but after paying out for the screens the company refused to do any short runs to get us started, and we were in deadlock. I'd lost my screens and a great deal of money.

My business was in trouble. I realised that I was just not business minded enough and that my skills lay in inventiveness and problem solving so I initially advertised for a partner. "Ideas Woman seeks Business Brain". I had a couple of replies but neither were really suitable partners. One wanted to buy a business for his daughter but eventually bought her an Aromatherapy business. As things got more serious I had to sell the business outright to pay its bills. I would almost swear that the guy who bought me out was Duncan Bannatyne, later famous as a Dragon in Dragon's den. He was very much like him. But I couldn't swear to, or prove it and it's a very long time ago.

Anxiety

After I sold my non-competitive play business I was looking for something else to do when I saw an advert for social workers both trained and unqualified to work for a children's charity project on a new project in North Hull. I knew my playschemes experience would give me a chance of getting this job and so I went for it. What I didn't realise until the day before my interview was that I was already pregnant with Kira. The day of the interview I was so nervous because I didn't know whether to tell them I was pregnant but of course I knew I had to, so it was the first thing I said as I sat down for the interview. They gave me the job anyway. The team was a diverse one with 4 qualified social workers and 4 unqualified. But the project was a bit strange. It was one of several layers. On the surface our brief was to help families cope with day to day problems which may have led to physical deprivation or all different types of abuses. But there was also an underlying information gathering exercise and threat of removal of the children from the families. I felt we were misleading the families we were working with. I believed we were exacerbating problems rather than helping solve them. I found this very stressful and, after Kira was born when it was time to go back to work I had a powerful resurgence of my old panic attacks and found it very difficult to get myself into work. I didn't realise at the time was what I was suffering from was post natal depression. When a friend suggested I hand my notice in, I felt a wave of relief even though it meant that I was once again unemployed and technically a single parent.

My anxiety attacks were very disabling. I had social phobia and health phobia. The waves of fear would start as I woke and I was battling them all day. The attacks were so strong that I feared that this second time I might never 'come back', so I went to my new doctor with the problem. I told him I didn't want tranquillisers and he gave me beta blockers which did seem to help. I wasn't so resistant to beta blockers because my mum had taken them for 20 years after her first heart attack and since my phobia at the time did have a heart attack phobia element to it, it was probably a good choice.

Before handing my notice in I was signed off work for a month and when my doctor wrote "Anxiety Neurosis" I argued that I didn't want to be labelled neurotic. So he put anxiety state. I was content with that and also happy with the very understanding and sympathetic treatment.

As I left the surgery the doctor put his hand on my shoulder in a gesture of empathy. I think that simple act gave me more of a boost than any drug could. Once again I set about changing my diet and reading self help books. One book which really did help me was given to me by my friend Margy who had worked with me at Gasworks. It was called "Pulling Your Own Strings". I've read other books by the same author and the more recent ones I find a bit silly and overly spiritual, but this simple book really helped me sort out the things that were troubling me and what was and what was not important in my life.

Of course I wasn't the kind of person to sit around doing nothing and this was when I took up the guitar as catharsis and miniatures as therapy. At the time they were neck and neck in importance in my life. I also became a volunteer on an anxiety and panic helpline which helped me just as much as it helped the callers because I could see where people succeeded and where they failed. Those really were my first steps to drug-free freedom from anxiety.

2

Love, Miniatures And The Blues

My dad told me my first miniature work was OK but that he'd seen better at Miniatura. And yes he had. He'd seen the best at the time, Lesley Burgess. I didn't see her work for another year or two but was once more prompted to be better. OK was just not going to be enough for me. I think it was from her work that I hit upon the pivotal technique of caning after seeing a lemon slice which was probably one of Lesley's in a shop in Devon. I thought I knew how it had been done, but I didn't. My mistake paved the way for all my future work, re-enclosing oranges and peeling them back, which would never have been possible by the original method. Then I began realising the potential for caning and started enclosing and cutting away at cakes and meats and all kinds of fruit and vegetables and making cabbage and lettuce leaves with veins in them. I was excited! I had hit my element quite by accident. Problem solving in Polymer clay.

I remember the travelling best. Dragging myself out of the house. Sometimes just to gigs and blues festivals across the country, with my new-old steel (bell brass) guitar, my acoustic guitar, clothes and the panic attacks I never told anybody about. Sometimes to the twice yearly miniatures fair at Exmouth (near my mum' and dad's new place in Devon). This time with two suitcases full of miniatures and my Samsonite travelling workshop. This was a small hard briefcase which I had re-purposed to hold just enough tools and materials to keep me busy for two eight hour train journeys to and from Devon to visit my mum and to go to the Exmouth fair. I made little wooden vegetable crates, chocolate boxes and fruit punnets as I travelled. Sometimes I'd even combine miniatures and gigging and I'd have two guitars, a suitcase a shoulder bag and the mobile workshop. And the leather 'don't mess with me' jacket that I always used to wear to make me look less vulnerable than I was feeling.

Kira's dad was very good about being left with the baby and often with my other two children who were growing up rapidly by then. We were good friends but maybe never meant to be more. I had married and divorced the love of my life and didn't really expect another.

But I can't say I was really settled.

Around this time I started to go to more major miniature fairs like Alexandra palace and Pudsey. Miniatures became my business. Although low paid, it got me out of the single parent trap. I wasn't living with Kira's dad and we had both been on unemployment benefits. I was getting busy with a little voluntary counselling on the side as I was recovering from my own panic attacks and felt able to help others doing the same. I also began to teach miniatures.

My first lesson was a trial though. My mum's local group had told a neighbouring group that I was coming. Over 30 people turned up to my very first class! There was no room for panic here with 30 or so eager faces and 300 or more eager fingers all waiting to have a go. It cost me a fortune in clay because I didn't charge properly in those days. But it was worth it as an experience. Straight into the deep end and I hadn't drowned.

A little later I was invited by Alex Blythe (then

Curtis) to teach at a Polymer clay Guild weekend. I met Sue Heaser there and she taught me the Skinner Shade Technique in our 'downtime' - an idea which doubled my inspiration overnight.

Getting the Blues

I had started playing guitar when I was still married to my first husband. I bought a second hand red dreadnought guitar. I found it difficult to play and wasn't very good at it. I wrote several 3 chord songs though and even recorded some of them at the studio of a friend who one day brought his new little baby along. That baby is now my daughter's partner. Soon-to-be husband.

One of my first performances as an adult on stage and on guitar was in the Hull City Play. My then boyfriend Steve and I signed up to take part, along with Alan and even 3 year old Kira. And my eldest son Dominic even signed up as a stagehand. The city play was a project written and performed by the people of Hull with help from professionals who drew it together. We turned up at casting in March and 270 Hull people were cast to play over 300 parts. This meant that some people took more than one part.

The play was a history of Hull, both real and fictional. From floods in medieval times to wars wars and labour conflicts in the 20th century and of course the history of the fishing industry. There were emotional scenes of tragic losses of trawlers as well as the heroic visit of the trawlermen's wives and families to Parliament to demand new safety rules. Rehearsals started to take over our lives in spring of 1992 It was performed in June 1992 over a week.

It's impossible to recreate the emotion and energy of the play "Vital Spark" which was what's called a 'promenade production' which means the actors take over the whole space of the theatre, or in this case the vast City Hall. I have to say that this experience was very formative for me. I was still suffering from anxiety attacks and I had to get over many of my fears and phobias to perform. I didn't really understand those fears myself at the time but bit by bit I challenged myself to 'feel the fear and do it anyway'.

The community of players was so diverse and so supportive I don't know anyone who was involved who doesn't say that the experience changed their lives. Many claim that the experience helped them go on to do their own playwriting performing or public speaking. At least one of the cast went on to be a professional actress. It certainly gave me the confidence to sign myself up the following year to one module of a college performing arts course called Music For Performance. Once again this was pushing myself just a little beyond my comfort zone but it really did help me take my first steps in playing and singing in public. When my tutor said of one of my performances that he would pay to see a performance like that, I went home floating on air. I was far from the best singer in the group and, in my mid 30s, a good deal older than most of the class.

King Billy to Royal Willy

Our next move was to start going to an acoustic blues club on Monday nights. This was a bit of a disorganised affair in a tiny and rather unsuitable bar room with largely older folk-blues musicians. Eventually the owners had a word with us and asked if we would take the club over and move it upstairs to a much bigger room. We took a look at the room and it was ideal. We negotiated a £20 fee which we passed straight on to whichever musician we 'booked' to lead the session. It was a simple formula. An open mike night with no mikes. In fact no amplification at all. One musician at a time was booked to lead the evening, giving each experienced member chance to prepare a twenty minute to half an hour set to encourage the rest to fill in the remainder of the evening. There was never a shortage of people prepared to do so.

Although the old timers had their noses put out a little bit by us taking over, they were the first ones to be booked and were regularly booked from then on. The money wasn't good but it paid their expenses. They could see our advertising was bringing in new audiences and so we gained grudging acceptance. When the King Billy (William) closed for an update we had to move and we found a place fairly close called the Royal William. They were happy to have our already successful night and agreed to the same conditions. The folk blues now blending with some serious delta blues and a bit of more modern blues rock taken back to it's roots by being performed acoustically. It was now a real melting pot and some seriously good new performers were cutting their teeth and learning their craft in the difficult acoustic medium.

We had to be very strict about the acoustic rule. It was amazing how many people thought they should be able to amp-up at an acoustic event. Of course it was different at the second club we were asked to run at the Blue Lamp on Sundays. We already had a potential audience and a mailing list and Steve did sterling work cycling around the city hand delivering advertising leaflets. I was telling my brother about my new interest and my occasional performances and one day he turned up (from Germany) at my house bringing me a present. A beautiful green electric acoustic guitar. Of course even I wasn't allowed to amplify it at the club. The Blue lamp nights were also pretty successful for Sunday nights and we even managed to bring in some American blues stars like Catfish Keith and Paul Rishell and Annie Raines. Both Catfish and Paul and Annie agreed to do workshops during the day before their gigs. This helped their earnings and was also very good kudos for the club.

Becoming a Blueswoman

I still wasn't technically a very good player and what I really wanted to be able to play was slide guitar, and particularly delta style slide guitar on a Dobro or National steel guitar. There was only one person to learn from and that was Dave Whatt. Although there were other people who played slide guitar, all more or less competent but some more 'clattery' and just not deep delta blues enough for me. Dave had a mellow deeply bluesey sound and he was known to give guitar lessons. I really couldn't afford them. I think I managed to get Dave to give me a lesson whenever he needed a haircut and actually a few more that were never paid for. I suppose Dave recognised my passion for the sound at that time and took pity on me. Dave had a battered old no-mark acoustic guitar which he painted black chopped a hole in and dropped a resonator into. It had a wonderful sound.

Dave taught me how much power and control you needed to play slide well. It took two or three lessons and loads of practise and frustration, but finally I understood how you needed to think the place you were going to with your slide in advance and really control it with solid muscle control. This gave a great 'attack' to the sound and was one I appreciated and tried to emulate. I started to notice when slide guitarists didn't do this, and realised It really was fundamental.

He also had a really important lesson to teach on performance which I have never forgotten. He told me simply to play high and low, fast and slow and loud and quiet. By which he meant a performer should vary the texture of their playing in order to keep the audience interested. This sounds obvious but so many of the beginner musicians that played at the acoustic club didn't do it. As soon as the audience got noisy they tried to compete and started to complain that they needed amplification. What was wonderful to see though was that those who really worked with the audience got listened to. And Dave proved his mantra over and over again as he played with various other musicians and was always listened to. This lesson can be applied to all of performing, teaching and indeed life. All need a variety of texture to keep people's interest.

Of course I needed a resonator guitar. I don't remember how I got the couple of hundred pounds I needed to buy a wooden bodied Monarch (Dobro copy) resonator guitar. It was OK, but not a proper steel (bell brass) resonator. One day just a week after I'd got the copy, Harry Gurevitch told me he knew someone who was willing to sell a Dobro just like his and he wanted 500 pounds for it. There was nothing for it, I had to sell the guitar I'd just bought to a friend and then I sacrificed the last of my industrial sewing machines and somehow raised the money for the beautiful 1970s National style Dobro.

Dave must have been a good teacher because I did learn something, at least enough to get away with writing some blues songs based around some of the 'licks' he taught me and I started to play them at fringe events at the blues festivals of Colne and Burnley. Sometimes I played with a really good Blues Harmonica player called Tim Haigh.

Tim had a Sonnyboy Williams style, and started coming round to teach Steve to play Harmonica. Steve developed a pretty good technique but had problems with rhythm. Tim however really did have the Blues. And a thirst to match. He could play through rather a lot of alcohol but had a habit of falling asleep afterwards. One day, in conversation with Tim it transpired that I'd actually babysat for him when he was under two years old. I remembered it too. I remembered his mum told me if the baby screamed I was to dip a dummy into a jar of honey and give to him. I then knew what Tim's Blues name should be. "Honey Child". Tim won the Burnley harmonica player of the Year in about '92 or '93. We were ecstatic for him.

We went to the festivals ourselves in the next years. I don't think we bought tickets for the main stage but attended lots of the fringe events especially at Colne where I got to play in the Acoustic Cafe run by Max Haynes, a blues historian who liked a whiskey or three. The next year he gave me a proper 'spot' and a very nice review.

"Angie Scarr (Plays) Beautiful rural style Blues on wooden bodied and steel guitars... Angie has a natural feel for her steel and plays some of the most exquisite Bottleneck you're ever likely to hear." **Mississippi Max Haymes** (blues writer, historian and promoter.)

In '95 I entered the Detour Magazine Acoustic Blues Song of the year competition at Burnley Blues Festival. The competition had been won the 2 previous years by Kevin Thorpe who had also entered a really good song, Blues in a Bottle, this year. I didn't expect to get anywhere with my simple little ditty Bad luck Man, but I deliberately went to watch a friend of mine Chris Scott perform just before I went into the competition. I wanted to grab some of his power and energy and put it into my own performance. And maybe it worked because I won!

I couldn't believe it. The prize was £100 which I handed straight over to Luther Heavysides (Pete Howlett) in part payment for my new Tony Revell guitar. No I couldn't afford a perfect Tony Revell. They were going at over a thousand pounds at the time. But I was offered a slightly water damaged one at a quarter of the price. What a bargain. What a beautiful sound. And here it was in my hot little hands largely paid for. By selling (sorry Howard) my green guitar and topping up with my winnings. That was a good day.

The song was a "tribute" to my first husband who had always pooh poohed my attempts to play guitar and write songs as self-indulgent. The last words of the song were "revenge is sweet". There could never have been any better nor gentler revenge for that put down than to win a song writing contest with a song about his negativity and when I played my encore the irony was powerful. I sang that line with a real feeling of sadness … and triumph.

I was also getting interesting, though low paid support slots with musicians I really wanted to play with. I was once invited to support Honeyboy Edwards at a gig up in North Yorkshire. I was starstruck. I think he was probably in his 80s if not 90s. I got chatting to the old dude himself and asked him how he kept himself so fresh. His answer (verbatim) "Young womens. I got me one thirdy fii(ve)" "You old dog" I said "That's younger than me!"

Business

Around this time I decided I needed to become self employed as a miniaturist even though this was to drive a wedge between my unemployed boyfriend and myself. The government was making it possible to pull yourself out of unemployment by offering a top up called Family Income Support. I needed some help though, as although we had our first proper computer, it was a bit of a 'dog' and we didn't yet have a printer. We'd all done without Xmas presents that year to buy an ex British Gas computer with problems. My son Alan was getting to grips with it, helped by going to a computer club at the Lonsdale Centre. I'd persuaded the volunteers there to allow Alan to join even though he was a bit young for them because he clearly had a talent. That computer not working and the 'geeks' at the Lonsdale Centre were very formative for Alan and, it turned out, for me too.

I decided to go along and learn word processing and spreadsheets to help with my advertising. There, swivelling in an office chair, eating chocolate was a young computer geek who looked strangely familiar but I had no idea why. He became my helpmate on some of my projects including a very early website right back in the early days of the internet, and he made the offer to record my CD. I had met Frank, my second husband, though I didn't know that yet.

When Frank first started 'flirting' with me his first line was "You know those lies you're always telling? ... They're true aren't they?"

He'd looked on "Alta Vista", a search engine on the embryonic internet and found out that I actually was a blues musician with a radio programme following in America. He found out from Alan that I really did travel round the country selling miniatures and that I had indeed started an antique clothes business when I was 17 and that I did make parachutes without strings for a living for a few years. I agree that none of it sounds very plausible.

No more Blues

I sometimes played with another harmonica player Pat Missin. Pat was a technically brilliant musician. I'm not sure he had the tortured soul that Tim had, but Pat had a wider knowledge of styles and an ability to do just what I asked for. Sometimes I had to rein him in because he had a bit of a jazz habit and loved to solo. He was relaxed about my control of it and I don't remember us ever having any 'irreconcilable differences'. It was a real pleasure going on the road with him even though his car was a heap of bits held together with gaffa tape and cable ties. One gig we did was at a big diner in Derby. We arrived on time in spite of the old Marina only allowing us a couple of gears.

Immediately we realised we'd been booked erroneously. The manager looked at us with our two guitars and a bag of harmonicas and just a couple of small speakers and asked where the band was. He'd booked us from my advertising though. What had he not understood about the words Acoustic Blues? I wondered. On my advertising I appeared solo, so Pat was more of a 'band' than he should have been expecting. We set up on the non-dining side of the central bar and played our first set to a small but appreciative audience. But it seemed some people wanted to watch and not eat. In our break Pat ran outside to talk to the AA man who was attending to his car while the manager came across and suggested we didn't play the second half and that he only paid us half the fee. Oh no, I wasn't having that. This was one of the few places I ever played where there was a contract and I used it against him.

As Pat came in with a big smile on his face I met him at the door with a similar grin. We apologised to the few audience members who were still hanging around and picked up our gear and made off with our full fee and an early night ahead of us. We gave each other a high five and repeated Pat's Mantra "Did the gig. Got paid".

In the Danger Zone

Spain was a country I knew from my sister's tales of holidays on the "Costa Benidorm" was bathed in sun and alcohol and rude Spaniards. And I never had any interest in going there. But when I met a homesick Spanish guitarist, I played the blues with him and in between listened to tales of another more romantic country where people said hello in the streets and parties were about listening to tall tales from cheerful people over less alcohol and more natural food. When he left my heart followed him to Santander and on to his home in Andalucía and I vowed in my mind that I would follow him there too. And I did. The 'handsome Spaniard' got me 3 gigs in the Seville area.

With my two guitars in the overhead lockers and my then boyfriend Steve tagging along, I made my first visit to the part of the country where I now live. I spent a strange week gigging and hugging people, eating baby clams at the seashore and driving through beautiful sierras and getting used to the idea that not only had I current boyfriend, but my obsession had a current and very beautiful girlfriend.

I also had another important factor keeping me "home". My little daughter Kira was only seven and very much a daddy's girl. I wasn't about to drag her and Alan off to another country on a whim. And though I got over the hopeless non-relationship with the Spaniard and instead chose a new life with the wonderful man I now call my "last husband". I continued my relationship with the country and the language and, happily also a friendship with my earlier Spanish obsession who became, and continues to be, a very good friend. Out of this obsession came some of the songs on my album.

Another of my songs "Your Subtlety" was my answer to the songs of another married musician on the scene, who was equally obsessed with me. It seems we were all getting into danger zones. Lots of material for the blues.

Even now I still find it difficult to believe that was me writing and playing with such passion. I didn't have a lot of confidence in my own abilities but I was getting good reviews at the time.

So when Frank from the computer club offered to record my songs for a self produced CD, at a time when hardly anyone recorded at home I couldn't resist.

Frank's recording studio was his mum's front room with dodgy 1970s carpets and knocked together studio equipment, but somehow I managed to think myself into the role of recording musician and go for it. I often turned up late because I was battling another anxiety attack and had to force myself to leave the house. It took a couple of months to record and then all the tweaking Frank did for which he demanded I was present. Though I didn't really understand any of it. I rather think he could have done the mixing without me.

Danger Zone was recorded and released entirely independently with financial help from several supportive friends. I guess it was like a Kickstarter scheme, before Kickstarter existed. It too gained some rather good reviews.

... remarkable and compelling ...

Al Handa - Delta Snake [online] Blues News Nov 97 (USA)

... what an absolute pleasure ... Totally lacking in pretension ... simple yet fascinating

Keith Fitton - Blueprint Magazine Nov 97

... a natural grasp of the delta blues idiom ... Some of her compositions may well become the blues classics of the future

- Just you wait an' see!

David Kidman - 'Tykes News' November '97

... An album which constantly impresses through it's fresh and often invigorating take on acoustic blues.

Sean McGee - 'Rock and Reel

Things weren't as easy as just a few good reviews making me a rising star though. I had a real problem simply picking up the phone to sell myself as a solo female artist. The idea of saying "book me, I'm good" was terrifying. I guess all solo artists have this in a way that bands who aren't so close to their own fragile egos but are selling a whole band probably don't experience.

The problem I had believing in my abilities and that of my stage fright failed to go away even though I was booked for and did play the main Stage in Burnley in '98. At the same event, I did a talk called "A woman with a guitar" about the way women were treated in guitar shops and the problems of getting gigs and about all I'd learned about performance from Dave. But it only took one poor review of that performance and an ungenerous summing up of my abilities by Thurston Binns (another local event organiser) totally to undermine my belief in myself. Either that or I became simply too happy for the blues. Or too busy with the miniatures. Either way these were my last performances and last reviews. I was an Ex Blueswoman and I never did promote my CD. Even though I'd been offered a recording contract on the back of it, which I turned down. The record producer was, it seemed to me, just collecting song rights.

Weaving through all this was a very sad timeline when I lost first my father then my lovely mum with whom I'd shared the miniaturist hobby. I often say that was also when my life turned right around. At the age of nearly 40 I suddenly realised that what I most needed in life was the kind of relationship that my parents had enjoyed. One of joint goals, equal effort and mutual respect and one where alcohol was only present on high days and holidays rather than every day.

When Frank came into my life all the pieces came together too. All the things I'd been trying to do but failing because I didn't have the skills that he had, suddenly became possible. So, my first video which I'd filmed with Steve in 1996 and which was still sitting on the shelf in 1997 unedited, suddenly became a reality, quickly followed by several others. I was getting used to this teaching lark.

3

The 'Love Shack'

My relationship with Kira's dad had been failing for some time mostly because to my mind he just didn't have a direction. When he expected me to find the funds for his trip to my mum's funeral it was the last straw. I was grieving and I was bitter. It was the right time to part although it felt like the worst time and there may be some truth in his idea that I left him in order not to share the inheritance from the sale of my mum and dad's house. Steve had been the right partner at the right time. I hope he would say the same. We took care of each other just sufficiently to get us over our previous painful relationships. He was and is a nice guy. Just not the love of my life. Nor was I the love of his.

I had no idea whether I was doing the right thing at the time; I wasn't at all sure how I felt about Frank. As soon as I got back from the blues festival where Steve and I had parted, Frank came around … and stayed around.

Instead of the gigging equipment I had my eyes on and could finally afford, instead of the new car and driving lessons I would have loved, instead of the shoes and handbags (not really. I never was that kind of girl), I bought "The Shack" as we called it. Short for The Love Shack from the B52s song. I didn't buy The Shack because I liked it. I bought it because it was so cheap it could be bought with the quarter of the price of a 'proper house' that I'd inherited. I think I paid about eleven and a half thousand pounds. Property prices were low and in that area they were about to go even a little lower. It was also a move just around the corner so we could literally carry my goods and chattels round with the help of a few friends and family. We spent everything we had. At least it was a step out of the poverty that having to pay rent was always going to cause us. It was a badly designed house, cold and uncomfortable.

The Shack was a late Victorian corner shop, a little less than a 90 degree corner, which meant it was smaller than it looked. Just one big and one small room on each of 3 floors. We got it cheaply because the owner had got sick of being taunted by the local youth. Being on the corner it was a bit of a prime site for kids to hang around. I suppose he must have challenged them once and it became an issue. I hoped we wouldn't have similar problems and initially we didn't.

Before we moved into The Shack Frank took me for a trip to Spain. This was Frank's first generosity test. Frank had never been abroad before and we visited Seville. It turned out Frank loved Spain too. We took a trip out to the ceramics area of Santiponce (pronounced Santiponsay) on a scorching hot day where the bus left us by a cotton field. We trekked back to the ceramics warehouses and bought some Spanish tiles which I ended up wrapping in newspaper and carrying on the plane as hand luggage with a straight face, pretending they didn't weigh a ton. This was in the times before X raying hand luggage. The Spanish tiles ended up as a surround for a perfect arched cast iron Victorian fire which I had taken out of a skip on Coltman Street and put into the empty bedroom fireplace. This was one of my first DIY challenges.

The shop front was boarded up, and initially we had no idea what to do with it. We knew we couldn't put the glass back in because of possible vandalism and so we settled on painting the boarded up panels initially. I decided not to paint it a plain colour in case it attracted graffiti so I put in a background of cement colour and then we went over that with a sponge dipped in brick red paint to make a brickwork pattern. I wasn't sure whether it was cool or awful. But it was better than plain boards for a year. And if there were any Graffiti it would look like art. Strangely it must have confused any potential graffiti artists because we never got a full on 'work' just the odd teeny scribble.

Then I set about repairing all the upstairs windows that were cracked or broken and there were quite a few. I had to learn to take out Victorian sash windows, to cut glass to size and to tack and putty up the new panes. On some of them I even had to replace the sash cord. It was all very daunting at first but by the end of the job it was second nature and my puttying became very neat.

Because the building was so tall and thin it was very cold. The windows were single glazed and there was no central heating. The fire in our bedroom was functional but sometimes a bit smoky and there was a small wood burner in the tiny living room on the ground floor. I still remember how cold the bedrooms at the top of the house were and we had to resort to electric blankets and hot water bottles. Kira particularly suffered from Raynaud's syndrome in those days and I was constantly having to massage blood back into her poor cold hands when she came home from school.

Wood was hard to come by for the wood burner and often my hands were red raw from chopping up old pallets and anything we could get our hands on. One day Franks brother rang us up with the weirdest offer ever. He was working in a local hotel that had a convention of fire walkers planned. It had been rained off and did we want a truckload of logs? Oh yes we did! The hotel was so keen to be rid of them that they even brought them round and offloaded them for us. Our back yard was packed with logs and we were going to be warmer for Xmas. Frank and I took to singing a stupid made up song about "loggy the good log" (deliberately off key) which amused us but drove the kids mad. For a short time there was barely enough room in the back yard for Sooty our rabbit, and the guinea pigs.

We'd had a couple of reverse custody battles with my ex over the pets. In the end it was agreed that I'd have the rabbit and he would have the dog as the shack was too small for a dog and Frank was not a dog lover but he was quite fond of rabbits.

Pretty soon the logs ran out though and I tried using coal and coke in the stove. Of course coke was too hot and ruined it completely. Once again fate was to step in. My friend Annie Ryan was changing her gas fires and offered to sell me one of the ones that she had in her house on Coltman Street. It wasn't going to be cheap at 100 pounds but it was definitely going to be worth it. So we borrowed the money for that and the fitting from Alan, who was by that time working part time for a company called IT In The Community, building computers from parts. Alan was, at the time, still at college. He never did finish his college assignments, by this time he was enjoying the work more and just slipped seamlessly into working in the computer field.

Frank and I hadn't completely left music behind by this time. We put together the first Indiegrrl compilation which consisted of several emerging female independent musicians from America and little old me from the UK. It was fun receiving loads of new music in the post and we accepted everyone who sent a disc. It wasn't up to us to decide what was good and what wasn't. We did spend some time working out which were the best tracks and what order would put each of them in the best light. Frank tweaked the levels and added his little bit of magic. We asked Kira to draw a cartoon cover and I thought she made a really good job of it. Unfortunately the American girls had different ideas and Kiras cute little woman carrying an oversize guitar was rejected in favour of something more 'Lilith'.

Starting writing

I'd always harboured the desire to write a book. The only problem being that my techniques in Fimo couldn't be explained in any other way than visually and every process was self destructive of the last. Non-digital photography was so hit and miss you couldn't keep dropping your work, running off to the developers and having to start all over again at the beginning if one picture didn't work. And you couldn't just leave several canes in different stages and hope they would all look like part of the same process. They just wouldn't.

The moment digital photography caught up with my ideas, just as soon as a 2. 1 mega pixel camera came on the market. I went to into Debenhams' photographic department and asked them if they could order one. They could. I had it ordered straight out of the warehouse . I couldn't afford it of course. It was 600 pounds which was a lot of money in those days. Especially to a family with a supported income. I bought it with my Debenhams credit card. It was the best investment I ever made.

Just for comparison 15 years later you could get the same number of mega pixels in a cheap camera for around 30 pounds. I started photographing and writing in 1999 while we were still in 'The Shack' and the writing continued through our next crazy house adventure.

During one of our trips round the country we'd visited Marion and Edward Fancey who ran the Dolls

House and Miniature Scene magazine. Having recently received copies of my 3 videos, which I'd sent to the magazines for review, Marion wanted to ask me if I would write for them. Until this year there had only been two magazines, hers and Dolls House World. But suddenly there was a new kid on the block in the form of The Dolls House, and clearly Marion was worried. The new magazine was getting good distribution because they were part of the GMC group. I had to admit to Marion that I was just starting to write a book to be published by GMC and though I didn't see any conflict of interests I had to retain the rights to my own writing in case I needed to reuse any of it in the future. For me it was an ideal arrangement because I would be seen and advertised across 2 platforms. I chose to write mostly for DHMS and occasionally for The Dolls House when it would aid my book sales.

Marion's idea was that I should write a series of articles which would be called "Challenge Angie". Sue Heaser was taking a break from writing for them and so at the time they didn't have a polymer clay writer. I was delighted with the idea. A challenge is what I like best.

Marion was going to publish a request for challenges and meanwhile I had ideas that people had already asked me to have a go at at fairs and classes. Even though I was comfortable with writing step by step projects for my book, I had no idea if I could write in an interesting enough style for a magazine. I didn't want it to be just step-by-step. There were already several of those every month across all the magazines. Plus that was what I was doing for the book. I wanted to find my own style. I knew what bored me and what interested me in magazines and I knew more personality was often what was needed. How difficult could it be? I'd been writing songs and poems for years and telling tall stories for nearly as long. So, never one to be daunted I set about my first challenge. The boar's head.

I wanted to give some historical background to the projects and I found a time team film with a Tudor feast and paused the video. Frank captured a screen shot for me and I worked mainly from that but also asked Aileen Tucker for info, as I knew she was very thorough in her research. I asked Aileen to help me several times more over the next couple of years and she was always generous with her information. I'll go so far as to say her contributions helped make the series which I'm happy to say became more and more popular. Every issue which had one of my projects in began to sell out and the magazine was more than holding its own against the competition.

At one point Marion rang me and asked me if I'd do a cover give-away. I won't say what I was offered per cover but it was a pitifully small amount. Even though I wanted the prestige of having my fruit slices on a front cover I couldn't put the work in at that price. We agreed on a slightly higher amount and then I got started making lemon, orange and lime canes. It's really difficult to believe looking back that I was originally going to slice and then bake the fruits. Until then I hadn't even thought of making pre-hardened canes. What I lost in being underpaid for the job I gained in the light bulb moment I had very shortly after, when I realised baking in advance was the only way I was ever going to get the job done. From that moment on I baked my canes in advance and started to sell them that way as 6cm canes. Though I got in family and friends to help with the endless slicing, all our fingers were sore and even blistered. As the canes cooled the slices often jumped all over the place. There were fruit slices everywhere. I mean everywhere! I could walk out into the street months later and see little orange and lemon slices stuck in cracks in the pavement.

But slicing wasn't the end of the job, we also had to count the slices into tens of thousands of tiny bags ready to stick on the magazines. If I were to do it again I'd certainly mix them all and put 'a pinch' in each bag instead of counting. We were exhausted by the end of the job and vowed never to do it again. Unfortunately I didn't stick to that vow and did two more cover give-aways. Even though each was for a smaller circulation as, not surprisingly, Marion and Edward chose to sell the magazine as it reached its highest circulation figures. Edward had not been well and they needed a rest.

Writing for the magazine had been very good for me. We hadn't been paid by Marion and I was a bit too 'green' to ask. I was grateful to Marion for my first proper exposure and the great advertising it produced. It got us invitations to teach and exhibit in other countries. One of the first trips was to Sweden where the group treated me like a celeb and introduced me fully to Swedish customs. I was enchanted with Stockholm and my Hosts Gunilla and Gunnar. I didn't sleep at all that night because I'd had two cups of real tea. I think I started with a cabbage class but It could have been a swede class I do remember finding out that Swedish people never ate swedes, not surprisingly. I do wonder where the name came from. During a lovely meal, where I'd had maybe a second glass of (very expensive in Sweden) wine, one of the girls passed me my sweet. Strawberries and cream and we all marvelled at the lovely pattern in the sliced strawberries. Hmm I said, I reckon I can do that. I think it was the alcohol talking because when I revisited the idea for one of my last challenges for Marion I realised it really was a tricky one. But I got my spatial awareness head on and worked out how to do it and it became one of my signature and most often copied canes.

Unfortunately the first edition of the magazine produced by its new owners was absolutely dire, it did improve steadily and eventually became really good again. Though I did write several more articles for them over the next few years I'd lost my rhythm. If truth be told it was probably as much to do with house moves, travels overworking on making enough stock and finding it increasingly difficult to discipline myself into setting up the table for photographing my work.

Another of my bright ideas

One day, both suffering from colds and in bed snuggled up together I had a bright idea. My sister was coming to visit from Australia, so I hinted at Frank that it might be a good time to have a "big celebration". Nope, Frank didn't get the hint, probably because I'd spent the first part of the 18 months we'd been together telling him I would never marry again. So I had to drop heavier and heavier hints until finally he got the message. He got the message, but he still didn't ask me. I was determined that it wouldn't be me who did the asking this time. Finally I had to put the words right into his mouth and tell him how to use them. Not a terribly romantic proposal but when we look back on it it still makes a good story.

Our wedding was simple but rather beautiful. We had no money but we did have a short miniature teaching tour planned just before the wedding. Taking in Devon and Wales and Somewhere near Cheddar gorge. We came back from the trip with a couple of hundred pounds which actually I owed to my son Alan when he lent us it for the gas fire. He generously wiped the debt as a wedding present, and another totally unexpected gift of a similar amount from an uncle who I rarely saw but who we visited in passing in South Wales. This was to become our honeymoon money.

We had only a few days to prepare for the wedding. During this time my sister Stephanie arrived from Australia with her daughter Alex. The community centre where Frank was a volunteer gave us their recently repainted hall free of charge for the reception and it just seemed that everyone was prepared to muck in to help. We girls went to Humber Street markets and blagged being a trader because I was in business. We came back with armfuls of freesias, roses, star lilies and gypsophila. And a stack of flower foam and baskets. The floor of the tiny living room in The Shack was covered in flower stems and ribbons, bits of oasis and people especially my sister and my niece, making huge flower arrangements for along the centres of the long tables in the hall which I covered with a huge roll of white cotton fabric bought from the well known Hessle Road shop Setam's, for next to nothing a metre.

My cousin Allison made us a big chocolate wedding cake filled with cherries in cream and decorated with falling leaves and musical notes. It was beautiful. And delicious. Quite a lot of the rest of the food was made by Frank including a pile of chimichangas. No, I'm not sure what they are either. Our friends Frankie and Pete came along as the two piece Mambo Jambo to be the entertainment for a pathetically small and delayed fee. They were brilliant and upbeat and the audience loved them, especially Franks granddad who was in his 90s.

My daughter and her friend Daisy acted as flower girls, dressed in burgundy tops and black trousers. Kira was already not into over the top pretty dresses, which was a good thing because our budget was just not up to the princess look. But they did look very cute. My wedding ring was hand made as a wedding present by our friend Phil, who is a jeweller. I handed him a silver ingot and a little tatty gold pendant that were from my mum's jewellery box. He created a ring to my specifications. Silver, lined with the gold and engraved with circuit board markings, filled with gold. So subtle that it's barely visible but it had and has real meaning to me.

The thing which made me happiest of all was to see how many of my relatives took the long journey to attend especially my brother Derek and his wife, and all my girl cousins. Of course Stephanie's visit was somewhat hijacked. I thought it was a nice idea but from some of the things she said I'm not sure that she was totally in agreement.

I cried during the short register office 'ceremony' as I looked into Frank's eyes and saw that he meant his vows and all the leftover demons from my previous marriage melted away. Another surprise guest to my wedding was my ex mother in law June, who generously decided to join us and I was very pleased that she did. She hadn't been to my first wedding to her son because she and his father wouldn't be in the same room together. Although it was a little bit strange, I wish she'd been able to make it to the bit which would have been more fun and maybe less emotional, but she decided not to come along to the reception. I think the moment of my joy was just a bit painful for her.

We melted away from the reception with a bottle of Champagne brought by my eldest son, and the top layer of the wedding cake, and took the first train to anywhere. Of course the first big city after Hull is Leeds so it wasn't surprising that the first train to anywhere was to Leeds. So Leeds it was. No hotel booking had been made. We decided to wing it and we thought we'd try the impressive Queens Hotel just outside the station. We asked for their cheapest room but when we told them we had just got married and how we'd landed there quite by chance they upgraded us to honeymoon suite. Very nice it was too. We spent just two nights in Leeds living off champagne and wedding cake before getting back to real life. There were still bills to pay and mouths to feed.

The Love Shack had a wedding present from several of our guests. We'd asked for carpet squares in a particular colour from B&Q in the hope that if each guest brought one or two squares we'd be able to cover our hardboard living room floor. In the end most people found that a difficult task and a lot gave us money instead. This didn't matter as one of our guests Sean Sullivan, who we called 'Mr 3d' for his fantastical ideas around holographic images and the like, paid for the rest of the floor tiles that we needed, so in the end the wedding present money went to buy a CCTV camera system which didn't last long as a local 'scrote' climbed up and destroyed it. I guess I could have predicted that!

Here I wrote the last two or three blues songs I ever wrote because I hung up my guitar forever shortly after moving. But Worries On My Mind, and Four In The Morning were written about relative poverty and the discomfort of living on a street corner where every other night time passer-by was either dealing in or buying drugs. And Mr Hometown was the frustration of being held back by hometown ideas.

Our life was on the up though, and we were working hard on ideas for a book, having had good sales of the videos. At the same time I was writing articles for Dolls House and Miniature Scene.

It wasn't long before we decided enough was enough living in The Shack and we had noticed that after the famous murder of Shane George on Coltman Street, the house prices had fallen sharply again after their rally in the 80s. The houses on Coltman Street were large impressive Georgian and Victorian houses which had been subdivided in the '80s into flats. The street was crying out for a more stable population, and those who did own whole houses down the street had the benefit of beautiful large and comfortable well built properties. We decided we wanted one. I had always wanted one since I first moved to the area and rented a flat.

The 'Mansion'

We did a naughty 'wangle' to buy the Coltman Street house. We applied for a home improvement loan. Nowhere on the loan forms did it say that improving our home couldn't consist of buying a new one, and selling the old one. So we didn't tell them our plans, and they didn't ask.

At that time I very much had my eye on and asked about number 114 which was owned by the council and which they wanted to offload but couldn't get through the red tape. It was a beautiful old late Georgian property once owned by well known local Shipowner and philanthropist Christopher Pickering. who lived there in the late 1800s. I wasn't the last person to be frustrated in their attempts to get that house. The story of 114 has had a happy ending/beginning though because it was eventually bought by an equally passionate renovating couple who went on to be stars in one of the TV programmes (Renovation Home) about the subject.

So with exactly 10,000 pounds budget we started going to auctions whenever a house on Coltman Street came up. But I was frustrated. Deals kept being made before the auction for around the same amount of money as we had. At one of these auctions I bumped into a landlady from the street. I'm not sure if she was buying or selling but I asked her if she knew of any properties which might be for sale. She told me to ask about the house which was between hers and her daughter in law's rental properties and she gave me contact details for the owner. She knew he wanted to offload it but wouldn't speak to her as they didn't get on. There were dire warnings not to tell him that it was she who had given me contact details.

And so it was that I found myself in the attic room of 123 with the then owner, having absolutely promised Frank I would not make any decisions without him seeing it, negotiating the purchase. It went something like this: "Well, what do you think?" "I like it. There's only one problem. I only have ten thousand pounds". "Then ten thousand pounds it is". And a handshake. Yes. I'd just promised every penny we had for a house with no running water, a bit of a slide on the back and loads of damaged internal walls. On the other hand I'd just promised a teeny amount for a huge Victorian house with a stepped and pillared entrance, largely in structurally excellent condition having been re roofed twenty years before. "It was the roll of networking cable in the attic that did it. It was a sign" was my excuse to Frank. But we both knew I'd made an excellent deal.

I later found a buyer for another of the same man's properties, earning a central heating boiler as commission. And so started our first major reform. We took the boards off the windows, hung up net curtains and started to live in the house which had formerly been converted into four separate flats. It was still in quite a state. Electricity was only available in flat one. So, until we got an electrician in, all power was distributed through long extensions from Flat one. Water was only available from the attic flat, Flat 4 and so all water was temporarily plumbed from there.

But it was a fine house with some original features including stained glass panels in the inner front door. One urgent DIY project was to find out what was causing the heave backwards of the extension at the back of the house. Mrs Wilson (the landlady who had pointed me at the house) became my angel of mercy. She told me that someone had turned an ancient stop cock on, which was supposed to have been completely disconnected and left it on for days on end. The water had quite simply undermined the back of the house. She'd had the water board in and they had cut the water off. We simply had to stick an indicator strip over the crack for a couple of seasons and if it didn't move again, which it didn't, we could simply patch the crack and move on with our lives. Which we did.

We had little time for more renovations in that first few months because I was contracted to write my first book which was started but still had the major work to do and a deadline looming.

The next step was trying to persuade the Publishers GMC who had just recently published Jamie Carrington's book Making Character Figures, that my step-by-step digital photography would be up to standard for one of their books. They had never used digital photography before and didn't even know how to handle images in the digital domain. We didn't know that, and assuming that they would be way more advanced than us, happily sent off our images untouched. Disappointingly that is the way they left them. The only corrected and optimised images were the ones used in the cabbages and beetroot projects which we had done ourselves for the synopsis.

I had a comic series of phone calls where my editor asked me if we could print out our images and send them to them to scan back in to their system; because we were getting a better result than they were. I tried to explain that we had used a 'cheapo' Epson for our example images, but we hadn't realised that they'd never used digital image editors before and didn't know how. Of course very soon Mr "I've been doing it this way for 30 years" retired and by my second book there was some younger talent in the company. I did enjoy working with Kylie aside from the conversation about simulate vs emulate. Kylie had changed it all to emulate and I tried to explain the difference. In the end, for the sake of peace I agreed to 50% of the simulates being changed. She obviously checked because in the end they were all changed back.

Funnily enough I never met anyone from the company face to face and I wonder whether this was also the first book they produced entirely remotely from the author. In fact I never met them at all until I was in talks for book 3 around 15 years later. Talks which I'm happy to say broke down amicably leaving me free to be a self-publisher. People don't realise just how small royalties can be with a rather cleverly worded contract.

Nevertheless the book must have been more than passable because it came out in summer 2001. I'd already persuaded them that the 2000 copies they first intended to print wouldn't be adequate because I already had orders for a quarter of those so they printed 4,000 and it went on sale in the summer of 2001. When I got my book in my hot little hands I thought, that's it. I've produced something worthy ... I can die now.

My first book was finished in the big house which we variously called Love Mansions (after the Love Shack) and then Sun house, after the Blues Musician Son House. I started off working in the room next to our bedroom which had been the kitchen of flat 2 but which we later converted into a luxurious en-suite bathroom. Frank built me a light box which looked a bit 'Heath Robinson' but which worked a treat. Four flats became one generous house and I was the lucky owner of a whole flat for working in when Alan moved out at the age of 18. I had a clean workshop, a dirty workshop and an office. And a toilet and kitchen all to myself. Nevertheless we still had locks on each of the former flat front doors and we used to lock ourselves in flat 2 at night.

We were already members of the neighbourhood watch presided over by Roger Hamilton who was a tireless worker for improvement although we didn't always agree on methods, we knew Roger was very invested in the project and over the next few years we all put rather a lot of time into organising a website for the street with the help of the Web Factory where Frank worked, including a house by house listing of the former residents of every property in the street only up until the 1930s (in order to protect the innocent … and not so). At the same time, Frank and the web factory were also working on a project the called Walkabout Hull which pre-dated Google street view but was very similar in concept.

We found out there had been some famous people living on the street over its lifetime. As well as Mr Pickering who Pickering park was named after, there was Alfred Hollins, a blind concert organist, pianist, and composer; who was soloist with the Berlin, London, and New York Philharmonic Orchestras, who wrote an autobiography which included his first recollections of his childhood home, our house at 123. His childhood friend next door at 124 (The numbers run sequentially in Coltman Street) went on to be a British Ambassador in Spain. The director of the Doctor In The House series of films had also lived there and Hull Truck Theatre Company was 'born' there in the early '70s.

We started organising a street party once a year to try to reverse the negative image of the street. With some success. There were always those who wanted to believe that the street was fundamentally a bad place but it was and still is an attractive Georgian and Victorian street with several listed buildings close to the city centre of Hull and a certain number of long term, stable residents. Its problems were largely due to historical factors including the two world wars which changed it from a wealthy merchant and shipowner's street through many falls from grace into guesthouses, some of them later had a reputation for being, well, 'bawdy'.

The street fell into real disrepair. Only a third of the houses were occupied when the council took charge in the 80s as I first moved there. They gave grants to builders and landlords and especially builder-landlords for conversion into largely private landlord-owned single and multi-occupancy flats and a few council flats leaving very few private houses. I'm sure the town planning department had their reasons and initially it seemed a good idea in order to save the fabric of the street. However nobody seemed to have taken account of the fact that, to provide a balance of permanent residents, some larger units were needed. Also some truly innovative and artistic ideas were thrown out at the planning stage at that time. The deciding committee stating that they didn't want to 'gentrify' the area. One, a fully glass backed Georgian fronted house was too 'out there' an idea and was rejected. Whereas a two thirds size nasty little pseudo-Victorian style terrace full of one bedroom 'rabbit hutches' was approved on the plans without any reference to scale.

We had some support in our efforts from the Council, the police and the landlords and, by and large from the whole community who were thoroughly sick of the reputation of the street becoming a self-fulfilling prophecy. That is to say, because of the tendency of people to think of the street as a 'bad area' in the past, not many people wanted to live there who had any options. Therefore there was a low uptake even of council housing. As a result the street became unbalanced towards people who were deprived either financially or socially. Of course that is how, as a recently separated single parent I 'washed up' there.

I hope its obvious that the street wasn't solely peopled by down and outs, just that there had been an unequal balance towards people with problems. When we started the website project, someone brought me an old Hull Daily Mail from the 1980s, where I'd been interviewed about moving myself and my children into the newly refurbished street. I loved the architecture then and still loved it a dozen years later when two of my three children had grown and left home. I was also contacted by an old man whose Dutch parents had bought a house there during the war. He told stories of his childhood as an immigrant in the city I wrote up Rik Heidstra's story for the webpage in the hope that some of the disquiet about another wave of immigration might be calmed by the realisation that Hull has always had a very large immigrant population and would in fact have died without it. What we hoped to help do was re-balance the street so that it had a healthier balance of both flats and larger long term residences.

My book arrived in August of 2001 and it was all hands to the pump to get them out to the more than 500 customers who had pre-ordered. It was so exciting and of course we had a reasonable income from that first print run. The book sold out before Xmas that year and had to be printed again becoming one of GMCs best sellers. And that pattern continued with a reprint on average every year for the next seven or 8 years. By that time I thought maybe it was time to write another. Because we needed funds for yet another crazy house project.

The Church

During those years the house renovating bug hadn't left me. In fact it had consumed rather too much of my business time and I was having difficulty keeping miniature stock. Perhaps I'd never charged enough but my work sold quickly and not really for an adequate income.

One day I was sitting in our part renovated Coltman Street house, when I looked across at the empty Methodist church building on the other side of the street, the previous owner of which, Mr Atkinson, had recently died, and I simply said to Frank. I'd like to buy that.

Well Frank had got used to his crazy wife's madcap schemes by this time, and I know he had little doubt that it would happen in spite of our tight finances. My dad used to say that my mum was the vortex into which he got sucked and I realise I probably do the same to poor Frank.

I approached the grieving family as tactfully as I could and offered to buy it. I'd spoken to my bank about a loan and by this time my credit rating was reasonably good. The owners wanted 20,000 for it. Which was probably what it was worth at the time in that market. I got it for 16. Unfortunately that meant passing up any chance we had of buying the house next door when that too came up for sale very soon after. This was a problem which would come back to bite us in the future.

The Detroit disaster:

One of the great things about being a teaching miniaturist is being invited to exotic places and having the cost of that trip guaranteed by the payments of the students in your class. We've been far from wealthy but we have travelled more extensively than most people on four times our income.

During the previous couple of years I'd been to America a couple of times, to the Philadelphia fair as an invitee of IGMA to do classes and have a stall at the fair, then to the New York Miniatures fair. Frank initially found the American customers more demanding than their European counterparts. Frank is not a deferential person. He didn't appreciate people stuffing baskets full of items under his nose while he was counting and insisting "I'm ready now". On the other hand he soon got used to the fact that once they had asked a few prices they had the habit of simply sweeping the stand clean, and so he forgave them somewhat because if the first day was rushed and stressful, the second one was a breeze.

We'd had a lovely time on the New York visit. We arrived late in the evening and, as usual after flying, I had a dreadful headache. Frank and Kira went out into the city that never sleeps in search of food and found the all night Chinese buffet shops which were a real novelty for us. They brought me back the most delicious selection of food and as my pain killers kicked in we sat cross legged on the hotel bed, after midnight New York time, picking at the tasty takeaway. I had sold out classes which paid for the trip. After the fair, we took Kira to down-town Manhattan and she absolutely loved visiting the places where some of her favourite TV shows were set. including Central Park. She was a complete 'Yankophile'. I, however, soon had my view of America thoroughly tarnished.

One morning while working in my office I got a call from my son Dominic. "Put on the telly mum!" And we witnessed 9/11 in real time. It was horrific. These were places we'd been and were due to go again next spring for the Philadelphia IGMA show. I had absolutely full classes. I'd even had to agree to some overflow classes in Long Island to keep everybody happy. Frank wasn't bothered about going again, but my son Dominic (then 25) certainly was. So I decided to take him. He could help me carry extra materials and stock and I'd take him to New York as a treat after the show and before the extra Long Island class.

Everything was in place. The bags were packed, the stock was checked and listed for customs and we were very excited. Of course it was post 9-11 and the world and New York was still in shock. I'd considered cancelling the trip as I thought people might be afraid to travel. But I was assured that nobody thought that way.

We had travelled by a rather circuitous route, (Humberside/ Amsterdam/ Detroit/ Philadelphia) as it was very much the cheapest and easiest we could find at the time. Plus Humberside is a small airport very close to where we lived. The more normal route via Manchester or London would have added overnight stops to each end of our trip.

I arrived at the Immigration desk in Detroit in a rather anxious state. This was due to the airline being unable to tell me where they had put my hand luggage which did not fit in the overhead locker. Half of my miniatures, representing nearly two month's work, were in that bag. I was very tired and irritable because my son and I had been seated apart and I couldn't remember whether I had been given a receipt for the luggage. In fact I had to insist that there was a bag missing even when they were putting us back on the plane. My bag was eventually returned.

Yes. They did put us back on the plane. The very plane we came in on. I now realize why we were singled out for the treatment we received.

I believed that my innocent anxiety was one thing that may have lead their Homeland security officers to suspect that we may have been something we were not. Thereafter I think they felt they had to build a case for excluding us. This was instead of taking time to check the details at all. It was several days later that the truth hit me. We had been victims of racial profiling, and apparently our experience was becoming more and more common.

The colour of my son's skin and his Muslim (sounding) middle name. There was a no fly list at the time and if you had a suspicious name you would be pulled out of the line for further examination

When I gave Dominic the middle name 'Karim' it sounded pretty. This was 24 years before 9/11. Although his birth father was from Pakistan I was a single parent then and have never given my son any religion, let alone a radical one. The nearest I got to being politically active in those days was being a member of my local Neighbourhood Watch and promoting my street.

Then I remembered we were also asked about Dominic's middle name in Amsterdam, by some USA guards who were stationed there at the time "just out of curiosity" we were told. "Because they had a cousin who was called Karim" This didn't seem important except in the light of what subsequently happened to us. Now I think the story about the cousin was probably more appropriately named "Bull".

The officious HS officer, who I remember was called Todd asked me if I was prepared to be interviewed. I said "yes, of course". I had nothing to hide and no idea that this was a prelude to him pressing a spurious case that Dominic was trying to work illegally in the country where the truth was that although he was going to help his mother on the most informal and unpaid basis, our primary objective for Dominic was to have a mother/son trip to Manhattan. They didn't even interview Dominic and they did take some important words out of my statement. They asked me if Dominic was intending to work and I said no. They then asked "then why is he coming with you?" And I said "basically to help his mum out and then to have a holiday". They took out the word no and the next question so it read "is your son intending to work while in the States. My answer in the transcript they had was "basically to help his mum out".

I did make a complaint through my then MP Alan Johnson, and asked them to dig out the videos to prove my assertion. And I did receive a letter from a Mr Cronin to say they would investigate. Sadly that was the last I heard about it. Racial profiling, I think, was simply too politically sensitive a subject at that time. I felt terrible hurt for my son, who lost trust in the system as well as a very well earned holiday. And my finances, just on the cusp of buying the Church building, were in ruins.

I was also disappointed to find that the books and videos I had left with the IGMA class organisers and asked to be given to each student as an apology were in fact charged for as a proportion of the money returned. This left a very bad taste, and I never renewed my membership of IGMA. Neither did I ever return to America. I did think about going again when Obama was in the presidency but of course after Trump was elected I didn't see me ever setting foot on American soil again. Nor wanting to. The truth is I'm still angry. I behaved faultlessly, as did my son and the one thing I really can't stomach is injustice. Incidentally Dominic has been to the States since, several times But he always gets pulled out of the line for an interview whereas his other travelling companions never do. He now works in a job where his credentials have to be impeccable so these days his problem is short lived but still irritating.

One sweet story came back to me just shortly after 9/11 which proves the truth of the idea that its a very small world and that people are affected in ways you just can't imagine. An American trade customer emailed me and told me she'd received a lovely thank you card from her retail customer who lived in Manhattan. Her customer's post office happened to be next to the twin towers and was badly damaged and closed by falling debris. A few months later, after the clean, up a dirty, sooty parcel was delivered to the customer with a note attached apologising for the damage. Inside, totally untouched was a bowl of my miniature apples. Apparently the lady's customer was very emotional at the survival of her little apples through The Big Apple's darkest hour.

Creative Thinking

I can't remember where I heard the tale about old man Atkinson's method of keeping his building secure from the local wildlife ... and by that I mean the thieving junkies, but I did hear that he had a shotgun rigged to a tripwire inside the back door of the church building. Thank goodness his daughter must have known about it because by the time we visited to inspect it there was nothing to be seen and we lived to tell the tale. Maybe it was just a story he put out since he never came across as a hard man. Wiley, yes, but not a killer.

The sign on the front said "Nazarene Wesleyan Evangelical Church" -something of a mouthful.

I simply remembered the church building in its last

incarnation as a place where the mainly black members of the church sang their hearts out on a Sunday afternoon. Even though I don't 'do' religion, I found it a beautiful sound as I passed by back then. Now the building was silent. There were rumours about why it had closed down but maybe it was simply too expensive to keep up. There was still a pathetic little blue box in the main hall with the words 'Building Fund' painted on it. And, of course ... It was empty.

We did find out one possible cause of the church's financial problems shortly after we got possession of the building and plumbed in an inside toilet and sink as well as a kitchen sink. Not for the first time I scratched my head about what was causing the damp problems around the building. And, not for the first or last time I found out it was an old water connection that had not been properly cut off when the new water connection had been fitted during the renovations of the street during the 1980s. I found out this time because the back garden was sodden and my first water bill was for over a thousand pounds. I wonder if the Church members ever paid a bill of that size? They probably never would have thought to ask why.

Because I was involved with the community and its history, I already knew that there was originally a house on the back of the plot which was probably damaged during the war and subsequently pulled down. So I called in the water board and had them confirm that water which was flowing into the church, was flowing right back out again into the rear plot through an old 'in' connection from the former house which presumably was the rectory. I was very firm about whose fault the connection oversight was and insisted that the pipe was fixed and the bill wiped. Once again we'd bought a building for a song partly because of water problems.

Once again it was an easy fix. I heard that the Church was actually built during the first world war by the women of the community. Now it was another woman playing at being a renovating expert.

Having sorted that problem out, the next thing to look at was the roof. It was steep pitched and covered in slates. Although there were a few slipped tiles, it was nothing major, on the facing side. At the other side, where the building adjoined a terrace house, a deep gutter which was full of leaves and badly perished, was letting water in. The answer, according to builders, was to remove the roof and re-do the gutter then re-lay the tiles at a cost of many thousands of pounds. So I slept on it.

The answer, it turned out, was for me to crawl on my belly like the biblical snake. Clean out the old gutter, apply a liberal amount of sealant and simply push a new box section gutter in over the top of the old one. The job, as they say, was a good 'un'.

The inside of the building was next. Fortunately the leak in the roof had hardly touched the front hall, just a few little dribble marks down the right hand side wall. So the floor was in largely wonderful condition. It wasn't anything 'posh' just thick pine planks. We hired a sander and took another of Frank, I and our friend David (always known to us as Popdog)'s 'never again' long weekends of killer work to strip down the thick black paint covering a large part of it. It was impossible to get the thickest paint off the edges so we re-painted the edges with a pale grey floor paint and I varnished the centre strip with a nice matte varnish. It was lovely, and for our pockets it was expensive. As we were removing the old altar and preparing the floor we discovered the baptismal bath under the floorboards. All tiled out. We had our own swimming pool! We never filled it. The floor boards from the alter were made by my artist (and dab hand at joinery)friend Dave into very strong rustic looking benches for wedging clay. I loved those benches and two of the three have followed me everywhere I've gone and even now sit in my workshop supporting my pasta machine and all my polymer clay pounding.

I had expensive tastes. I wanted Italian leather sofas in the back meeting room. So leather sofas we got. Leather on the 'never never' as my parents called credit. Four of them in a rectangle. In my mind the building's new incarnation was to be a craft centre and shop called 'Creative Thinking' I have to say I never completely fulfilled this dream as it ended up being a little beyond my capabilities pockets and ultimately interests. But it had started well.

During the renovations I had bought myself a lovely little square section scaffold and climbed it like a monkey. My son Alan helped me paint the ceiling. I grew to love climbing that scaffold and I was the fittest I'd ever been in my life having lost 2 stone on an Atkins-like diet.

I learned the value of wonderful lime putty in old buildings and I generously slapped lime plaster into places where previous 'bodgers' had attempted to use hard cement with no success. My friend Margaret who was already in her mid 60s helped me to tile the kitchen floor with quarry tiles and we bought in a pair of Ikea Kitchen units. Which, funnily enough we still own and which form the basis of my kitchen in Spain having moved around with us in several moves in the intervening years and been slightly flood damaged in storage. The famous Boyes store on Hessle Road were re-fitting, so seeing some of their old units being moved out I asked the manager if I could have them and hold of several display units and storage benches which we fitted around the walls.

As soon as we had the floor, the walls painted and had bought some fold up tables and renovated some of the church's old bent metal chairs, I started to let people in once or twice a week for craft sessions. These were very much led by what the community wanted. In March 2003 we opened the church building up formally as a craft centre and started looking around for ideas of other classes to put on as well as my own and various other community craft sessions. Shortly after I had managed to buy a second hand kiln I was offered a second one. Two kilns was a good idea because we could be stacking one while firing and cooling the other. Vicky, Alan's girlfriend at the time was a very talented girl and produced some really very good pots.

Because nobody who came could afford large quantities of materials I spent way too much money on clays and glazes and other craft materials which I would charge out to the class members as they needed them. We also charged £2 a session for craft sessions. We did have a very generous offer once again from Mrs Wilson who was really supportive of our community efforts and offered to buy us a potters wheel. Of course I accepted the offer. We had a visit and class from a local potter who happened to be the sister of changing rooms star Linda Barker. She was just as nice as her more famous sister. Another famous person I met around that time was just a small time reporter from the Yorkshire post, who came to interview us about the changes on the street. Well, he was small time then, but he was clearly talented. I see a lot of Richard Bilton now on Panorama where he is one of their major investigative reporters.

I put on several miniature weekends and days over the next few months. Mostly teaching my own classes but we also had Diane Harfield teaching a very beautiful corner garden in Cold Porcelain.

One of my most successful fairs around this time was Pudsey which was just outside Leeds and run by Doreen Vincent. I was lucky to get a stand there as it really was (and I believe still is) a popular fair and very busy. It was another fair where our income was often limited by the number of people who could get around our stand at any one time. Fortunately our site on the stage, although it was small, was easy to see and we had lots of space in front of us. My first book was still selling well and so we were beginning to pull ourselves round from the previous year's losses from the 'Detroit disaster'.

Summer at Lillaskuggan (Little Cloud)

The second trip I made to Sweden I had managed to persuade Frank on the beauty of the place. I had enjoyed the warm welcome given to me by the lovely Gunilla and Gunnar the first time I went. This time we stayed with Cristina who I already knew and the trip was a delight. The little boy she'd waited so long for and swears she conceived in London around the time we first met at Alexandra Palace was now a couple of years old and it was absolutely wonderful to share this time with her family, complete as it should be. We stayed in her little cottage in Lillaskuggan (little cloud) which turned out to be a former hunting lodge in the kings hunting park.

A more historic and idyllic situation would be hard to find. The cottage itself sat between trees with a glimpse of the lakeside. Well, it wasn't actually a lake, it was the sea, but Stockholm is made up of so many little islands that it looked like a lake. The inner walls of the antique cottage were covered with stretched canvas, painted in a particularly Nordic blue palette of duck egg blue with lines and flowers round the edges and corners. It was like everyone's dream Swedish cottage. I tasted the pleasure of basking naked in the 4 am sun through the open bedroom window. And the pleasure of messing about in boats. Cristina and her husband's boat to be precise. We set off from their own jetty which they built the previous winter over the surface while the sea was iced over. How clever!

Cristina's husband played guitar and allowed me to play some too and was very charming about my playing. The long weekend was over far too soon. When we left, Cristina gave me the gift of a book called The Harmony of the Stockholm Skerries. Apparently it was written by a friend of hers. I still cherish this book and it brings back many memories.

I don't remember much about the classes from that year. Unlike the previous year when we'd been in a community school and I'd "bragged" that I could work out how to make a strawberry cane. Well, there were so many other memories this year We had also been on a water Taxi with Sigrid and Pia and before going home we popped into Stockholm and watched a game of Kubb being played in the Kingsgarden. Kubb is a traditional Swedish open air game where 2 teams compete to knock over the other teams 'pawns' before attempting to knock over the King. It looked like fun. Then we went to the town to eat in one of the many pop-up cafés which had been put there for Stockholm's 750th anniversary. Then we went and found ourselves our own Kubb set. We weren't quite sure how we were going to get it home though. It was solid wood and heavy. This was another rather heavy item that went 'hand luggage'.

In August we tried Scottish Miniatura again because this time it was in Edinburgh. I decided to take Kira with me and we went by train. Edinburgh was lovely and it was nice wandering the streets with Kira but sadly the Scottish fair was not up to expectations in Edinburgh either. I remember one conversation with a customer who was buying a pack of blades for one pound. I smiled at the lady as she handed over her pound and said "they're difficult to get hold of aren't they". Her friend piped up. "I get mine from the chemist." "Yes you can get them there but I think you only get 3 in a pack" I said "Och noo" said her friend. "I get fayve for a poond". "Then I shall get mine from the chemist" said the first woman and snatched back her pound coin. I'm loath to confirm stereotypes but I have to say that this kind of thing only ever happened in Scotland … and Holland.

Fortunately Birmingham Miniatura was much better, as usual in those days, proving itself worth the very high table fees and the irritation of the jobs-worth parking attendants. We always enjoyed it mainly because it was busy and profitable but also because we got to meet other miniaturists from all over the world. It was at Miniatura we first met John and Hazel Dowd. Hazel was and is a doll dresser and was, at that time way ahead of her peers in publishing her projects on the internet due to having a son who worked in IT and she and John both being naturally creative and inquisitive.

I'm eternally grateful to John for persevering and getting through my nervousness and scepticism. And always encouraging me in my early years in the Miniatures scene. They told us about Minis 4 all which was a new group they'd set up and one year talked me into doing a coconut basket class the day before Miniatura and a few years later I would go to a couple of their annual weekends and enjoyed them immensely. Hazel was very nurturing and so was John and I often teased them saying "yes mum" and "yes dad", but I really appreciated their support and advice and was always really happy when I found we had close tables.

In November we decided to try going to Madrid. It

would be our first Madrid fair and maybe only a few years into this fair. The fair was pretty good. Not like a Miniatura but it paid for itself plus a bit and we had the feeling the hobby was on the up in Spain. I enjoyed practising my newly learned Spanish even though it really was just a 'smattering' of the language that I'd picked up from my gigs in Spain a few years before.

4

Selling Up Or Selling Out

We'd given our all to Coltman Street and in many ways the street was better for the community efforts. However I was tiring of the relentlessness of the work that just a few of us put in. The Church was by then functioning as a craft centre called Creative Thinking. We had a few regular users who formed a kind of craft club a couple of afternoons a week. They paid a monthly fee which added up to £2 each per visit. and they had access to pottery and craft materials at cost price. In addition I'd been giving classes and inviting other artists to give classes as well. Plus we had started to let the place out to a dance group for the handicapped. But I was losing money hand over fist as soon as the council slapped business rates on the building. Things had started to look a lot less rosy.

I realised that if I wanted to keep the place open I'd have to turn it into a full on community craft centre and go 'grant grubbing' for my running costs and my income. That just wasn't my area of interest. So, when a local businessman came along and told me that he wanted to buy it to turn it into a karate centre, I was only too ready to believe him and I sold the building for forty five thousand pounds, having spent probably five on the renovations and wasted a few thousand more more on un-sellable craft stock and business rates. Still it was a profit and one I was very happy to take. The businessman was a bit 'sharp' though. He knew what I needed to hear in order to get me to sell, and what he actually wanted the building for was a tyre refitting franchise. I was disappointed but not surprised, and by that time we had our eyes on sunnier climes.

Denmark

We'd already had a busy spring with the Minis 4 all weekend at the end of February then Miniatura in March and Pudsey in April.

Marianne invited us to do Farum fair at the end of April. This was our first trip to Denmark. The fair was pretty good and the fact that she'd organised some workshops for the day before helped us be sure it would pay its way. We found we loved the students we met. Danish people are kind and funny. Our Hull sense of humour seems to owe something to the Nordic races. I particularly remember that was the first time I met Gerd who became a very good friend. We also discovered that a Danish pastry in Denmark was a completely different thing from one eaten in England.

The day after the fair Marianne and her husband Max took us out for a day driving around the area. Max was already suffering from brain cancer but at this point he was quite well and in good spirits. In fact he made us laugh quite a lot.

First they took us for a meal and when Frank went off to the loo, Max leaned over to me and whispered conspiratorially "I can understand some English. And I understand you quite well. But him … " he said, indicating Frank's departing back, with his thumb, "not one word". I was amused by his candour and I've told this story several times since. I come from a family of pompous prigs where accent and grammar is concerned. As a child the Hessle road accent is one I was particularly cautioned against using. Frank's Hull accent is quite strong. In fact, if truth be told, it's strongly 'ezzle rerd'. Yes, I have picked up Frank's accent a little more than my father would have liked. We often joke that dad would be turning in his grave to hear his daughter's accent these days. I can just imagine him saying "Well he's a nice enough lad, but why does he have to talk like that!"

We were then driven to Helsingor to take a look at the castle Kronburg. This was the castle immortalised in Shakespeare's Hamlet as Elsinore. Max told us about how the Danes once owned the western part of Sweden and he shook his fist at the Swedes over the sea in Helsingborg for stealing his land. When we left Max, who had recently been learning how to work in miniature with silver, gave me a tiny spoon with a twisted handle for Kira.

We never met Max again and sadly he died later the same year leaving us with sweet memories of the short time we knew him. When we got back to Copenhagen Frank and I decided to go into the Tivoli gardens. It was nice enough but we don't know why it was so very popular. I suppose it's "of its time" but it seems to me that its time is gone and yet it's not yet old enough to have a really historic charm. Frank was totally smitten with Copenhagen's Danish pastries which, I had to admit, tasted so much better there. They aren't called 'Danish Pastries' in Denmark though; there they call them Vienna brod (bread).

Spain

We set off for Spain with the completion on the sale of the Church building just days away. I was determined to strike while the iron was hot otherwise I knew the money would just disappear. This was our one chance to own a little bit of sunny Andalucía. We knew we couldn't afford a house in good condition. We knew we would be rolling up our sleeves once again. But at 47 I still felt I had another project in me. Though maybe not more than one.

So we set out with the express intention of buying a house without a roof. Yes, this was a mistake but you live and you learn. Maybe a smaller house that was more watertight would have been a better idea. But on our budget we certainly weren't going to get much.

First we had a miniatures fair in Javea near Alicante and, just before it, one day of classes. We stayed with Iris Broughton who was a member of Minis 4 all and who offered to put us up in her little house in the hills outside Javea. She and her husband had bought and renovated the tiny property as a holiday home. Her husband had passed away a couple of years earlier. Iris had a very positive attitude and visited the house regularly. She picked us up from Alicante airport in her old car which Iris said liked the rumble strips on the side of the road, and so it did. I don't know whether that was because it had right-itis or Iris liked to keep to the very edge of the road. Possibly the latter because the car was a beast and her house was perched at the top of some quite scary narrow roads with steep falls.

When we wound our way up the hillside to Iris' house our first view was a picture. It was a tiny house but had a pretty garden full of sweet peas which were in bloom when we arrived. The house was off grid, at least as far as electricity was concerned and it ran on batteries powered by a generator. So the only electricity in the house was on 12 volts. It was a quirky little place with a reed ceiling which, it turned out, was full of rats. Iris called them fruit rats, which I'm sure they were. But they were rats all the same and the sound inside the roof at night was quite unnerving. One thing we learned from this visit was the realisation that we would be better off in a community, albeit a rural one, than having a house so far off the beaten track.

I was teaching in a bar where a young Argentinian worked. He carved amazing sculptures from wine corks in his spare time. I remember those sculptures much better than I remembered the class or the fair. I do remember that the fair was good enough for me to consider doing it again.

House hunting

Then we were off to Andalucía. I think we must have picked up a hire car because I seem to remember we crossed the country by car. Firstly we contacted a few estate agents on the way towards the triangle between Seville, Huelva and the Sierra de Aracena which was our preferred destination since my Spanish friend had shown it to Steve and me on my first Spanish adventure. We started off in Estepa and were shown several properties by an English Estate Agent. She was a bit too smooth. A bit too friendly. Just a wee bit too patronising. She took us to see three houses. All terraced and all a bit kooky. One of them had been inhabited at some time by 'druggies', obvious by their 'droppings'. No needles, but tell tale plastic caps were still there. The whole terrace looked similar and it was a definite no no, even though the views were spectacular.

Another was in a tiny street and was extremely narrow, but otherwise was quite interesting. The third we were told was a "no-brainer" which she'd saved for us and was absolutely recommended for our needs. And it was cute but it was very small and there were piles of frass (woodworm dust) everywhere. At first we were interested but after an overnight full of dreams of wood boring creatures I rang up the estate agent and explained my reasons for passing on that one. Instead of being understanding and offering us other properties she curtly told me that was a "stupid" reason not to buy.

So bye bye we went.

We moved straight on to our preferred 'zone' and stayed in a hotel in Aracena. Aracena is the town at the heart of a national park of the same name. El Parque Nacional de la Sierra de Aracena. We fell in love with the area which, in spring, reminded me of Devonshire for its lumpy bumpy-ness. This was exactly the sort of area I wanted to to live in, but it was a bit expensive being a tourist area for the Spanish of both Seville and Huelva capitals. This was real rural Spain and although there were a few English residents dotted around the area, they were definitely the sort of people we could get along with.

The town is famous for its cave system known as the "Gruta de las maravillas", its slow pace of life and its Jamon serrano (ham). When I first tried it I did what any Brit would do. I headed straight for the cheapest pinkest leanest meat, little knowing the delights that were in store when I discovered the smooth melt in the mouth parmesan flavoured quality of fat from the '5 bellotas de Jabugo' ham from the pure race pata negra - black footed free roaming acorn fed pig. The area is a delight for ingredients, year round. Famous for not only ham, but goat cheese, honey and chestnuts, and during the rainier seasons, wild mushrooms,

There were several estate agencies and we saw two of them. One was run by a very nice Irish girl. They showed us two properties. One was a tiny little outhouse on a fabulous plot. It was literally a one room shack with a toilet off it. It was on a beautiful sloping site with almond and mandarin trees and a stream at the bottom and with its own spring. It was a lovely little huerta (vegetable plot), but no good at all for living in and I was sure there'd be no planning permission to enlarge it. In addition to being expensive the national park had strict planning laws. But sellers knew that foreigners often don't realise this and at that time the market for any kind of property was brisk. The second property was really interesting. It was owned by a Belgian hippy family and they'd clearly built it piecemeal. It was on another sloping site and it was weird but homely. We were also sure this was an illegal construction, but we really would have considered it except that the owners sniffed foreign buyers and hiked the price to way outside our reach. So that was out too. Even if it hadn't been expensive I still had in mind that I wanted to be in or at least on the outskirts of a village because even in my late forties I was aware that retirement was going to be looming soon. Well I thought it was. Of course at that time retirement, for me, was still expected to be at age 60.

The next day we had an appointment with another estate agent but at the last minute he cancelled. It was our last day and we'd just heard that the buyers in England had completed. The money was burning a hole in our pockets. I was almost resigned to another trip but I thought we wouldn't waste the opportunity. And prices were going up almost by the day. We really did only have enough money for a wreck. I decided we should go for a drive and just look at the surrounding villages. Our method was just as simple as our honeymoon choice had been. It was to take the first road we saw out of town and see where it led us.

And so it happened that about 10km outside of Aracena on the road towards Huelva, I saw a pretty little village from a distance. It was just splattered across a little hillside with another slightly bigger hill sheltering it. "Ooh Frank" I squealed "I hope the road goes that way!" It didn't seem to at first though. It twisted and turned for another 8km but finally we did arrive at the little village of Campofrío. It was time for a coffee at the bar in the central square. Outside the bar was a little fountain and we sat on the edge of the fountain and contemplated our next move. I really wanted to talk to someone but was way too shy.

So after the coffee we decided to walk around the village, and of course we were looking for 'Se Vende' (for sale) signs. Would I feel cocky enough to phone a Spanish number? It would certainly make for a cheaper deal if we cut out the exorbitant estate agent or 'corredor' (a Spanish local who knows everything and puts people in touch for a fee). We did a tour of the village. It was small but cute and as we got back round into Plaza de Andalucía just before the main Plaza (Espana) we saw our house. It was tiny and low and very shabby and sat behind 2 smelly rubbish bins. Not promising at all, but it had a Se Vende sign and we thought it was shabby enough to be cheap, and it was very central. So we started trying to work out the faded number on the sign.

Suddenly an old bloke in a cap rapped his cane on the stones behind us making us jump. "Gruhuhu-e-a" he said. "Perdona, no entiendo". "Ye-ya-eh-o" he said rather louder "ah-ah-eh-a!!!" I started to pick up that there weren't going to be any consonants and that I needed to imagine some in order to continue this conversation. It turned out that he was offering to take me to see another house … or failing that la dueña (the owner) of this one. I told him OK. This one. He threw himself into the back of the car. With his stick over our shoulders he rapped on the windscreen to indicate we should drive, and which way. Fortunately there was only one right turn and one left turn. In fact it was less than 100 yards before we were back outside of our car in front of the local school.

The old fella took his stick to the Hammerite-d front

door of the house opposite the school. After a second even louder rapping a little old lady came to the door. Well, I say old. She was probably only a handful of years older than I am now. What a thought. Anyway this was our first meeting with Maria Luisa who became, over time, like a Spanish mother to me and who we now call Mama.

She was the owner of the house and after a short conversation with Antonio-the-stick she also jumped into the back of the car and we returned the 100 yards back to our house,

Well, It wasn't "our house" yet. We still had to see it and decide to buy it. If it wasn't promising from the outside, it was even less attractive inside

As we stepped through the front door we could see there were problems out the back. Daylight was shining in from the other end of the house and there was no back door. It looked like a recent collapse had been cleared up and what seemed to be the kitchen area had no roof at all, and not much in the way of walls. Still the front was OK … we thought. Or did we. I'm not sure we were even looking. We were taken over by the romance or by the English habit of leaving our brains behind when we came out house hunting.

Maria Luisa led us through the back of the house and down an overhanging, prettily rustic but mostly destroyed walkway to a little door in the left hand wall. We stepped through a kissing gate type door into the back garden which was very small indeed and dog-legged off to the side of the main house plot. There were 2 more buildings. One a small half level 'nave' (like a workshop) and another two storey house. It was enormous but completely collapsed. So much so that we didn't dare enter it. The site was pretty big. It was clearly a lot of 'real estate' for your money but really, not a lot of house.

Why on earth then did we fall in love with it? To this day I don't know. But we did. I think it was the site which is central in the village. Maybe it was the weather, the chatty neighbours, the view of the hillside. The totally enclosed garden? It was all of these things. What it wasn't was any kind of liveable home.

Of course we did make an offer. But it was rejected. A higher amount was asked but we had to refuse as we just didn't have enough money. The owners then came back with a counter offer which was lower and included a deferred payment of 4,000 of the total for 2 years. So all was agreed. We used a lawyer of course (a friend of a friend) and returned a month later with a deposit of 2,000 while the checks were done.

In May I had a fair at Soest in the Westphalia region of Germany. I had been going for a couple of years and it had become a favourite of mine, as well as usually pretty successful. The pretty tourist town of Soest was all historic half timbered ancient houses with lovely little bars and restaurants. I also realised it was my brother Howard's 50th birthday that year. Since we barely saw Howard in a decade because he lived in Frankfurt, I called my other brother and my sister to see if there was any chance of us surprising him on his 50th. Derek said there was, but Steph was in Australia and it was a very long and expensive journey.

We gathered together a picnic basket full of English "goodies" for a birthday present. I even had a tablecloth embroidered with a happy birthday message. Howard, known these days as Howie was totally unaware of our plans and very surprised when we turned up at his girl-friend Geraldine's flat on his birthday. Geraldine was, of course, in on it. I stayed on at Howie's a few more days and then a friend Iris Bodenbender took me up to Soest in her lovely red sports car.

Very soon, it seemed, it was the middle of July when we had promised Antonio and Maria Luisa we'd return to Spain to buy the house. We decided to take my daughter Kira with us so that she could get a feeling for the place. I was beginning to realise that Kira was feeling some negative thoughts towards Spain. My fault really. I'd had conversations with her where I told her yes, we would go there one day but she wasn't to worry, we wouldn't go until she was older and living on her own. I hadn't really realised how her 15 year old mind would calculate that as too soon and she started saying rebellious things like "I don't care. You can go now if you want". Even though I was still constantly making mistakes as a parent I did realise that her words belied her real feelings. I wished I'd kept the Spanish dream to ourselves for a while longer. My habit of telling the truth had often been more destructive than I'd intended. It was too late to worry about that now. The cat was out of the bag. I hit upon the idea of taking her dad Steve with us. Steve was newly single and in need of a holiday so we said if he bought the plane ticket for himself, we would pay all the accommodation expenses so that he could share a room with Kira. It suited everyone and did make it a lot easier for Kira.

We arrived in Malaga in the middle of a July heat-wave and had to stay overnight in a Hostal near the airport chillingly named the "Hostal Terminal". We'd stayed there before but the name always made us laugh. Every time we stayed there we joked that this time was bound to be our last.

It was late when we spilled out into the still scorching streets in search of some food that Kira and Steve would eat. Both being extremely picky almost to the point of phobic. As we crossed the deserted street a large beetle scuttled across in the other direction. It was like a scene from a movie. It wasn't a cockroach, but it might as well have been.

The day before the house purchase we'd had to fiddle around at the bank because they couldn't give us a cheque without moving our balance to the Aracena office. Tired and crotchety, we'd headed off to Fuenteheridos to show Kira and Steve one of our pretty little local towns. Fuente meaning spring and herido meaning injuries or wounds, the waters are reputed to be healing. It was hotter than hell outside though. I was already beginning to realise that in order to keep everyone happy I was having to pay for endless rounds of ice cream for Kira and Frank and beers for Steve to keep them not only hydrated but in reasonable moods and I was also going to have to do all the translating because nobody else was going to make an effort to speak even a word of Spanish. I was hot too and very frustrated and at one point threw a strop. I slammed the money on the bar table and said "You guys work it out between yourselves". I went down the steep steps to the "Fuente de Doce Canas" (Spring with 12 pipes) to cool my head, my throat and my temper and yes, it felt healing to me. Fuenteheridos was to become a very important source of drinking water for us over the next few years and the fast flowing taps of cool clear water always do clear my mind of stress.

The next day it was off to the notary's office in Aracena, We were supposed to meet with the English guy, (or was he Scottish) Craig, whose guest house we were staying at in Castano del Robledo. He and his wife had starred in one of the TV episodes of "No Going Back". Their lives really were as complicated and chaotic as they looked to be on the programme. We really should have taken note of the repetition of the phrase "This wasn't the way it was supposed to be" and maybe drawn a few parallels. We didn't, and today we were embarking on our own journey. There was to be no going back for us either and, although I was getting better at Spanish, this was way too important to leave to chance. So I asked Craig to come along to give us some translation support and bunged him an extra 50 Euros for his effort. Craig turned up eventually just as I was getting very nervous indeed.

We were due to meet our lawyer there too. But there was a hiccup. He was late too. Very late. Our appointment time was passing and if the doors closed it would be for the weekend. Not just a normal weekend but a long weekend. A "puente" (a bridge). This is when Spaniards take extra holidays to fill in between planned fiestas and the closest weekend. It looked like we were going to be stuffed and so were the sellers. Even these crazy Brits weren't about to complete without our lawyer.

Finally we heard that he was on his way and we asked the notary to wait, which he kindly did. It seems our lawyer's girlfriend had been mugged the night before in Seville and had been in hospital with a dislocated shoulder after having had her handbag dragged from it. We'd been warned before about gangs who operated in the quieter plazas in central Seville and had always been very careful when in the tourist areas, once ducking back out of a little plaza near the Alcazar when we saw a suspicious looking group of men, one of whom carried a long stick.

The sellers came along as a family. Maria Luisa, her husband Antonio and their granddaughter Natalia who must have been around five or six at the time. They were all dressed in their Sunday best. Our bankers cheque was ready and the process began. It was quite informal but legally binding. And of course we understood hardly a word. We had wanted to do everything totally legally.

No under the table payments or anything like that. There was a problem though. Legally all payments had to be made by cheque from a Spanish Bank account to prevent money laundering I suppose. That was okay, but there was the small matter of the deposit we'd already paid ... in cash. It looked like we were going to fall at the last hurdle.

Suddenly we came up with an idea. The price of the house went down by the 2 thousand. We were paying the full price there and then. Only mildly naughty, and needs must. The sellers were warned that they may or may not ever get the extra 4,000 from us that we'd agreed as a delayed payment, but that they couldn't take the house back. They said they trusted us and all went smoothly. We got our keys to the Spanish dream/ nightmare. Of course we did pay the money we owed, almost exactly 2 years later.

We went down to the bar with Antonio, Maria Luisa and Natalia and bought them a drink. We already felt like friends.

It wasn't long before a tiny, permed little old lady from down the street took us to one side and had a bit of a grumble. She told us the house should have been hers and it was wrong that it had been left to Maria Luisa by her uncle. I nodded and shook my head at appropriate points. We'd checked. It was the seller's when we bought it and that's all that mattered. But inheritance law here is complicated and one house can be owned by a number of people. Often houses lie empty and crumbling because family members can't agree, or simply can't be found. And old disputes have a long half-life.

We were a bit disappointed when we went to the house to take a look. We'd asked if all the antiques could be left for us, but it seemed old Papa Antonio had had all the antique terracotta urns removed from the property before we arrived. We forgave him because it's very much the Spanish way to stiff your neighbours in any way you can. And Antonio didn't know us from Adam at the time. He was pretty suspicious of us for quite a while but over the years 'Papa' showed us the soft side of himself and his toothless smile could light up the room. He was a big man with a big heart. And Maria Luisa we learned was a small fairly timid woman with an even bigger one.

There wasn't much left of the bits and bobs of antique-y stuff except a wonderful old door lock with a huge old key and a copy made in brass. This bore a label 'Don Rafael' and we soon learned that Don Rafael was the uncle who had left the house to his favourite niece Maria Luisa. We also found a huge picture of the old family and a box of receipts dating back to the 1940s. We passed those on to Maria Luisa. She told us Rafael's grandmother had once lived in the house and lived to the grand old age of 105, which was a good omen we thought. Later we heard more about Don Rafael and everyone said he was a particularly careful, tidy man who never married. The house was a shop throughout all this time and many village folk still remember shopping there, and just hanging out in the shop.

We were now owners of a substantial plot of paradise. But the torrential rains later that year were to make it even less of a house and more of a plot as the old adobe (mud block) walls crumbled away. Still, out of sight, out of mind. After the house purchase was complete we took Kira and her dad down to Punta Umbría. There was a hot Saharan wind coming in from the sea but still Punta always held a charm for me from my first visit for its long golden beaches and its wonderful seafood and many heladerías (ice cream shops). Its still our favourite seaside town and we nip down the hour or so trip a handful of times a year.

A little later that year I took my first trip to Northern Ireland to give some classes to the miniatures group in Jayne Mcclenaghan's church. I know things have changed a bit, or rather a lot but I still had to get over the idea I learned during my childhood in the late 60s and early 70s that Northern Ireland was full of bombs which went off on a daily basis. The truth was very far from my preconceptions. And where Jayne lived was a peaceful, small, rural town. Much like the west of England. Green and lovely. I did see banners painted on the sides of houses, a reminder that people still held passionate views and that problems were just held at bay through sheer force of community will.

It reminded me how important putting time and patience into our community was. By now however, I was feeling we'd done quite a lot more than our fair share. I know it is a common problem in communities that a very few people do all the work. I also knew not to go for any 'top jobs in the community and was quite happy to have Roger as the Neighbourhood watch figurehead even though we disagreed more often than we agreed. Roger was tireless and even though he had a terribly bad back had often helped us out in the garden of both the house, and the church building. I kept having to rein him back in both his physical exploits and the habit he had of extrapolating relationships between the historical occupants of the house just because some names were the same. Many was the time we argued and I refused to call someone a relative until more proof was produced. After all, that historical data wasn't going anywhere now.

I felt I owed Roger some gratitude and respect at least though. So I passed on two of the four almost new Italian leather sofas. He really deserved them to rest his poor back. The other two went to my son Dom for the new house he'd just bought in Leeds. I was beginning to feel it was time to step even further back from Community work and get on with my businesses. I certainly had taken on too much with the craft centre, especially during the street party where it became the place where we displayed old photographs and history. The street could have done with keeping a place like that in its very heart, but I had to keep reminding myself that this was no longer my worry. The pull of Spain was strong and the recent arrival of techno-greeks in the house next door was driving us to distraction. Not for the last time we wondered which was going to be better, soundproofing, or selling up.

5

An Insanely Busy Year

The second week In January 2005 we made our first trip in what turned out to be a really hectic year for us.

We visited Puebla de los Infantes, Spain, for the wedding of our new friend Cristina (daughter of the lady who sold us our house) and her novio (fiancé) Juan Manuel, a well builder. How many of those do you get in England? We had imagined that the weekend would feel rushed. Spain worked its magic, especially with the siesta dividing morning and evening and the "two days for the price of one" feeling kicked in instantly.

Maria Luisa took me by the arm maternally and sat me next to her in the church. Being a humble little woman she decided against the big mantilla and posh frock that was usual for the mothers of bride and groom and opted for more simple attire. I had agonised over my clothing because the last time I'd been in a catholic church was when I was 7 and it was almost the law that you wore a hat in church. I'd bought a hat but of course it didn't suit me. Nor did the winter trouser suit that I'd bought for my son's 'passing out' and thought would do for the wedding too. The day was fine, warm and sunny.

The wedding itself was simple and mercifully short and, it goes without saying, the bride was beautiful. The wedding feast went on all afternoon and evening, with a seemingly endless number of courses of things I had never tried before and Frank was never going to try. I learned the lovely expression 'tiquis miquis ' (fussy) and have found it a quite useful 'get out of jail free card' in awkward social situations when someone is trying, yet again, to foist ham - based Andalucían specialities on strictly vegetarian Frank. My first experience of a Spanish wedding was unforgettable and I particularly remember being taken on to the dance floor by one of the young musicians. I didn't protest too loudly!

The next morning we were lucky enough to meet up with the family and take a traditional Spanish breakfast of churros con chocolate. Or in my case con cafe-con-leche. Churros are an unsweetened doughnut mix which is piped in huge swirls straight into the huge cone-shaped fryers. Chocolate, pronounced like 'latte', is a thick, sweet hot chocolate drink almost always taken with churros. Then we took a trip across country towards Córdoba hoping to meet up with Quique who was fairly recently married. We were waylaid by the sight of Almodovar castle and the stories of how it was rebuilt. The weather was amazing and we picnicked on the hillside on the most delicious rosemary flavoured olive oil crisps, Spanish made Havarti and chocolate bars. I pointed out that all we was missing were the "lashings of ginger beer" but a Fanta de Limon was almost as good!

We reached Córdoba mid-siesta. At 17 degrees in mid January it felt like heaven. It was such a rushed visit we really can't say much about it except that we'll be back to see its wonderful historic buildings and bridges. And our Hotel (Tryp) was very comfortable and really inexpensive. We didn't get to meet up with Quique, who, it turned out, lived an hours drive away, where he was suffering with a very bad cold. I don't suppose it was improved by the record low temperatures Córdoba experienced just a couple of weeks later. It seems true winter in Andalucía doesn't happen until late January.

Sabrina had contacted me about the first Miniaturitalia which she was organising in Milan. I had helped her with some translations and agreed to go in February. Our 'neighbours' at this fair were John and Hazel. So of course much fun was had by all, especially in the evenings which were spent imbibing too much 'Grappa', an Italian drink introduced to us by Jan Van den Doel and enjoyed, maybe a little too much, by all. We had brought Kira with us to Milan, with the promise of taking her to Venice for the tail end of the Carnivale. She spent most of the weekend in the hotel room. She was a bit on the teenage-grumpy side. She said she was doing her homework and actually I could believe it. It was exam year for Kira and she was a very hard working girl. I found out later she was having a very hard year emotionally as well, in very many ways that I didn't know about at the time. Carnivale was a bit overwhelming but camp enough to be fun. The weather was absolutely freezing though so although I did buy Kira and me a mask and cloak each, we went out for a short promenade with our teeth chattering the whole time. You couldn't move for people posing and people clicking and it was difficult to fully enjoy the ambience for cameras.

Later that same month we were back with the Dowd family again, this time at the annual 'live' British Miniatures Weekend for the online Minis4all group organised by John and Hazel. For the BMW weekend I decided I wanted to come up with a new idea that used Liquid Fimo and moulds and which couldn't be produced as easily with any other material. I'd already used it for moulding false teeth using white tinted Liquid Fimo for the teeth, baking lightly and then adding pink for the gums. I always get creative when something is very much on my mind and my old teeth were costing a lot around that time. This time I wanted to do this as an exercise in producing an idea for the first time and experimenting live. A sort of live "Challenge Angie" of my own making. That meant no previous practise and, of course, a new idea.

By the time we arrived at Walsall I still hadn't got that new idea. I'm not used to panicking where miniatures are concerned ... well, what would be the point? So after a first evening of good company and creative ideas flowing I went to bed and slept on it. Great for creativity ... fatal for sleep. In the middle of the night I did my "oh dear I'd better get out of bed and write this down before I forget it" routine. Sometimes sleep wins the argument and I know I've forgotten as many ideas as I've realised. This time I knew it was important so I jumped out of bed and scribbled "rocket lollies" on a piece of paper. Then I went back to sleep.

The beauty of mould making is you can make moulds using just about anything as an original. You can model originals using a firm material like wax for instance. Or, as I do, just using Fimo. You do have to bake the master before making the mould. You can 'archive' work you've been doing by making a mould from one piece of work and then make a second and improved next generation. You can do this as many times as you like and each time make a new mould from the improved master. This was how I made the master for my 'false teeth' and also for ice cream. I borrowed a Phillips head screwdriver for the first master and then explained how to modify it. The three layer rocket lollies were a great success with the students adding as many ideas as I took to the group. Whew I'd sailed close to the wind on that one!

This Arnhem fair (Holland) was my first drive abroad. In fact it was my first very long drive anywhere having passed my driving test just the year before, and I'd only had my new 4 yr old car month or two. I really hadn't a lot of confidence yet and I was doing it on my own! I travelled across on North Sea Ferries with once again the lovable Hazel and John Dowd, who were beginning to feel like family. John was, of course, regaling us with very entertaining stories, as is his wont. Over a few years I did hear a few stories more than once but he never lost his sparkle as a raconteur. Still, I wondered how often Hazel had to hear the same tales!

There was an annoying piano player in the bar. At first we thought it might be nice to have some entertainment. But as the conversation increased in volume the piano player cranked up his volume too. At one point in the evening John threatened to go over and thump his fist on the piano and say in his slightly Merseyside accent "Yaow are too Laowd". He had us all in hysterics. Maybe the large glass of wine helped. I was beginning to consider John a bad influence along with Pat Kay, a feisty Lancashire butcher's lass who was getting to a certain age (maybe around the age I am now) and was also fond of a large wine and a laugh. Pat could also tell an entertaining story or three.

To be fair John had cautioned against drinking too much and I thought it was because of the swell. I was horrified by how early we were woken up. We'd lost an hour of course and I think we were woken at 7am European time which was 6 British time. But I'd failed to take into account the change to British Summer time which meant it was 5am to this Englishwoman! I could now see why John said don't drink too much as you could certainly still be drunk at that time of day driving off the boats.

John and Hazel offered to be in a convoy with me and I'm sure they saved my life, or at least my psychological balance on that trip. A couple of times I lost them and called Hazel through the bluetooth headset that I'd bought as a precaution. It really proved its worth although I'm not sure I ever used it again. The fair was held in a great big hangar-type building with a cafe in the upstairs part where I gave my workshop. It was a seriously smoky hole as all the cigarette smoke from the diners mixed with that rising from down below in the hall. A couple of years later smoking was banned. Good job too. It's no surprise to me with exhibition halls like that that many musicians and performers die from cancer. Certainly after a couple of smoky visits followed by laryngitis each time, I was quite prepared not ever to do the Rijnhalle again.

As Frank wasn't with me I'd asked around if anyone could help. Klara, who often helped Anja Van den Doel (a wonderful paper flower maker and friend), came to help me at the fair. Along one wall of the Rijnhalle was a raised platform with several food outlets and Klara introduced me to the so called "Danish hot chocolate" which was normal hot chocolate with a huge blob of vanilla ice cream plopped in and a swirl of cream on top. Sucked through a straw it was a really interesting experience, hot and cold coming through the same straw! I never found "Danish hot chocolate" in all my visits to Denmark though. Our evening get-togethers were always fun. Several of the exhibitors, including me, relied on Jan (Anja Van den Doel's husband) to book our hotel rooms and organise the evening meal. He was pretty good at this job, having great organisational skills and a Dutchman's eye for a bargain That year we were staying at at a lovely rural hotel in Nijmegen called the Golden Tulip. The evening meal after the first night was just around a kilometre down the road. It was far enough to drive and so I took my car. I was so unused to being a driver that during the meal I completely forgot that I had my car with me and not only had one glass of wine but also ordered a second before I suddenly realised. I'm ashamed to say I did drive back to the hotel and I know that I shouldn't have. Maybe I would have been under the limit but its by no means certain and I am very easily affected by alcohol. I've never made that mistake since, fortunately. The very next Arnhem fair we stayed at the same Hotel. One night I was actually stopped and breathalysed on the same road. Of course this time my reading was zero.

On the journey home I had a bit of a crisis. My car boot suddenly popped open, scattering papers all over the carriageway behind me and frightening the life out of me! I was really worried about losing my rear convoy, John and Hazel having given me dire warnings "not to go to Den Bosch". It was before widespread use of 'sat navs' and we certainly didn't have one. But John had seen the crisis unfold and pulled in behind me. Boot down, pull off and we were away again. I was so glad we were still together because the route into the coastal areas was absolute hell with trucks right up my rear end frightening me to death. It was a baptism of fire for driving abroad and of course I was glad a year later when we decided to take my little 'fez' to Spain, that my major driving experience had been in that car, and in Europe.

The one day Pudsey fair in Leeds was in mid April. It was and is a packed little fair and for us a very good fair being low on expenses and high on visitor numbers. I was already, in April, beginning to see a dive in my stock levels but I was starting to sell a few repeatable items like moulds and demonstrating their use kept me busy chatting and kept Frank busy with sales.

Farum fair was also in April and we opted to go for a second time. I remember that was the organiser Marion's last year. The loss of her lovely husband Max had knocked the stuffing out of her I think. And we missed him too. Once again I was asked to give workshops and we did a basket of coconuts and apples with autumn leaves. I also did some heart shaped cakes that year which was my first foray into teaching using semi-liquid Fimo. This was a lot more enjoyable than I had imagined and I was worried that it wasn't "Angie Scarr" enough because it didn't contain any caning techniques. I keep thinking I have to teach more and more complicated ideas every time but sometimes it's fun just to throw a load of ideas at the table and sit back and watch the class create.

That's very much what happened. The principle was that we'd all learn to make just the right thickness of 'icing'. Not too runny so that it all fell off the cake, but not so thick that it had to be sculpted. In this case we were thickening the Liquid Fimo with Deluxe Materials Shovelled Snow and it was a bit of a non-Newtonian mix. That is to say it had a habit of appearing thick but then suddenly deciding to run when touched. It was a lovely bright sugary-looking mix though. Once we'd got the mix applied to the moulded heart shaped cakes we just had fun with fruit slices and beads etc. The girls were very inventive and I pretty much sat back and watched the fun.

We had booked into a guest house on the side of the lake. It turned out to be a log cabin. We found it a bit dingy downstairs in the basement and a bit strange, being covered in dusty Norwegian troll dolls! The owner was a very petite pretty lady in her late 60s who was having a romance with a former sweetheart from her days as an air hostess when he was a pilot … and married. He was now a widower and she was once again a giddy girl! But the basement of her house where we slept was downright weird for us bright light loving Brits. It was all what Frank refers to as "woodity" and every lamp was half covered with another piece of wood which made it cosy … but dingy. It didn't help that tacked all the way round were strange troll-like dolls. I learned later that our hostess was actually originally Norwegian and that was the kind of style I should expect from Norwegians. It wasn't to my taste at al, although the rest of the place was delightful.

The fair wasn't as good as the year before because we were in a gymnasium and there wasn't really any 'traffic'. I decided to give Farum a miss from then on for a few years.

Since I'd been to Alicante the year before and enjoyed it I decided to give it another go although this time without the additional workshop. It was actually in the heart of Alicante, where the town was much nicer than I'd imagined. This was another fair done without Frank but I had my very kind new friend from last year Iris Broughton to help out. The fair was modest but fun to do and the first night back at my hotel, which was also very modest, I had my first taste of the dreadful predictive text on my new Nokia phone. Frank had warned me not to use the phone but to text instead. Unfortunately all I could get was Sporrr Sporrr and some other gobbledygook. The more I tried to use it the more ridiculous its words became until I ended up rolling around on the bed in hysterics just trying to write "How do you turn off the f***ing predictive text?!!!"

After the second day's trading some of us had a pre-dinner walk along the promenade. This promenade was full of illegal traders with sheets on the floor that they could just gather up at the first sign of the Policia or Guardia. Hazel, Iris and I bought a scarf each from one of the girls, and were quite amused to see the game of cat-and-mouse between the traders and the police. If the police arrived the traders scattered like leaves blown in the wind.

We then looked for somewhere to eat and that was

the first time I'd ever encountered the other side of John Dowd. The hungry side is not a pretty sight! Fortunately a Dowd properly fed with almost burned steak (and nothing else will do) is a very happy and delightful animal. We decided to try a suckling pig between 4 girls. Hazel, Pat Kay, Iris and of course me. Although it was the most delicious pork we'd ever tasted, the sight of that tiny piglet made us feel very guilty and we all vowed that we'd never have it again. But I can still taste it and I'm having difficulty with the never again bit!

Then John, Hazel and myself went down to the beach with a bottle of very sweet Moscatel and really got rather drunk. Now I rather suspect Hazel imbibed less than John and I, but she was certainly as jolly as we were and I named them 'the old reprobates'. A name they seemed to revel in and carried with them for a few more years until John's heart attack forced him to calm down a little bit. But not too much. I think John, like me, hardly drinks at all. Let loose in the world of miniatures and miniaturists he can keep up with any one of us.

After the fair was over I had decided to use a few extra days away from home to relax and think. Each day I went down to the Internet café, read my email and sent up my work from the day before. Each afternoon I went down to the beach with a swimming costume, a pen and paper and enough money to pay for sunbed and parasol hire. It's a hard life! I did finally get down to the basic plans for my second book so I still claim it was a working holiday.

Soest in Germany was the start of my ridiculous itinerary for June, which saw me doing 14 flights in 28 days. I'd been invited to the AMEA conference in Tasmania and yet I wasn't going to miss Soest fair, so I enveloped the whole Australia trip within a German one. Once again I flew into Frankfurt and visited my brother Howie.

Because Frank wasn't coming with me on this trip Howie came up on the train with me to the Stadthalle in Soest to help me out. It was a really lovely excuse to spend more time with my brother again. We'd been very good friends as little kids but really had grown apart in the following years. In fact all my siblings had scattered (was it something I said?) in the intervening years and we rarely saw each other anyway. Even less so after our parents died. I'm convinced that absence makes the heart grow colder in reality. Certainly it's very much easier to be real friends when you have time to re-draw your boundaries with family that you haven't seen for years and my family were so far apart and so rarely saw each other that we didn't have any kind of shared narrative left.

Soest became my favourite miniatures fair for all the time it was in that tiny beautiful town. Yes, the Dowds were there again and this time the drug of choice was ice cream! It had become a bit of a "thing" that all the traders ended up, after their meals at different bars and restaurants, in the ice cream parlour in the central town square. This ice cream shop had all the normal choices but also made some mega large ice cream sundaes, ice cream pizzas and even ice cream spaghetti complete with red sauce "a la bolognese".

After the fair and probably several kilos heavier, I went back to Frankfurt with Howie for the first flight to Australia for the AMEA conference. This year it took place in Tasmania. My 2 week, whirlwind, 4 state tour of Australia started in Sydney where after a double-hop through Dubai, I took a day of rest for the total spatial and temporal confusion of the jet lag. I then took another very small plane out to Hobart in what the locals call 'Tazzie'. On the plane I met up with some New-Zealanders who recognised me and told me what I should expect. Hobart is a pretty town which struck me as British seaside-like, which of course it is. Its picturesque Victorian clap-board houses were very colonial-looking. The weather was very English too, a bit cloudy blustery and drizzly.

Jan Jones picked me up and took me around the views of Hobart and we took breakfast there. Jan was incredibly busy during the conference (as was her sister Merrie and the rest of the committee). But Jan still took time to be the perfect hostess. After the workshops and fair she took me out for a day trip round her area and to the wildlife park where the wombat lives, along with Tasmanian devils, which really were as horribly vicious looking as their name suggests, kangaroos and koalas etc. as you would expect. One thing that surprised me is that if you're lucky enough to get to stroke the drugged looking Koalas, you find your hands smell very strongly of eucalyptus. Apparently it is quite toxic and the quantities they eat would kill a man and certainly seem to stun them. They really looked like drugged up animated teddy bears.

My first visit after the Tasmania Conference was to Andrea Currie's place in Melbourne. I taught classes in her own teaching room at her home and I really think that her home teaching room influenced me in my later decisions about my Spanish house. Andrea and her family looked after me so well. I'd been nervous about the trip but Andrea and her husband made it all so much easier than I thought. We went for a trip round Melbourne and pressed our noses up against cake shop windows. Andrea had been on a very successful diet so we didn't actually go in. Pah!

One ulterior motive for my accepting the invitation to Australia was was to get to see my little 'sis' on her own home turf in Perth. Though I've never quite forgiven Steffie for leaving England just after voting for Margaret Thatcher's first term! When you're apart for such a long time the relationship takes a bit of re-making like any other relationship. Steffie and I had been apart for most of two decades. She was living partly in Perth outskirts and partly in a little house deep in the forests of "Dwelly" (Dwellingup) with her new, older partner (later her husband). I had a couple of days of classes booked in Perth.

Steph came with me on the first day but I had to ban her from subsequent classes after the first time as, just as my mother had when she was at my first ever class, she kept stepping in to help, explaining the next stage before I'd got to it, and totally ruining my timing! Steffie had unwittingly taught me something new about teaching. I felt really bad about saying she couldn't come. I needed to find a way of explaining why. That meant I really had to think about what was happening and why a class didn't work if one advanced student was trying to lead the way.

A class is a performance and you have to treat it with care as to when you reveal the next step and never forget that it's the element of surprise that makes it exciting. Yes. I banned my poor sister, who was only trying to help, much to her consternation, but at future classes I learned how to deal with the 'advanced' member of the class. I found usually they tripped themselves up making a big mistake because of racing ahead, leaving them with egg on their face and me to get on with teaching my way! In fact in the end I decided that this approach too was uncomfortable for the poor unwitting "stooge", so I took to explaining at the beginning of the class what would inevitably happen to the most gifted student. Then when it happened that person usually smiled benignly, knowing they were clearly the most gifted because they had fallen straight into the trap.

After the classes were over we could get on with the 'sister time' we so needed. I love the sea and couldn't resist a splash when Steph took me to the seaside town of Freemantle. Of course June is winter in Australia, the temperature was on the low side but bearable. The surfers were probably having more fun than British surfers in June! Steph came back on the fairly long flight to Sydney with me to extend the time we'd have together.

The class was held in Liz Barnes' place in the suburbs. Liz showed me some of her lovely decoupage work with postage stamps. One that I particularly remember featured a tree frog. It was really cute. I'd never really encountered decoupage before and was surprised at how beautiful it could be.

The next day Steph and I went for a day in town. The eateries along Darling harbour were a fishy feast, displayed on cake stands overflowing with seafood. I wasn't into the idea of oysters so Steffie snaffled all those, but I couldn't get enough of the fresh prawns. We went shopping on our full bellies and bought some opals for me and my daughter Kira. I also found a cute stuffed wombat which became a great aeroplane pillow and made the air crew laugh on the way home. Steph and I parted in the airport for another five years.

Summer in Campofrío

That year we decided to spend a whole three weeks in Spain. My excuse was that it would give me the time to work on my book. Franks excuse was that he could work on a website generation program. Three weeks of bliss. Work done … very little! We flew into Malaga, picked up a tiny little ford Ka rental (which we found we rather liked) and travelled the coast road and then inland to Ronda where we spent an evening enjoying the beautiful and dramatic scenery. Our first stop the next day was Mazagon near Huelva. Huelva is the capital of the Andalucían province of the same name in the most westerly corner of southern Spain. We met our new landlords, picked up the keys and signed the contract for our rental house which, until then, we'd never seen. It was chosen for us and the price was negotiated by our friend Quique. We settled on 270 Euros a month and initially we signed a contract for 6 months but we ended up staying 5 years.

Really it was an awful little 1980s box of a house. Pretty from the outside but totally impractical. It had been built with the cheapest of materials and it was cold in winter and hot in summer. If that sounds like the expected situation it's worth remembering that Andalucíans know very well that good insulation is key to a comfortable existence. Not only did the house appear to have no insulation at all but also the fireplace was set at right angles to the room and produced almost no heat, no matter how heavily stoked the fire in winter. In summer we quite simply baked. The windows were cracked, badly fitted in metal frames and the doors were gappy with broken handles. The blinds were showing their 30 years too. Maintenance just didn't seem to be something the owners had looked at and the gas cooker reeked of gas. But we were to find out all these problems way down the line.

As soon as we'd offloaded our luggage in the rental house we went to visit 'our' house. We had by then already realised it was going to be a demolish and rebuild project, after the really heavy rains of the winter before. Of course, while we wanted it to stay up- it fell down. Now we wanted it to fall down- it' had stayed up.

Typical! We knew it was time to make a decision. The father of our lawyer from last year was an architect and we asked him to come over and take a look at our house and give us his opinions on a renovation. He told us it was possible and we asked him to measure up and give us his ideas. Overnight after dreaming of crumbling walls I rang him up and cancelled the contract. What we did know by now was that whatever we did, we were going to need some money. Frank persuaded me that we should put the Coltman Street house on the market. There was some sense to his plan because the house we'd paid 10 thousand for was now worth 120 thousand.

I very reluctantly agreed. We were still struggling at times with problems on the street. The new owners of the house next door to us had put some druggies in one of the ground floor flats and we weren't sure we had the stomach for a fight to get them out. We'd also, not so long before had a few problems with noise next to our bedroom from some nice but loud students we called the "technogreeks". They'd moved out but to top it all the local council had decided to house far too many men in one of their properties causing some racial and sexual tension with one of the local families. Although we had organised a successful meeting with the council, the police, the community leaders and the family to defuse the situation, it was indicative of how difficult and sensitive such tensions can be. There's nothing like the fear of loss of value to motivate you to sell. I loved my house on Coltman street. It was going to be harder for me than it was for Frank who wasn't really a DIY-er at the time. He was not as heavily emotionally or physically invested in the 'palace' we'd been making.

We also had some new and rather smelly tenants in the Campofrío house. They call them 'Golondrinas' here. Well, they would, if they could speak the King's

Spanish. Unfortunately they take out every consonant that might help you to understand what they're saying and like everything else it comes out just a string of impossible vowels. Golondrina would sound something like goia (or goya). A bit like an Essex local saying 'something like that' comes out as 'so-i-ay-a'. They're just like that here. Maybe Essex people would find it easier to learn the Andalucían accent. Well I say Andalucían, but if truth be told every village has its own dialect and often even other Spaniards don't understand them at all. Here in the village there are some people whose accent is so thick that even their own neighbours don't understand them. Add to that the words picked up from Portugese or from the original English owners of the Riotinto Mines and you just don't stand a chance.

A neighbour gave me a 'palabrario' of local mining words which are often tainted with English. For example they have a word pronounced Ka-keh which means a type of cake! Not to be confused with Kaki (Sharon fruit). Frank says that if you understand the first word of the sentence you stand some chance. But if you miss the vital clue, you drown in a sea of vowels. Then they shout at you and speak faster in an attempt to help you understand. Since Frank doesn't like to make a fool of himself he gives up at that point. And that point comes far too often and far too early in almost every conversation and is the main reason why it took around a dozen more years for Frank to start to speak with any fluency at all.

Another thing that the Spanish do where the language has moved on because of social media, is simply re-do the spelling. So the word "estoy"(I am) simply becomes "toi" and would be spelled that way in graffiti or communications. Even people of my age do it, showing that it's not just text speak. "Na' is Nada (nothing) and 'no-ni-na' is a complete bastardisation of the language and means 'nothing at all'.

Our new tenants the 'Golondrinas' were swallows. Tiny low flying, swooping black and white birds. Very pretty to look at but they poo everywhere, their poo is very rank smelling, and they set up home wherever they want including inside 'our' house.

Under the eaves of most of the houses here are their little mud and spit nests. They are really cleverly constructed, rather like the pots that one of the guys at the ceramics club we had at 'Creative thinking'. They make really tiny balls of mud all squashed together and stuck to the 90 degree angle of the eaves. Their 'houses' are often decorated with lines of other colours. Almost as if they were deliberately artistically embellished. Many of our neighbours squish plastic bags under the eaves to deter them from even starting to build. Others simply wage war by knocking down the nests as soon as they start to appear.

Our 'family' all had their hairy little heads poking out of the nest and squawking whenever we were there, because mum couldn't get back to them with lunch when we were around.

Apart from that everything looked pretty much the same as it did when we were there last. Except we hadn't yet had the courage to look right in the back garden because last time we were there the wall of the big building looked really dangerous. And also I forgot to bring any sensible shoes and the dry grass is spiky.

Frank and I spent the first week just getting our basic needs together for the rented house. That included silly little things like a big mug for my tea, a bathmat etc. Then there were the larger expenses like shoes for me as I'd only brought sandals, and sandals for Frank who only brought sensible shoes. We needed a table each to work on, computer leads, a printer and a computer monitor. It seemed everyone had converted to flat screens except Frank. We spent most of the time taking little trips out to Aracena for some other little necessity for our new rental house, including gaffa tape to tape over the broken window panes which years later our landlords denied were already broken. Our favourite shop at the time we affectionately named 'The Bizarre'. A lot of shops were called Bazar and this one was called Bazar Carmen and looked for all the world like Baitsons auction house crossed with a pound shop. I bought piles of enormous white bath towels for five euros a time which was about £3.50 in those days.

We did manage to take in the Fiesta de Santiago (St James to us, or Sant Jacque in northern parts of Spain and France) which is always on the nearest weekend to the 25th July. Because Campofrío has the oldest Bullfight in Spain (after a scrap with Ronda over the title), as part of the fiesta, there is usually a bullfight. Sometimes there's a different session where the little sisters of the bulls get their own back. The 'valientes' of the pueblo, or more realistically the idiots that got smashed the night before and are still drinking, run around the bullring teasing the heifers and imagining that they are brave bullfighters. We called one plucky guy 'greenpants'. The score was equal. He ended up on his face his jeans dragged down revealing his undies. His friends diverted the heifer and all was well. We rather suspected the whole audience and the participants hadn't been to bed the night before. The mood was distinctly merry!

We had our first and last experience of an actual bullfight. I understood the spectacle and the fiesta atmosphere but I couldn't take what I saw as the torture by the picadors and the machismo of the bejewelled skinny and somewhat camp looking toreros, prancing around with the ears of the bull held in the air. I never went to another. The village is very proud of its bullring. It's certainly very rustic looking and over the next few years suffered some serious rain damage. Around this time the council started a project to build a bullfighting museum in the village. Not surprisingly that project never came to fruition, partly because of lack of funds and partly through lack of political will as the subject of the bullfight became more and more controversial. Whatever my views on bullfighting I think its a shame the project floundered. History and cultural tradition should always be respected, in a museum at least.

The fiesta culminates with the parade of Santiago (Saint James). The village folk parade an image of Santiago, who looks unnervingly like a young version of my ex-husband, through the streets of the village to the sound of a brass band and fireworks. The procession around the village took over an hour. We sneaked away to the Bar Encina for one of Cecelia's amazing solomillos (sirloin of Iberico pork) served with long sweet green fried peppers and chips for me, and just a plate of chopped local tomatoes, simply garnished with chunky sea salt and the delicious local oregano flowers, for Frank.

We were back in time for the end of the parade and the fireworks. Total cost including more than one round of drinks was around 8 euros in those days. I soon learned that my favourite drink was Tinto de Verano, red wine and lemonade over lots of ice. So easy to drink two and end up slightly tipsy! I'm a cheap date. All drinks cost one euro then and still, a dozen years later, usually just one euro, though some have very recently gone up to 1.30.

While we were in Campofrío, Juan Manuel and

Cristina came over and took us to see Las Ventas de Abajo, a deserted hamlet somewhere near Campofrío which we've never been to before or since. It was strange to see a village which was entirely deserted although someone had been doing up one building. We returned to Malaga via an overnight stop at la Puebla de los Infantes. It was a vertiginous drive up the side of a mountain into a plain that looks for all the world like an ancient caldera. On the road I saw that the cactus were in full fruit so I nipped out of the car to collect a few. I should have listened to Baloo and used the claw! I was picking needles out of my hands all the way to Cristina and Juan Manuel's place. This was before Cristina and Juan Manuel had any children so we stayed at their new house.

In August we were back in Spain yet again. This time at the Cubelles (pronounced 'Cubeyas') fair. We were invited to attend this fairly small fair near to Barcelona in this little seaside town. We accepted mainly because we wanted the excuse to visit Barcelona. We stayed in a really nice family-run hotel called Hotel Cesar in Villanova I Geltru. We really recommend it. If you visit and are offered a 'gastronomic offer' take it. The food is excellent and very good value. Even Frank, who is notoriously hard to please found several different dishes that he liked. We were deciding that in general Andalucía's gastronomic offerings were not as good as the ingredients they were made from, whereas in Barcelona the reverse seemed to be the case.

The fair was not busy, but not a disaster either. It was also very enjoyable especially as we spent the 3 hour lunch/siesta break on the beach. I washed the sand out of my hair each day in the sinks outside the 'loos' before the evening opening. We found ourselves hoping we could find an excuse to go back the next year. It was our first time in Barcelona and we absolutely loved it. We visited all the major tourist destinations including Las Ramblas, Park Guell, Casa Battló and the Sagrada Familia. We were enchanted and I could really understand why it was such a hot tourist destination. I vowed to bring Kira back there because I felt sure she would enjoy the culture and especially the subculture.

If you're visiting, watch out for the card sharks! We watched a very professional team take 150 euros from a gullible 'punter'. Even the 'members of the public' who appeared to be on the side of the punter, could be identified as plants when you knew what was going on. At one point the 'plant' stood up to the card shark demanding he gave the other guy his money and giving the punter a false sense of security for the bigger gamble to come.

Cecelia, my neighbour and brilliant cook from the Bar Encina once cautioned me against trusting people by telling me the Spanish saying which is like the first rule of con-artistry: "Hay un tonto para todo los dias. Solo hay que encontrar el tonto de hoy". There's an idiot for every day. You only have to find today's idiot. One day soon we were to become that day's idiot.

Strolling through Barcelona there were many memorable sights, smells and sounds but the most evocative was hearing a strange resonant melody from a distance, turning the corner and seeing this guy (Pedro Collares de Moraes) playing what looked for all the world like a small silver spaceship. It turned out to be a type of hollow steel drum. We sat for much longer than we intended and I particularly found it hard to tear myself away. I did buy a CD but I have no idea where it went.

There are some things you just got to do just because you can. I made a mould of the Gaudi paving stones using a HUGE amount of Silicone mould material. It was a waste because I never did anything with it.

Warning. If you have emetophobia please fast forward a couple of pages.

Leaving 'The Street'.

At the end of summer 2005 we did get a full price offer on the house and we prepared to leave behind all our hard work and the memories we'd built up over those last 5 years. I also very much regretted leaving the lovely kitchen Dave Whatt had made to my specifications, which had cupboard doors made up of a dozen or so drawing boards I'd bought at Baitsons Auction House for 50 pence each. Sadly the new owners lost no time in ripping my kitchen back out and re-converting our single house back into a number of flats.

There was our last street party and I put in a couple of hundred pounds towards it in an attempt to pay back for the help Mrs Wilson had given us over the years. There was a little regret leaving our big beautiful house. When Frank and I shut the door for the last time he gave me a hug and said "You created a beautiful home there Ange". That brought a big tear, but we were clearly following a "no going back" line.

Memories flood back of the battles with floorboards, plumbing and particularly with the garden where once again Roger helped me to remove the Japanese Knotweed and I proved you could keep it away with constant vigilance. I remembered the children's games Kira and Daisy used to play out there ... the silly songs. I remember building up a bank of soil and planting a screen of raspberries and a slope of strawberry plants which produced more fruit than we could ever eat. Then making a tiny little pond with a waterfall that I could look out on and listen to while I worked in my 'clean workshop'.

My first attempt at being a 'brickie' when I rebuilt

a pillar for the gate to our enclosed secret garden. The time that gate was carelessly left open and some local opportunist thief had crept through and put his hand through the back window to retrieve my beloved yellow chainsaw. And the bad smell in my office for a couple of weeks which at the time we were convinced was a dead rat under the floorboards until we ripped every one up and, not finding anything; put a whole bottle of anti-pong under there. These days I can't help thinking that smell should have been reported to the police, whenever I see one of those serial killer programmes … Ahh yes. That idea makes it easier to shut the door definitively on that period of our lives.

Then it was Arnhem again. This time Frank came with me, which would have been a relief but Frank didn't heed my dire warnings not to have a pint or two of cider before bed and as the swell became very pronounced (it was the worst crossing I ever experienced) the cider came back, all over the bathroom and part way into the bedroom. After which the queasy but semi-conscious Frank fell asleep, leaving me to clean up. I wasn't happy at all and the effort, the irritation and the heavy seas meant I didn't sleep at all that trip. This was the first of several times I had to clean up after Frank, not only at sea. He has developed a stomach which refuses even to try to hold on to anything which is undigested come bedtime. But he has no problem falling asleep straight after. In the last few years I've had to learn to be very strict with him about late night meals and drinks which is sometimes really difficult after late fairs. But we now know what triggers it and also I've put my foot firmly down about cleaning up afterwards!

This wasn't the last time either that Id have to look after someone who was feeling sick at a miniatures event.

Kira had become our best helpmate at Miniatura

and we paid her properly for a girl her age at a fiver an hour for 2 eight hour days, a nice little income for her and really well worth it for us. She was good with the customers and hard working adding up, packaging and taking money for the smaller orders.

This time we had bought Kira a sandwich from Sainsbury's on the way out … she'd chosen tuna and during the night after eating it she began to become a bit queasy. This got worse in the car on the way to the NEC. We assumed it was just car sickness so we gave her mints and carried on. Poor Kira spent the day in a worsening state and we had to take her to the sick bay where the poor little thing was sick over and over all day meaning not only didn't we have our best helper but I had to leave the stall for most of the day to look after her. We always said that on a good Miniatura, if I was demonstrating all day, our income was only limited by the time it took to process orders. Not having our little helper was a blow. Not having me as the saleswoman was a double blow. It was an appalling Miniatura but I assured Kira she was not going to miss out on her pay even though we'd missed out on ours. I wrote a very strongly worded letter to Sainsbury's and received by return of post a cheque for Kira's pay, which was what I'd asked for. It didn't cover our losses but I didn't ask for or expect that. Kira was happy enough but I know she'd rather have worked the weekend. And the customers missed her too.

Then it was time for my second Auning fair in Denmark. It felt like it would be a rest compared to the rest of the year. I went on my own, as fares to Denmark were quite expensive. And vegetarian Frank didn't fancy the in-house food. We were guests of the Family in their 'Kro' a guesthouse with added meals for the traders. The meals were cooked by Birthe's husband Jonny and he was a great chef. The food was really excellent. In Denmark it's common to have two courses at an evening meal swapping between starter and main and main and sweet course. All very well but I have a sweet tooth. Or at least I did in those days. All these wonderful Danish meals and crispy gooey Danish pastries between classes were not helping my expanding waistline any! On the other hand the customers were amazing and they half cleared my stall on the first day. I rang Frank up that evening and moaned. "There's nothing left on my stand but rubbish!" I needn't have worried, by the end of the second day my happy customers had cleaned that up too!

Not feeling myself.

By this stage in the year especially after Auning, we were very short of stock and I needed to try to keep production up for Pudsey on 12th November. I was working until midnight most nights and was absolutely wrung out. But we were committed so we went and I demonstrated. I was beginning to realise that with this many events there was a law of diminishing returns, but I thought if I redoubled my demonstrating efforts we would do OK in book sales. So we set up the tiny stand squashed up on the stage which was my customary spot. I had time to wander around and was rather annoyed to see another girl demonstrating peeled oranges with unbaked canes of her own making. I would have minded a little less if she wasn't showing an incredibly dangerous method of cutting the peels back. A little later someone come up to me and complain that the soft cane she had bought … from me (she said) at the last fair, didn't work. I didn't sell unbaked canes at the time so I knew something was going on. I took the other trader to one side and had rather a sharp word with her.

Later in the day I was in the swing of demonstrating some technique or other when a lady came up and smiled at me. "You're getting quite good aren't you?" she said. I smiled and thanked her. "You're nearly as good as that Angie Scarr" she continued. I thought she was joking so I laughed with her and replied "I hope I am as good as her". "Well, you're certainly getting there" She said. I continued what I thought was the joke and turned to Frank to bring him in on it "do you think I'm as good as your wife? What do you think … will I do?" The woman looked confused and at that point I realised she hadn't been joking. I leaned over and whispered to her with a smile "I am Angie". "No you're not" she said, clearly irritated "I know Angie very well and you're not her". "Well I was the last time I looked" I replied, thinking this had gone a bit too far. "Well", said the woman before turning on her heels and stalking off. "If you're Angie Scarr you've put on a LOT of weight!" I had, it was true. But I like to think that I had the last-laugh imagining her checking the programme to find that I was actually me and feeling perhaps a little embarrassed at her behaviour. I like to think it. But maybe she's got bigger problems than that.

She had a point of course, in between fairs and workshops, I had barely moved from morning until late at night for making miniatures, and writing about them. I only moved for cups of tea and the inevitable half pack of biscuits. Well, a cup of tea is too wet without a biscuit, or a piece of chocolate. And the second half of the pack is way too dry without another cuppa! I wasn't very self disciplined. So it wasn't long before my weight was mentioned again, though this time rather more kindly, especially as I was by now in my late forties. Aileen Tucker, who'd often helped me with snippets of information about the history of food had a daughter who worked with her on the business "Merry Gourmet".

Gail is a tall likeable girl rather like Miranda Hart in behaviour and with a similar slightly public school accent. We'd become friends over the years and she would often come over and buy a few mini prawns to add to her Tudor table settings. The next Miniatura she saw me and came over to greet me warmly. "My" she said looking me up and down "we are blooming aren't we!" - she paused for a half second which was enough time for me to realise what she was about to say. "Are we … ?" My reply was ready. "Yes … we're fat!" It's not often I say exactly the right thing at the right time and usually I have to make up replies like this later in my mind but I was pleased with this one. I had, at least started to develop a healthy attitude from my 'miniatures therapy' if not a healthy body. I was now no longer afraid of travelling which had been one of my previous phobias. How could I after all my recent trips!

The year ended with Madrid fair in late November and our house move to an expensive rental house in Swanland just in time for Xmas. That was a crazy year! I don't know why I thought Swanland was a good idea. I think it was because it was so far removed from the world of Coltman street, and partly I wanted to give Kira a glimpse of another life too. Plus it was a little way down the road towards West Yorkshire where Frank was getting more and more of his work some of which was teaching Cisco and Linux and some maintaining networks and writing database driven websites. The place we rented was way too expensive though and I soon wished I'd chosen somewhere cheaper. Sadly Kira was not at all fond of Swanland and chose to spend more and more time with her dad rather than take the long bus journey to her school back in Hull.

It turned out we weren't that fond of Swanland either, or of the bungalow itself which smelled very badly of curry. It had not been cleaned by the landlords prior to our moving and had moths in the carpets as well as significant damp and the garden was badly overgrown. Our later experiences with the landlords left us with a very depressing memory of Swanland which otherwise is a very pretty village. It wasn't the last time that a landlord left her property in an appalling state and then complained when we only partially improved on it!

I'm not sure how we did it, but we fitted in an end of year trip to Spain to see if we could find a builder, and we did. Quique suggested a builder who'd done a few jobs for him. Quique had just bought his own flat and after the 'promotor' (Spanish term for new construction owner) of his new development had 'bogged off' leaving several jobs uncompleted including the communal roadway. This former associate was the one who had finished the jobs, perhaps for a small, or large, extra gratuity. I should have heard alarm bells ringing even then, and yet we thought Jesus, pronounced hey-sus might just be our saviour.

Now I don't want to be too unkind about Jesus. But to be frank ... he was what my dad would have called a 'spiv'. He had a good team of men who came all the way down from Extremadura and who were known to us as the "Badajoz boys" and the architect he worked with was very thorough and professional, if a bit pricey. Jesus had a taste in expensive clothes, shiny shoes and big cars and was, he felt, 'on the way up'. He didn't realise we were just exactly what we said we were, on a very low and shrinking budget. Jesus was determined to milk the rich English for all they had. And we were naive at the time and it took us the next year and around 30,000 pounds (at that time nearly 45,000 euros) to wise up. I certainly wouldn't call him a thief; but he was 'sharp'.

6

Demolition And Design

If we wanted our commitments to lighten up for us during 2006 we were going to have to make cuts. I was already frazzled but things were about to ramp up to even more ridiculous levels.

My first fair of the year was supposed to be Milan in February, but having seen the price of airfares it was just impossible for us to go. Although the first year had been reasonable, there was no way we could afford 700 pounds in fares, plus the expensive hotels and food. So we cancelled the fair and waited for news that the demolition had got under way.

The problem we had was that we were waiting for the licence to allow us to demolish the old building. Then suddenly we were told demolition had happened while Jesus was still waiting for permission. I was irritated. This put us in danger of a denuncia (a legal report) or even a multa (a fine). And one of the owners of the house on one side knew it too. Jesus had found their address to talk about the shared walls only to be threatened with a denuncia if we didn't make good. This was to be the first of many such threats and I started to think of that neighbour as something of a bully. Of course at this time I didn't realise that Jesus was in the process of trying to get a large amount of money out of each of us at the same time, and my neighbours probably quite rightly sent him off with a flea in his ear. I did learn that some people just liked to use threats of a denuncia fairly randomly and at first I found them worrying, so I got into the habit of taking photographs of everything at every stage for proof that we'd always either had right on our side, or done the right thing. Or at least we'd always attempted to do the right thing.

We'd already met up with Pepe the architect and had agreed on a design. Here is a 'Spinglish' translation of the note we sent in very rudimentary Spanish, outlining our needs to our architect. What we hoped we were saying was something like this:-

"We want a house that's a little unusual with the living room and kitchen on the second floor to care for and use light and because I think we want the possibility of using the ground floor cool and open to the public to invite people for approximately 10 weeks of summer. During these weeks we are going to remain on the second floor.

Things we like: -

Light, air, simple things, simple tiles and white.

Simple and spacious bathroom. All quite cheap but not the cheapest. (Of fairly good quality/ functionality) Although we like wooden windows I think I can not afford the price - therefore I prefer to use metal or plastic. Windows should be quite spacious in offices and laundry room as well.

We use a lot of electricity and I think I need quite a big supply with lots of plugs.

We want a cinnamon (I meant conduit) for computers all over the left side of the house and offices and also into the living room on the second floor" This was accompanied by my scribbled idea of how the two floors might look.

Our architect must have understood what I was trying to say because he came up with a first design that was almost ideal and only needed a couple of tweaks to make it perfect. Also he'd added a light well which I hadn't thought of but which is the most attractive aspect of the house. On the first plans there was an outside seating area under a full roof so I thought that should come back inside and form part of a larger kitchen. Spanish people tend to have small kitchens and their dining tables in the living room. I also wanted the units in the kitchen changed round so that the sink would be under the window. I also asked for a second set of balcony doors at the front instead of an ugly short window. I should have asked him to simplify the exterior doorway and window surrounds, which he'd designed in rather grand Sevillano style. In the end we just left those adornments off in favour of a much more humble village house frontage. I rather like the idea that the house looks small and simple from the outside but opens up to have the rather grand light-well in the middle.

Architects here are paid by a rather large percentage of the proposed cost of the building. This meant that our Architect was going to cost us 12,000 Euros, paid in 3 instalments. We paid the first third immediately and agreed to pay the second when we had a basic building and the last part when we had our Licencia de Primer Ocupacion (first occupation licence). On top of contracting the architect, by law we needed a building inspector who would cost us another 4 thousand (also paid in thirds). That was a total of sixteen thousand Euros.

We agreed on the design and some time later we received our big blue box which contained the entire plans and specification book for the project. We paid for 5 copies. One copy stayed with the architect. One went into the bowels of the school of architects. Of course Jesus had a copy which he needed, both to give us our quotation and to carry out the works according to specification. One copy went to the council, and one to us. Now I believe the only one which is not mislaid is our own copy.

Wow. This was to be our new home. It was so exciting. Of course we should have been more circumspect. This was a palace. Where we went wrong was believing that the architects pricing scheme had any basis in reality; It didn't. We looked at the architects estimate which was around 70 thousand euros in total and said "yep, we can do that." Yes, that, we could have done. What we couldn't do was what it all actually turned into.

We were already running low on funds from the Coltman Street house sale and only just had enough left for the foundation slab which itself was 20 thousand euros (doubled from the ten on the architects estimate). Without a presupuesto (estimate/quote) there was no way we could apply for a hipoteca (a mortgage). And for every bill we paid in advance our finances looked less healthy.

My nemesis shows itself

After the demolition the builders started making good and building up all the exterior walls to our enclosed site. But water behind houses was now becoming a recurring theme. Before the demolition water flowed under the house through the rocks which was why I was really happy to have plans for a great big slab of concrete straight on to the base rock that was detected by the technical survey just a metre or so beneath the house, with all the sewers and very complex roof drainage set into it. So that was all OK. I'd got water covered. Or so I thought.

During the building of the party wall between our house and Pepa's I was called round to the house to make a decision about drainage. Drainage? I thought that was all in the plans, but no, there was an extra problem. It turned out to be a very Spanish problem of ancient water drainage rights from one property through the next and onward down the hillside. When I arrived there was a bloody great pipe sticking out from Pepa's side of the wall through to ours and this, we were told, was to carry all the drainage from the roofs and patios uphill from us. Where was it to go? I challenged Jesus about it. We'd been away and he was obviously listening to Pepa's demands and Pepa's money was talking too. I could tell he was angling after and getting more work from her and to keep her sweet this monstrosity had appeared in my garden This gave me more than a little cause for concern and I decided the only answer was to consult the local municipal architect. The architect was just about to leave and a new architect replace him, but we didn't know that at the time so off we went to see him.

I sat there with Frank, Jesus, the architect and the secretary of the council and talked the problem through. As far as we could understand it, the architect's only suggested solution horrified me. He wanted me to divert the water back up from the garden, under my house and out into the main sewer. That was just not going to happen. For one thing the tube was already too low to drain back up to my house efficiently. For another, at least one of my neighbours had a habit of putting their washing water bleach etc. into this water course, another would wash all the blood away from the Matanza (home pig slaughter which was still legal at the time) into it and yet another had a big uncovered hole in the ground into which her patio drainage water fell, along, I imagined, with any stray thirsty dogs, cats or rats. I could just imagine dead (and live) rats and possibly cats and even children could end up trapped under my garden or even house. It would then fall to us to dig up the drainage to effect any rescue. Not only that, but I might end up discharging any amount of toxic and hazardous materials thrown into this drainage by my neighbours and because my house was the point of discharge I could end up being the culpable party. Oh no. That was definitely not going to happen. There was a similarly dead-in-the-water idea (pun intended) to discharge it into our well but the possibility for overflowing in wet years was extremely high, given that this water course was designed with tiny and humble little pueblo houses in mind and that most of the houses had had their roof areas increased 4 fold since its inception. Plus we were thinking of using well water as a partial supply.

I tossed and turned that night drowning in imagined waves of sewage and flood water. I woke up in a cold sweat knowing that we had only two options. One was to stop up the pipe and cause Pepa problems of flooding and headaches for all the neighbours upstream of me. This could very clearly result in a denuncia or three. The other was to pass the water along as near as I could get to its ancient course which I already knew of from the little rows of stones that I found in the garden before the demolition, clearly designed to channel surface water across the garden and out through the neighbours back wall. Originally there had been a little drainage hole in the neighbour's back 'nave'(outhouse) but the repair of his wall had stopped that up so we had to pass the water through the wall just a foot or two further along my wall into the empty field beyond. There followed a rapid and clandestine digging up of my garden and burying of pipe, as I knew that if we asked permission there would follow a world of pain and paperwork and denuncias all the way up and down the line. It was a double bind with only this possible answer. I knew legally my argument would stand but I also knew none of us neighbours could afford the legal hoo-ha, and I certainly didn't want to be the one to cause it. That would be a very quick way to become very unpopular indeed. I also realised that once again the previous owners of my property had come unstuck because of water and the old second house on the site had fallen down because of the undermining caused by all those extra large roofs.

I knocked on each of my neighbours' doors uphill and told them that they must each deal with their own run off as soon as possible and that I had found a "temporary solution" for a few months. So my garden grew over the new pipe and although I accidentally damaged it in a couple of places I did find that my garden toad was very happy with his new superhighway. A few years later I realised the neighbours were still putting contaminated water down their run off when my cherry tree died off on one side near one of my breaks, leaving the other side alive as normal. Some things are just better ignored but I realise some day I'm going to have to replace the plastic pipe with a cement one.

These jobs were expensive and every time we visited, which was regularly, we were slapped with another big bill. Four thousand euros, Four thousand euros again, another two thousand euros. We paid up but we started to distrust Jesus as the work didn't look that expensive. That's when we found out our neighbour Pepa had also been paying. I'd very nearly had enough and I warned Jesus he was pushing it and that from then on not a brick would be laid until we had the full presupuesto. Meanwhile I did authorise the laying of the extremely expensive slab.

Back to work

Meanwhile we had the normal round of fairs to complete before we could come back for a summer in the sun. In March once again we attended Miniatura at Birmingham N. E. C. This was our biggest fair of the year sales wise, but certainly wasn't our favourite. Birmingham was an uninteresting place and the whole offloading thing was such a chore. One great thing was that we had Kira with us. It was always nice to spend time with Kira and she was becoming popular with the customers. Plus she enjoyed earning proper money. The only problem we had was that since she was still a couple of weeks off her 18th the security staff insisted she sit in the car while we did all the offloading and setting up without her. But there was one thing about Birmingham that Frank really did like and that was the Balti-house we found that year. He was a happy little vegetarian.

In April it was time for Arnhem fair again and this time I thought we'd go for a full day making Salmon. This was a very popular class and was filled up straight away. By this time my tutorials, including this one, were starting to be copied on the internet. It was a bit annoying, especially when I didn't get a credit, but what could I do about it? I didn't realise then how copying was going to impact my earnings. I was doing OK and teaching was my life by now. I could never have closed up and kept my 'tricks' secret. What I did realise though was demonstrating at fairs really helped sales of the books. I started minimising the problem of hauling books around by leaving them with Marie Paule Hostyn, to bring to me next time we met.

In the same month we had Pudsey near Leeds (England). We were clearly still doing way too many fairs. I just wasn't getting time to top up my stock levels before the next fair which was Soest in Germany. When I got there, on my own again, there was a fairground in the town centre which made the sleepy little town of Soest a hive of activity and maybe even increased the number of visitors. It was certainly a busy fair.

I hitched a lift after the fair with Marie Paule and her husband Paul to Brussels in Belgium. Our next whole weekend was full classes at Marie Paule's Atelier and there was also a class on the Monday. I stayed with Marie Paule, a miniaturist who played with many media but settled in her latter years on ceramics with a twist, creating some really beautiful and unusual designed jardinières. We had a lovely weekend and my hosts took me to see the sights in Brussels. To be honest I didn't find Brussels that exciting, but the company was good and relaxed. It was lovely to see fashion doll dresser Helena Rijnen again too. At that trip Marie Paule and Helena and I got to know each other better and became good friends. I was always a little bit social phobic but in the miniatures world I found people who I really did get along with. With very few exceptions miniaturists really are some of the most wonderful, warm, open and sharing people in the world.

This year there was was another one day fair at York Racecourse at the beginning of June followed by Paris fair. It was all such a whirlwind that I barely remember it. I did seem to be seeing the results of my hard work in my wallet, although all the trips and building payments were leeching it right back out again.

Life in the rental and Kira becomes the boss

We had decided to spend the ten weeks of that summer in the rental house in Las Cañadas, the street running down from the main street to the ancient bull ring. While deciding what to do with the house, the most important thing for us was to see if we could 'hack it' living in Spain full time even in the hottest part of the year, especially as it was beginning to look like we might have to make some fairly momentous decisions about the house build.

The more time we spent away, the more I thought I would get around to writing letters. I did try writing to Kira who we'd asked to manage the posting from the business while we were away and who I missed enormously. Even though she had already gone to live almost full time at her dad's. It was a very hard time to be separated because the relationship was a bit fractious. But it seemed closeness wasn't helping as much as separation and her little bit of responsibility would. I like to think she grew up a lot during those 10 weeks. She certainly did make a very good job of managing the day to day things back at Angie Scarr Miniatures. And actually I enjoyed being able to treat her as an adult and an equal much like we did at Miniatura.

I knew myself well enough by now to know that I'd soon revert to email as soon as I got internet access from there. I did surprise myself and wrote more than I thought I would though. After all, I was supposed to be there to write in peace. In the first week we got the laptop set up with a printer and speakers in my 'office' and Frank was still waiting for the monitor he'd ordered.

In the end my letters turned into notes about the things that happened day to day, and as I never seemed to get around to posting a letter they had many additions and some became the observations that became part of this story. If I had something to tell a family member, I simply emailed it. Facebook and the emoticon hadn't really happened yet.

I wondered back then if the smiley things would actually enter written language. I always felt a bit naughty using them. My dad would have said (I can hear him now) that you should be able to communicate using the language itself. I'm sure he'd have hated emoticons. Just as he hated Americanisms … Come to think of it, so do I. I'm not unlike my dad and Kira is definitely his granddaughter. He was a clever, sensitive, intellectual old gipper, so that's not an insult to her, if you remove the "old gipper" bit. He wasn't always a gipper either. I remember him when he was under fourty!

Spain smells

During this first couple of years of owning our Spanish wreck, we were always pretty much just waiting for things to happen. We spent some time getting to know our new pueblo, visiting as often as we could. Some of the things we were learning about Spanish life still seemed a bit strange to us.

Hot water was almost non-existent in the rental because it was heated by gas from bottles, and the system seemed to have a gas leak so we just didn't bother. I'd developed quite a liking for several cold showers a day and didn't miss the bath at all.

Pillows are longer and thinner. Double beds normally have only one very long pillow. We couldn't get used to this because I'm a pillow-scrumpler on my side and Frank often wakes with a wet pillow on his, so we brought nice fat fluffy pillows from the UK.

It´s strange but true that each country smells different, from the ground up. Spain especially so. Whether it be the different perfumes chosen by the cleaning manufacturers, or just the pine or oak trees and dry or wet earth depending on the seasons. Shops smell different, not worse, just different.

Sometimes here after rainfall the air smells distinctly of eucalyptus and rock rose. A couple of days into our ten week stay we had an unexpectedly heavy summer rainfall and the aroma was distinctly earthy … But not English earthy. More the difference between almonds and toasted almonds … still almonds but ´toasty'. Our wet earth has a 'formerly scorched' smell.

Toilets smell different, definitely worse. Ranging from the slight whiff to the full on pong.

Probably the above depends on the weather which also has a largely predictable range from the mildly hot to 'phew'. The unmistakable aroma of Spanish loos with their little bins full of used toilet paper in the corners is partly a throwback to the times when plumbing used to be inadequate to carry tissue paper, and partly, we found out later, the regular omission of the very important U bend.

Our rented house when we arrived was full of lavender 'air fresheners'. Being a bit asthmatic I rapidly cleared them all into a little plastic bag and shoved them to the back of the bathroom cupboard so I could replace them when we left. Actually I did pretty much the same with quite a number of ugly knick-knacks' too. Plastic flowers and plaster-of-paris clowns and teddies. Ugh! I have a serious aversion to 'tat' and, don't tell anyone, but I don't collect anything at all, unless of course you include tools. I have a massive collection of very tiny cutters for example. But miniatures? no. I very rarely buy one tiny piece of someone's work that I really admire, but it gets put in a box and looked at maybe once in a decade. As for my own work I keep nothing if I can help it. Once I've worked out how to make something and made it to my satisfaction, my attachment to it is nil. So, moving into a house with other peoples 'tat', that's the first act, to bag up the stuff and bung it in the back of a cupboard until its time to hand back the keys.

Over the next few visits the reason for the numerous air fresheners became apparent. First of all I thought it was me, and decided on a several showers a day approach. After all the smell seemed to occur only in the corner where I sat in a low sofa nearest to the parts of my body most likely to whiff a bit. I finally cracked and moved the sofa to find the smell was at its strongest on the floor underneath it.

There seemed to be patches of mould and whitish patches too. Again this pong which was most like the smell of golondrina guano.

I´d smelt something similar before in the basement of a crash pad in Burnley, so I put it down to damp. With the sneaking suspicion that there might be rodents involved too, though I hadn´t seen any droppings. So I washed the chair cover, scrubbed the floor and hoped the pong would go away … It didn´t.

When we returned the next time the smell was there again. If anything it was worse. There were also some strange orange drips and drops on the sinks and some drizzles down one of the pelmets. The thought occurred to me that it might be lizard urine. Sure enough, one night in bed Frank saw one of the critters scuttling around the ceiling above the window. Behind the sofa was damp again and the floor had the same sticky en-crusted appearance. When I washed the floor edge where the old sofa stood I noticed a lot of tiny ants under the edge of the skirting tiles. Lizard food perhaps.

'Iggys', as we call the lizards, get away with surviving in our house, partly because they aren´t interested in my chocolate biscuits, partly because they´re so cute, and mostly because they´re rather partial to mosquitoes which in turn are rather partial to me. We even had a friendly little lizard who crawled into the lamp surround in our bedroom where he stayed scuttling around for ages as if he couldn't get out. We called him 'Kevin the special needs gecko'. He clearly did get himself into problems as he'd already lost half his tail.

So, out went the uncomfortable floor height sofa. In came a cheap but much more comfortable 'off the floor' version from Ikea and regular washing of the floor. They are not after all, interested in sofas per-se, just in dark corners. No cushions in dark corners ... no iggy stink.

One day I cleaned the front yard, ready for Fiesta. The central drain the Spanish yards all seem to have, wasn´t working properly so that all the detritus swirled round my feet. I tried to turn the tap off but made the mistake of dropping the hosepipe which then turned round and soaked me. Wherever I danced it followed. When I eventually turned the damn thing off I had to wade back into the 'bog of eternal stench' to retrieve my broom, brush away the top layer of water out into the street and take the top off the drain to clean it out.

I had to take a years worth of swallow droppings mixed with lizard piss out of the drain hole.

My Puma sandals which weren´t the most feminine, but were the only ones I possessed at that moment and which I´d already had to wash in the first fortnight here (using Listerine mouthwash to try and disinfect) now smelled of a cross between wet dog and rotting seaweed.

Having sat in the bidet overnight drying out from their second full body soak they still reeked.

I put them in the washing machine and gave them their own wash cycle and pegged them out in the 32 degree heat. A fairly mild scorch for that week. I still didn´t hold out much hope. And, as I guessed, there it was still. The faint aroma of 'Labradorwrack' which no doubt would be back to its full intensity when mixed with the 'low note' of Englishwoman's sweaty foot.

I found 'menorquinas' that year, a sort of simple flat leather sandal which I've worn in summer ever since.

A couple of days later Frank was sent out to tidy up the front garden and he thought he'd try using the Spanish mattock type tool. Nobody uses a spade here. So he set about the job reasonably diligently until there was a squeal. "What is that?" Frank shouted. Hmm I thought it was a bit obvious. Frank had put a big hole in the mains water pipe buried less than 20cm from the surface and there was now a rather impressive water fountain in our front patio. We couldn't find a stop cock so we ran around like headless chickens for a while. The only person I could think of to ask was El Mere A local guy who had a sideline in erecting aerials knew everyone and everything. I sent Frank off to fetch him while a neighbour taught me that an 'English key' which is the Spanish name for a wrench, could be used to turn the water off. Frank, El Mere and the local plumber Santiago came back and fixed the problem well enough. Actually slightly better than well enough, because for ever after we never needed to water the pomegranate tree. Neither did we have to pay for any water to keep that part of the garden just slightly moist.

Racial types

It seems to me more and more apparent that our racial type has very little to do with where we were born. There are some clear leads such as family trees where you can trace back as far as some previous scholarly member of the family has cared to dig and preserve elements of genetic history. These, following the male line as we do in England, are far less likely to be accurate as they are, for instance, here in Spain where you appear to take your father's name as the first part of your surname (of which the Spanish carry two). Your second surname is your mother's. I believe that's like racehorse naming. By 'stallion' out of 'mare'. Many people nowadays just use the one surname in conversation, non legal correspondence etc, but there seems to be no rule as to which you choose.

There are other leads which people seem to consider lesser, but which do call into question our present methods of looking at lineage. I, for instance, seem to have the slight intolerance to alcohol which turns me pink and giggly after only a very small amount. I believe this genetic 'problem' originated in Asia. I also know that there was a Spanish woman somewhere in my family´s past. Maybe that´s why I feel so at home over here, why I once found myself in Malaga asking directions from a man who was the spitting image of my grandfather, and why I seem to be the one whose happy to fit into the Spanish habit of sleeping whole summer afternoons away here, whereas in England I´m the workaholic in the family.

My husband Frank´s surname is Fisher. This I would quite happily accept as unequivocally British … to the core … as fish and chips. Except for one or two small things: His blue eyes and blonde hair are coupled with an ability to tan beautifully while in Spain, whereas our Spanish friend Quique has more English traits than both of us put together. Blue eyes brown hair burning skin and a dislike of the hot weather but not too fond of the siesta. My other related discovery was that Frank, normally rather on the work-shy side, with many an excuse not to get started and to sit in front of the telly for hours was in those early days in Spain well ahead with his work, totally self disciplined about starting times and didn´t finish until the job was done.

Could this be because Spanish TV wasn't of interest to him because he can´t understand it? Although the obvious answer, I don´t think that it´s the whole truth. Frank always complains of the weather in England making him depressed and not wanting to start working. I used to think that was just a lazy man´s excuse. Now I suspect that if you planted him in Sweden or Norway where the summer days are long and sunny and the winter days are short and gloomy he´d work all summer and virtually hibernate in winter. He seemed to feel active whenever we were here. In England however he barely got started at all. I saw a couple of potential problems on the horizon. When we finally lived here I wondered what would happen? Would I ever get my second craft book written? Would Frank settle down and find a slower pace of life suits him better or would the poor little hothoused Viking just burn himself out?

Presupuestos and mortgages

We cancelled the September Cubelles (Barcelona) fair because we were waiting for the builders to start laying the slab. More importantly we were still waiting for Jesus to give us the full presupuesto (quote). Jesus seemed to think that it was OK to spin this out and we weren't budging until we had the whole thing agreed. When it did arrive Jesus had quite simply doubled the architect estimates which, although we found out they were only a standard guide price for tax reasons it just seemed that simply doubling everything didn't make sense. There were some glaring overcharges and the addition of a number which he called 'gastos generales', or something like that. We weren't at all happy. It all looked very much an old school cut and pasted bodge job.

Jesus told us not to worry and took us to a bank along with the first version of his presupuesto. This meeting was a bit of a shock because we were told our mortgage to get the house finished using Jesus' presupuesto would cost us 900 Euros a month, largely because of the high cost of building, but also because of my age. We stood there with our mouths open and a real sinking feeling. There was no way we could even consider looking at finding that much per month. Certainly not reliably.

We told Jesus he'd have to reduce the presupuesto. While we were waiting for him to decide on this we OKed the pouring of the foundation slab even though it was over 20 thousand Euros worth of work. It seemed like pouring money into the ground. Twice as much money as it should have cost even for such an impressive slab. The neighbours thought we were crazy. Looking back, they were right but I was afraid of my nemesis and I didn't want any holes in the scheme.

The summer was glorious and we really didn't want to go 'home'. Yes we decided we could live here. We wanted to live here one day. We were however, beginning to get a bit nervous.

We got back to England in time for Miniatura in September. I'd sent some of my miniatures work ahead in 2 parcels. Unfortunately only one ever arrived. I really don't know why I didn't just carry it in my hand luggage. I was kicking myself. Half of my 10 weeks of production just gone, I was gutted.

That October my brother Derek and my sister in law Sue went to Campofrío for a month and stayed in the rental house. By all accounts, although the weather was changeable they had a good time. Derek kindly replaced a few of the damaged Persiana (shutter) sashes and fixed a few more dodgy bits and bobs in the house. I don't think the landlords appreciated just how decrepit parts of their house were becoming with fair wear and tear since the 80s. Mostly the houses were furnished with the bare minimum quality in door handles, plumbing etc. Derek and Sue had enjoyed the autumn windfall chestnuts up around Fuenteheridos and when we arrived back later in the year there was a big bag of them ready cooked and peeled in the freezer for us.

The final show of the year was mid November in Madrid at the Hotel Convencion. This was one of Tom

Bishop's fairs. I was getting to know Tom and his wife Eleni. My former irritation with Tom's authoritarian style was dissipating. He ran a tight ship was all it was and in the end I came to appreciate that.

Just before that, on the Friday, I did a day of workshops at a little Miniature shop called Pequeneces. The owner was lovely, and, like me, had a younger partner. It turned out they weren't married but they were sweet together. I suggested we'd come to their wedding if they had one. I don't know if we put the seed of the idea in their heads but shortly after they did get married. We never did get the invite though.

The green elephant

As there was nothing we could really do to the house or garden while we'd been waiting for a presupuesto, I'd already decided to buy Frank a rather nice birthday present which had been delivered to the rental. It was a big metal and polycarbonate greenhouse.

I must have been crazy. All I can say is it seemed like a good idea at the time. I always did like organising places for my husband to hang out. And Frank always professed a love of gardening. The problem was that the allotment we had behind our next English house, actually failed to convert into the piles of fresh fruit and veg I'd hoped for. This was not only due to the Hull floods as Frank claimed but also due to a singular lack of regular self disciplined work. Nevertheless I decided it was a good idea. So I bought a Chinese one and had it delivered to Spain at what I now think was eye-watering cost.

We went up to the 'Almacen'. The dictionary uses warehouse, shop, store. This one is actually the village builders' merchant, where I'd been introduced to Raúl who was very young at the time but who seemed to run the place.

We asked Raúl for a bag of sand, a bag of cement and a bag of cal (lime) all in a caretilla (a wheelbarrow) with a palo (a shovel). He told us to come back in 20 minutes. When we got there the sand (arena) was not there. He said he'd have to give us a tub of sand since he didn't have any bags. We were horrified. The tub looked like a large bath and it was going to be half full. Bear in mind that at this time (just after 10 in the morning) it was already hotter than the hottest days in England and we were sweating just thinking about having to shovel this into the wheelbarrow and wheel it up and down the hill in about 6 loads to the house. I sent Frank off with the wheelbarrow on the first run with the cement and lime, While I was to pay and take a box of ceramic tiles, for miniature work, home to the rental. Of course Frank tried the 'I don't know what you mean' tack, which I've come to know as 'I don't want to do it', but he had no option. When the poor boy came back drenched in sweat I was waiting at the top of the street having found the ceramic tiles too much.

We dropped them off, Frank pushing the wheelbarrow all the way having realised that we were now living in a world where machismo still ruled and he was going to lose a lot of face if I was seen pushing the barrow. When we got back to Transmejías, we were dreading the chore that was to come. Raúl was there, but no sand. He said the sand and the shovel were already at the house. He'd moved them there on his forklift … "You know the place?" Of course, I should have known, everyone knows everything in this village. And now we know it was rediculous even to think that we might have to move building materials ourselves. The village rumbles to the sound of the Transmejías forklift on a daily basis. People are really friendly here; I mean ridiculously so.

It's not just a village friendliness that you'd get in an English village. It's a full on welcome without a hint of suspicion. You do get people staring at you if they don't know you. At first it can be a bit strange and off-putting, but it's simply curiosity.

This was our own little self build project, We measured out and laid a brick base and then I rendered that, after a fashion. That greenhouse took about two solid days of mind numbing work, taking apart things to put bolts back in that weren't clear on the diagram, and I still have no idea how the windows are meant to hold in.

It didn't really matter. The greenhouse, like the allotment 'poly-shed' was another of Frank's wasted good intentions and whatever his many and varied excuses, he never really put in the hours of work it needed to be productive.

Back to reality

In October we were rather busy, or rather I was. I took another trip to Auning fair in the north west of Denmark. The usual suspects were there. The same people we used to meet at Farum near Copenhagen. There was metalworker Tony Knott, Silversmith, Jens Torp, flower maker Anja Van den Doel with her husband Jan, fashion doll dresser Helena and her husband Kurt Rijnen, Glassmaker Ray Storey and 'Grumpy Bob' Willans who I came to love, although he was difficult to get to know at first. One afternoon Bob had got sick of smokers' corner. It seemed as if Kurt and Anja were chain smoking the whole weekend. Bob grumbled at length as Bob was wont to do. I didn't like the amount of smoking either to be honest. At one point though, when Bob got hold of Kurt's cigarette pack and, while he wasn't looking, pierced each and every cigarette several times with a pin, I, as an ex smoker sympathised more with Kurt and thought this was a bit out of order. I needn't have worried though. Kurt loved his cigarettes, so much that with the strong draw he had on them he didn't even notice the difference. Since then Kurt has actually stopped smoking and I'm afraid we lost Anja to brain cancer.

What a lovely and funny bunch of people sat round the table to eat Jonny's delicious food that night. Birthe's and her daughter Tina are lovely too and the welcome was so warm I was sure I'd be back. This would have become a favourite fair. Unfortunately though, it only lasted a couple more years before Birthe and Jonny made their first attempt at retiring and they moved away from the Kro. In the event that became only a partial retirement because it wasn't long before the Miniseum was up and running again. You can't keep a good miniaturist down.

The food on this weekend may not have been vegetarian but my offering for the class was vegetable based. I taught celery and asparagus using the Skinner Shade Technique on the Friday before the fair which once again was small but impressively good. On the Saturday the customers took all my best pieces as they had the year before. On the Sunday, once again the stall was swept virtually clean and I had more fairs to do before Xmas. I just wasn't keeping up.

Fortunately the next fair was just the one day Pudsey fair. Even this regional fair could be a busy one for me so I was going to have to work really stupidly hard to have anything to show. That wasn't unusual.

November was coming up fast and time for the Madrid, Fair This time we had our car and the very generous offer from my friend Panti and her architect husband, to stay with them at one of the flats they had near the Retiro Park. We spent some time with Panti, a tiny but forceful character who never seems to stop buzzing for a moment. We only saw her husband in passing but Leopoldo is one very cool guy. Just like Frank is for me, Leopoldo seems to be the 'earthing' force for Panti. To say thank you I spent an hour or two giving Panti a private lesson. I think it was that year that it snowed on Retiro park which was very pretty from Panti's penthouse. It is usually bitingly cold in Madrid in November.

We had decided to spend the pre-Xmas period in Campofrío that year in order finally to get round to confronting Jesus about the presupuesto, the second version of which he finally gave us. I'd met up with a long term British expat, resident of Aracena, another Frank, who spoke almost perfect Spanish. I paid him a generous wedge to go through the boring presupuesto with me, but it was well worth it. We found so many errors and it was clear that Jesus had rushed this one too and just put the 'Gastos Generales' under a different subheading. I was, by this time, very pissed off and worried, and with his second presupuesto even more so. There was just a strong whiff of the unprofessional upstart wannabe about it. So, when he sent me a big bill for a wall that he'd done for the neighbour and which I had already said I didn't want and wasn't paying for, I simply refused to pay the bill. I knew it was going ahead but it was Pepa's wall which I didn't need and he'd agreed with Pepa to do it. He hadn't agreed it with me though. I'd made that absolutely clear.

Pepa wanted to rebuild it and I think Jesus had convinced her that he could get me to share the cost. I imagine she thought I was paying half because Jesus had told her I was and Jesus, although he'd heard me say no, wasn't taking that as no. He wanted Pepa's money … and mine if he could get it. This wall nearly turned out to be an even bigger problem. Or should I say smaller, because Pepa wanted her wall lower which would have given her more of a view of my back garden. I already knew that she enjoyed having visual access to our lives and I had to explain to her that if she did have it rebuilt it was her decision, but that I would be complaining if it was built any lower because, as I told her, English people value their privacy. This was not to be the last time I had to remind her of that.

I knew Pepa had paid some money to him, but I also knew the bill he presented to me was even bigger than hers as our side is lower at the base, therefore taller. I finally gave him the half of the money he asked me for and I told him he was lucky to get that. I had already warned Jesus in no uncertain terms not to present us with any bills that were not previously notified, so I took the opportunity to thank him for his work and to tell him that his attitude to our finances didn't fit with our actual finances. This was a hard decision but we realised we'd let the window of opportunity slip by. Jesus had gambled that we'd got or could get more money than we said and that we'd just roll over and pay what he asked. He'd gambled ... and we'd all lost.

We couldn't carry on without a mortgage and by this time because of the delay, by this time we couldn't get a mortgage.

7

The English Do-er-upper

Once we realised that we weren't in any position to afford a self build mortgage of 900 euros a month, we also realised that this figure was a minimum because builders have a habit of adding to the bill. At this point we nearly bottled the whole house build and almost sold the plot with its foundations and proyecto. We looked around in Campofrío for what else we could buy for around 100,000 which is the price I could probably have achieved for the plot at that time. All we had was a slab on the ground. A magnificent slab, on a very nice plot. But still nothing anywhere near a house.

We actually asked 116 thousand which is what I calculated we'd spent including trips backwards and forwards. Jesus did indeed come back with a buyer but didn't say who that was. Then he tried to beat us down from the 116 thousand we wanted so he could put more in his pocket. In retrospect I wish I'd continued to negotiate at that point because that was a very high point in values. but we knew Jesus was trying to milk us again and we were irritated! So we told him to take a hike and decided to carry on when we could get our finances sorted out. This was a very hard decision but we knew our only way out was to take a couple of years earning more money for our house build. So our project was shelved until we could make another wedge to throw into what was becoming a money pit!

One day, after we'd dispensed with Jesus' services

Pepa came up to me with a piece of paper with "50 euros" scribbled on it. I had no idea why and was only just beginning to get my ears round the Campurriano accent, so it was difficult to make out that she was actually asking me for 50 euros. "What for?" I asked. She told me it was for electricity and water usage while the builders were on site. I asked her where she got the idea that I was going to pay her for builders use of electricity. Apparently she'd agreed with Jesus to let them use her electricity but he'd reneged on the promise to pay for it and referred her to me. I was incandescent and practised my Spanish on her in a letter which basically referred to laws of contract and suggesting that her contract was with Jesus and not with me. I did feel a little sorry for her because I knew Jesus had been shafting her just as he had been taking me for a ride. Either way I wasn't going to pay another penny for, on behalf of or to Jesus. We needed to save every penny if we were ever to start the house build again. Besides It wasn't the first time nor the last I'd felt pressure from neighbours to look after their interests rather than my own and I'd been warned not to fall for it.

At that point I had another bright, or maybe a crazy idea. Next door to Frank's mother back in England, there was an empty house owned by another neighbour. The neighbour had bought it with an inheritance but had got thoroughly stuck, having taken down internal walls upstairs and then rather lost her way as to how she was going to continue. She'd also knocked some of the plaster off the downstairs walls in search of the source of obvious damp. Once again we were pretty sure we'd found our water damage conundrum!

We were looking to buy a do-er-upper for around 50 thousand but Anne, the owner of the house wanted 65 thousand. We settled on 55 sight unseen! We had enough cash left in the bank for the deposit and, fortunately could re-open a mortgage with our previous mortgage company because it had been under 2 years since our previous home was sold. There was just one problem. If we wanted to call it a renovation project, we had to have more deposit and pay a higher interest, so it had to be our home for the next 2 years to qualify. Though once again we'd be moving into a property that was barely liveable. Oh well. I was getting used to that.

One of the walls that Anne had taken out was an upstairs load-bearing wall (apparently slightly different from a supporting wall). She'd also taken another which wasn't load-bearing. The whole upstairs was one room plus a partly renovated bathroom. We couldn't get a mortgage with that wall missing so we had to get the keys from Anne in advance of getting the mortgage. Fortunately Frank and his mum knew her pretty well and she trusted us. Left in the house were some 6x6" timbers so we called up Dave (grumpy old surrealist, musician and artful-bodger) and asked if he would put back a partition wall at load-bearing standard. Which he did. I watched him build and plasterboard this wall and that experience was to be very useful two years later when we partitioned the third bedroom.

We'd been storing a container load of household goods since we moved out of Coltman street and it was costing us a fortune in storage fees. Some of our furniture was now in the house but there were still things that were too good to throw away but too expensive to store. I sold my beloved scaffolding and we did a car boot sale to dispose of as much as I could bear to let go. There was a beautiful mirror which had been backwards and forwards between my houses and my mums depending on where I was living. When she died I brought it back to Hull but there really wasn't a place for it in the new house, so regretfully it went into the car along with as much of the rest as we could carry. I don't like car boot sales as a seller because the public who come along early to nab a dealer bargain can be very rude and jostle you as you're getting out of the car, in the attempt to find the best bits. Rattled, I picked up the boot of the car and the mirror fell out and smashed on the floor. Of course I'm not superstitious. But ...

Water water everywhere

We'd been trying to cut down on Miniature fairs but the list kept growing. We even had an A team and B team experience that year when there was a clash between Arnhem fair and Miniatura. I went to Arnhem, arriving just as the hall opened due to a delayed train. Frank, Kira and our friend Dave (Popdog) went to Miniatura.

Then there was the new Paris Fair in its second year. Who could resist Paris in June? We certainly couldn't. A one day fair with a class up front to pay the costs, which gave us time to spend exploring Paris? Yes we were up for that. This year we spent Saturday making cut fruits, which has always been my most popular class. The workshop was held in a lovely glass building by the river but I wasn't very relaxed. The Fimo seemed dreadfully soft and wasn't behaving as I expected. And I'd left my red powder behind so I had to send Frank racing round Paris to try and find some red powder to complete the rosy apples. The fair itself had moved to an underground exhibition centre which was sweltering. Then on the Monday I did a very enjoyable cut red cabbage cane master-class at Cristine Voirin's house.

Then it started to rain. It rained and it rained and the Paris streets were awash, but more worryingly so were the streets of Hull where we'd left Kira to look after herself during her last week of college. Poor Kira had managed to get back to our house from college but the waters were still rising. In a frantic phone call home we advised her to stay in and move any valuables upstairs. Frank begged Kira to save the Sky Box of course, but I was more worried that we'd be totally flooded out and that Kira would run out of food and fresh drinking water if there were any problems with the electricity and water supply.

As it turned out the water came to just under our floorboards and mercifully stopped just centimetres short of total downstairs flooding. Given the state of our low lying soggy ground it was status quo for us although I did hear that some neighbours claimed for re-plastering, floor boarding, redecorating and new furniture and carpets for their downstairs rooms. We could have got away with it and we needed new plaster but I'm not a 'claimer' by nature. We were still in the same state as before the floods, with the bottom foot of plaster knocked off by Anne half way round the living room, pretty much like the rest of the people who then did have repairs but we were way too honest. Besides, our floorboards were new and in good condition because Anne had replaced them with treated boards. In the event it was a good job that we didn't claim as there would have been the added problem that when selling the house any flooding incident would have to be reported. It seemed that Hull had ceased pumping groundwater away and had built over flood plains over the previous few years and this was an accident waiting to happen. We lived near 'Tweendykes' and not far from 'Spring Bank' there were Lowgates and Lowlands, Hull was littered with clues that this could be a soggy area.

The back garden and the front street were completely flooded and all our stored stuff in our recently built shed was damaged including the kitchen units I'd saved from The Church building and the potters wheel. The kiln did seem to have survived though and eventually went as a wedding present from my son and me to Vicky, who was the person who most used it back at Creative thinking. One of the worst long term effects was that we had to tell Kira to stay indoors and not trail out into the sewage-filled lake in the streets to meet up with her friends for an end of school bash. Sadly the result was that she missed out on that life experience completely. When we arrived back in Hull we had to drive all the way round the city and sneak past the police barriers on the wrong side of the road just to get home.

We lived with the damp for a while. We were lucky though. Thousands of people were living in caravans. Many of them were still not back in their houses a year later. We had to stay in the house because of the terms of the loan and in any case there was no way we could do it up and sell it immediately. It was a busy year and we had spent all our money.

Although values had hit a peak before the flooding it wasn't looking so likely we'd be able to make the profit we'd first expected either. Kira was still sharing her bedroom space with my office which wasn't ideal. She had been having a tough time. It was her A level exam year and she was also going through some ups and downs in her personal life and her dad wasn't well either, which was worrying her. Looking back I'm pretty sure that it didn't help that her space at our place wasn't really her own either. She later told me that she'd decided to move full time into her dad's house after an argument we'd had about her job hunting. I was overworking dreadfully too so it was all bound to end in tears as harassed mother meets stressed teenager in what was essentially a cross between Kira's bedroom and my business premises. It didn't make for a happy mix.

On the 8 July I went to the Midlands Polymer Clay Guild where I met up with Gaynor Fryer and Pat Goodall McIntosh and I did a Liquid Fimo and Moulds Masterclass then we left soggy Hull for another slightly shorter summer in Campofrío.

2007 is generally recognised as the year the financial crisis or "La crisis" as it was dubbed in Spain, started. But for us ... well we felt that we were really not doing too badly considering. We'd pretty much stopped paying out for the house in Spain. We just had one little job to do and that was to have someone come and spray foam all over one of our neighbour's walls to protect it from weather affecting their adobe (mud) walls. Our mortgage payments on the English house were going down. I still had a lot of fairs. Frank still had income that year and I was well on with my second book which we saw as a necessity to boost our future income. We saw it as the book that would put the roof on our house and the moulds which we were making more of, we saw as one roof tile each. Every time we made a mould we'd say "one tile ... another tile". This helped me concentrate and work harder.

First I had a pleasant little obligation to fulfil. I took Kira to Barcelona to congratulate her on her very successful A levels. It was certainly time we had some mum and daughter time and we spent just a few days mooching around the city and around the little pool and bar on the rooftop of the hotel. I was right, Kira did love Barcelona's quirky little Barrí Gotic area and wide Boulevards of the modernist routes, and it wasn't too long before she was back for a rerun but this time with her partner. The ugly hump of A levels and emotional ups and downs was over but she still had challenges to face. Very soon she got a job though and started to feel back in control.

The nail art story.

I was in my workshop in the rental house one day when I got a call from a German guy who called himself Bjorn who told me that he wanted to order large quantities of my canes and so I must lower the price for him. Now this was blunt even for a German and I had never heard of him nor the nail art business and I had no idea what a good or bad business this was going to be for me.

I stood my ground "I don't have to do anything! My trade price is very good and it is what it is". And what it was was 50% off the retail price. Not a bad deal for most traders I thought. What I didn't realise was that Bjorn worked for a company that weren't any ordinary trader. They were a big player in the faddy and fashionable world of nail extensions. Bjorn was slightly put out by my reply but put in an order anyway.

I was used to orders totalling maybe a hundred or two hundred Euros from traders. Bjorn's order arrived and there was an extra zero on the end. Rapidly followed by another twice as big. I had to dig deep. I also had to get an assistant! I had to tell Bjorn I would work as hard as I could but as I was still finishing my second book and currently in Spain it was going to be very tricky for me to get the quantities on order to him as quickly as he wanted, but I would do as many as I could and make sure he always had some stocks. He was happy enough with this and there followed 18 months of ridiculously frantic overwork and ridiculously high turnover for a tiny one man (woman) craft business.

I confided to my friend Nicola Croad, who had also been approached by Bjorn that I was having real difficulties keeping up and she offered to take some of the strain. I was a bit worried about this because my work was of course easy enough to copy; after all I'd been teaching it for long enough, and why wouldn't I share the good fortune with Nic? But I decided in the end that yes, there was enough work for both of us, but that it was in my interests to encourage Nic to bring out her own different range. And of course that range should be something that I didn't make. I didn't enjoy making non-nature items, but she did. So I handed over the recipes for Fimo in chocolate colours which I'd just written up for my new book, and Nicola designed a very cute little range of mini chocolates which worked just as well for miniatures as they did for nail art of course.

Being constantly obsessed with the 3 dimensional "Nic" I said, "Why don't you show people how to round them off to make 3d chocs?" She did that and made a lovely job of it too, I also told her how I made mini Liquorice Allsorts in sheets and after a couple of attempts she made a far better job of producing canes for them than I ever did! I loved working with Nic like this because it was so mutually beneficial for us to support each other while staying off each other's 'patch'. And also Nicola is such a thoroughly nice person. We became really good friends. We had found the win-win. Nic then went on to design some other ranges herself and they sold really well. She made some 'funky flowers' which were based on having translucent background so that they would disappear into the nail varnish. Nicola was a much better salesperson than I and she contacted demonstrating nail artists and made some connections which were to change the direction of her work radically and eventually she became a nail artist herself. Meanwhile she also designed some Halloween and Xmas ranges and Bjorn's company lapped them up.

Of course, where there is money there are copyists, especially from the far east and both my work and hers was copied extensively. Other artists from the USA had the same problem and I started to see copies of their beautiful little characters and butterflies around. This was going to be the beginning of the end of our boom times. I was going to have some fun first though. When I knew that an order was from a copyist (the one of each item signature gave it away), I would deliberately send examples which had mistakes in them either in colour, or form.

All they knew how to do was copy but they were so very good at it that they copied my mistakes perfectly every time. Another signature fault of the far east work was that although the first generation copies were perfect enough to pass as mine albeit my seconds, they gradually passed the work down to less and less experienced makers who lost sight particularly of the original colour and this meant that the work moved progressively further from the colours of nature that I was recognised for, but not before they had enticed many of my customers away by their incredibly low prices. Mine were at trade in the region of an American dollar whereas the Chinese copies might come out at ten cents. Several times I found companies advertising their goods using my pictures. That really was out of order. There were even people in England doing it. I heard all the excuses. "Ohh I haven't got a good enough camera to take good enough pictures of my own work … I thought you wouldn't mind" and "Oh no it's your work. we're trade customers". I was hearing reports from around the world from my customers when they had bought from my wholesale customers. I even got reports and proof that my first book was being copied on to disc and sold on. At this stage I really didn't have time or money to chase this and the publishers didn't seem too bothered. And for now I was too damn busy to care.

I'd started neglecting the miniatures part of my work to service these big orders. I'd also thoroughly damaged my health working from what my dad would have described as "Sparrow fart" to midnight with breaks only to eat and occasionally get a little much needed exercise. I joined a Gym and went once a week for a swim and a massage which became essential. I don't know why but I never put these essential expenses through the business and lost out badly because of that getting a tax bill in the higher bracket which eventually because of subsequent events, I couldn't fully pay.

During this time I'd also made a mistake as an employer. I took on Kira's friend Daisy on a self-employed contract. I'd learned my lesson about employees from my experience of our friend who we called 'Popdog' whose excuses for non-arrival were legendary. So I offered Daisy, my daughter's friend, subcontracted work. On a self -employed basis. I paid her very generously for a seventeen year old at 10 pounds an hour, which rose to 11 pounds an hour when her work became perfect and I was earning well from it. The problem was that Daisy didn't need much money. Just enough to keep her telephone paid and for hair extensions. This meant she came in only when she needed the money. Daisy could have earned a fortune if she'd been putting in the sort of hours I was, or even half the hours I was. However she found a day or two a week was enough for her needs.

I was clearly not capitalist enough and we lost out because of it. I know now I should have trained someone else up as the competition would have kept Daisy sharp and I would have had a back-up. Daisy was really good at producing the goods even when we were away though. And her quality was excellent. I worked out what I could expect from an hours work from her and while we were away that year she had her own mixing machine and her own pasta machine and was able to keep working piecework even when we were away in Spain.

We really needed our own car now and that summer we decided to go down to Malaga to see what was available. We ended up finding out that cars were like houses here. They could be sold through different dealers and we thought we were going to see four different but similar cars, all with different photos and specifications. When it came to it there was just one battered wreck in a fix-up garage, and at least 3 sellers for the same one. This was distinctly suspicious. The whole street was full of fix-up garages. The car had probably been written off years before and left to rot in a ditch somewhere. There are some dodgy practises in the second hand market. The prices for second hand were astronomical too. About twice what you'd pay in England. We decided it would be cheaper to bring our car and, eventually to re-register it.

Names

We were getting to know our neighbourhood and our neighbours but names were a source of endless confusion for us. There seem to be only a choice of half a dozen male first names in Spain. There are the obvious ones Antonio, often shouted across the street Tonyo!!! We know several and have to give each a prefix or a suffix to describe them. "Papa Antonio"and "Antonio the head". Not to be confused with Antonio the stick who had bad headaches. That's when he wasn't giving us one! "Antonio the head" had had an accident falling off the wall at a neighbour's house. I'd happened to be around and kept his head supported and chattered to him to keep him conscious until the ambulance came. "What are you doing tomorrow?" I asked him "I'm dying" was his reply. "You aren't dying today. Not while I'm watching and you aren't dying when the medics are watching you" I said. My Spanish was getting better!" Antonio the head' was in a critical condition for several days and unwell for months, but fortunately I'd told the truth! That was it. He was "the head" for ever after.

José Maria (the male variant of Maria José) is another very common name often shortened to Chema. Manuels are also common, the diminutives being Manolo or Manolito. Even more often Juan Manuel which can be shortened to Juanma which when shouted becomes our favourite 'Wamma!" and Juma pronounced Hooma. Miguel- Migueeee! Or Luis Miguel – Luismi. And of course the most popular of all Francisco.

Frank is rather an unusual name for someone of my Frank´s generation in England, but here, in Spain there are Franks all over the place. So Spanish nicknames for Francisco abound. The obvious Fran, Franci (pronounced Franthee) Cisco and Curro are all common. Paqui is also fairly common. Even though it sounds very un PC to our English ears we've got used to calling our local policeman Paqui. Then there's Kiko. Don't confuse Kiko with Quique which is short for Enrique. But the most common diminutive is Paco This is the name that we chose for Frank's Spanish nickname.

My name Angela, when shortened to Angie, became fairly difficult for my adopted Spanish family (the people who sold us our house) to pronounce. So they always called me Angelie. Even though they now know how to pronounce Angie I've asked them to continue to use Angelie because I rather like it. Frank and I have privately adopted our own nicknames. Angelie Lela and Paco Loco ... A little joke between us because lela means something a bit like soppy and loco is of course 'nuts'. I have a crazy lady name in the village though

I'm only a little 'rara' (strange) in that I lay bricks, climb scaffolding etcetera. I've been catcalled by one truly nutty local who seems to have a little alcohol induced Tourettes "mujer albanil!" (bricklaying woman). Fair enough because we call various neighbours 'sweeping woman' 'sweeping woman's daughter' 'goat woman' etc when we don't know or don't remember their names. It's quite common in our village to call people an assortment of odd names the origins of which are lost in the mists of time. Some people get their trade fixed on as their name so we have 'El Pollo The chicken or there's a el Dique which we always translate as the ditch though we've no idea if that's correct We have a friend El Mere. For goodness sake how did that come out of his real name Hermenegildo. Oh forget it. Of course you would shorten that one!

Female names seem to be even thinner on the ground. One favourite is Maria Luisa. If you´re young you might be lucky enough to have it shortened to Mari Lou. Carmen, and Mari Carmen. Singers and dancers have a choice of Rocio or Flores. With a couple of 'Mar's meaning sea and short for Maria del mar (maria of the sea) thrown in. You can always tell when a girl is from Barcelona because they will almost invariably be called Montse, short for Montserrat. A famous Barcelona mountain.

The names I find the strangest are the ones with the deeply Catholic roots, like Inma which is short for Inmaculada Concepción (immaculate conception) which can also be shortened to Conchi or Conchita. Asunción (assumption) Puri short for Purificacion (purification). Then there's Dolores, shortened to Lola and its variants Loli, Loly and Lolita. But sadly the rather pretty name Dolores actually means "pains".

My "Paco" is truly 'loco' in the minds of the locals

because he's vegetarian. Not very unusual in Britain. Maybe not even that unexpected in the cities of Spain, but in rural Andalucía on the "Ruta de Jamon" (ham trail) where life revolves around the pata negra, Frank is truly 'un bicho raro' (a strange bug). To them, the idea of being vegetarian is totally beyond their understanding. I've lost count of how many times we've explained, very carefully, to local friends villagers and restaurant staff that Frank is a vegetariano 'muy estricto' (very strict), only to have his plate of mushrooms laced with ham. Or a bocadillo vegetal (salad sandwich) arrive chock-full of tuna. Patiently we explain that true vegetarians don't eat any meat. "Or fish?" They ask looking slightly perturbed. We patiently reply "ni pescado". The next question is always the same, an incredulous "Ni jamon tampoco?" (Nor ham either?!!!)

Name and address confusion

The spelling and order of our names always cause confusion too, partly because Spaniards have one Christian name and two surnames. So they think Frank's surname is 'Christian Fisher' and so paperwork gets horribly confused. But what they really can't get is the spelling of my surname. I explain patiently that my surname begins with an S. But S in front of a consonant in Spain is always pronounced es because it always has an E in front as in España. So a bottle of Sprite is an Esprite.

I am always Angie Escarr. In the hospital lists they've finally got it that Helen Angela is my first name but now they're at a loss to know what to enter in the second surname field. And so I'm Helen Angela Escarr Desconocido (Unknown) which here in Spain tends to suggest I am fatherless.

And if names are confusing to them so pueblo

addresses are confusing to us. Our house is variously Number 38 Calle Archipresto Delgado Lopez. Or maybe 38 Blas Infante as the name of the street on the left of us was changed. Then the top of the street before it divides into a Y became Plaza de Andalucía and at some time our address was registered in the Catastral (local property registration) as being in the Plaza. Opposite us are two houses, one on the plaza and the other next door clearly on the street off the plaza. Both are number 37. But neither is next to a 35 or 6. The one on the plaza is however next door but one to number 41. So we believed the one opposite our house was clearly considered to be next door to us in the numbering scheme. We are definitely Plaza de Andalucía. However, our neighbours to the right, who have different numbers on the Catastral, have actually numbered their houses 3 and 2. Out of any of the previous sequences! So our house is currently unnumbered but for clarity (clarity? Hah!) we sometimes call it number 1. We still have the old number 38 tile as a bedside coaster.

Palabrotas (swear words)

Equally amusing and confusing to us are which words are considered offensive in England and which are not in Spain, and vice versa. The Spanish F word 'joder' is used in the pueblo with impunity as it is these days in the UK similarly 'Puta' (bitch) no one bats an eyelid. But absolutely the most offensive word of all to us Brits which I can only describe as the 'c word' in Spanish is coño and is much used as a greeting even between elderly ladies "Coño hola!" One friend also calls her daughter and her granddaughter and her sister chuchi or chocho which I understand would translate to 'fanny'. Whereas what significance would an ordinary Brit give to the words "The Host"? None. Yet 'hostia' is considered one of the rudest of rude words and because of this it's been transmuted to ostra (oyster) this of course is now also considered to be rude. And for goodness sake don't go into a shop and ask "have you any eggs?" because that's a no no for reasons you can possibly work out. You have to say instead "are there eggs?"

I've made several amusing mistakes with the language. I've fallen into the pollo trap. No, you mustn't convert the word chicken to the female. It means the same as if you say it in the male form in English. I've also mixed internal letters a few times, like asking someone " quien esta la ultima en culo" meaning who is the last in the arse? ! What I should have said was cola - tail ... or rather queue.

I've often mixed up words with similar sounds but different endings. For example I've asked the price of a truck load of ants -hormiga(s) when I should have asked for hormigon -cement. The male to female endings can sometimes change the size with the gender. For example if you ask for a saco de arena you'll get a small bag of sand but if you ask for a saca you're going to get a builders supply. I don't know whether I get discount prices at the local builders yard because they've accepted me and taken me to their hearts ... or whether I just constantly provide them with the best laugh of the day!

We got back to England in time for fairs season starting with Miniatura in September then the Dutch fair in October and Madrid in November. I won't bore you. No I suppose I'd better come clean, I won't bore myself with trying to remember the details of another year of fairs. They're all fun but have all mixed themselves together in my totally frazzled memories of that year. By this time they weren't all profitable any more. At a rough estimate it costs a thousand Euros to do a fair including travel, accommodation and stall fees and sometimes you don't take much more and so end up with an overall loss in time and stock. Sometimes though, you get a really good fair that makes it all worth it, but I was beginning to find Miniatura and Arnhem were fitting into the former group. Madrid was only scraping a profit because we could stay at a friend's house and found cheap ways to travel. Plus I was starting to work very hard on the nail art canes and that was leaving me with even less stock. A problem which was going to be compounded over the next year.

8

Overworking Again

I was working 16 hour days 7 days a week by now, trying to keep up with Bjorn's orders and still producing a few miniatures for my dwindling stocks for fairs. The fairs diary was still pretty full. Sometimes we had to be creative. There was another Arnhem clash. This time I decided we weren't going to shoulder the expense of two fairs at a time. The ferry being horrendously expensive at around 350 pounds for the return trip, we were dug out of this particular hole by Joan and Joe Wearing, friends of John and Hazel. They agreed to stop by the house in Hull on their way to the fair to pick up our boxes of books and stock. They would set up a small table and give the extra space to Hazel who was our neighbour at this fair and who could always bring extras to fill another half table. It was an ideal solution. Their expenses would be partly defrayed by taking the difference between trade price and full price. They didn't want to take anything but I insisted. We'd saved a small fortune, plus it left me with more time at home … for more overwork.

I still had Daisy and my friend Margaret Curtis continued to come over for a few hours a week, totally unpaid. Although I could certainly afford to pay her, there was a tax problem in doing that. Also, to be honest, it was difficult to quantify the value of her work side by side with uber-productive Daisy. I would have been more embarrassed to pay her the smaller amount compared with Daisy who was only 17, than I was not to pay her at all so I have to say just a few of our building materials were paid for by Margaret's generous work!

Then, as if I wasn't already overloaded with work during this crazy year, another fairly 'bonkers' order came in. I was called by a lady from a company called Steven Jones Millinery. "Would I by any chance, be able to provide them with a fairly large order of fruit and vegetables for a 'costermonger' hat design for London Fashion Week?" Of course I could, how could I refuse? It was only recently I found the 'stable' that Stephen Jones came from when Frank was looking to see if Grayson Perry was Grayson Perry's real name. It is and Frank said "Ooh apparently he was thrown out of his home as a teenager and squatted with Boy George and some Milliner called Stephen Jones ... No idea who he is". "I do!" I said. If I wasn't already proud of my work being chosen for a London Fashion week project, I was certainly proud and intrigued afterwards. What an interesting squat that must have been.

My shoulders started to ache, my neck, back and wrists were giving me problems and I was getting really bad headaches. Frank and I joined a gym. We went once or twice a week for a swim and a sauna, and I started to have a massage once a week. These were the unpredictable expenses of working harder and earning more. I wasn't clever enough to put these expenses down to the business. I was earning a lot of money now, but I wasn't 'savvy', and I was getting into a higher tax rate and now had to collect VAT on all my sales which made the dreaded billing a much more complex job. I had a simple accounts system though. If it was made of paper and it had anything to do with the business, it was dropped in a box. I didn't have the time or the brain power for anything else. Fortunately I had a very nice understanding accountant.

Family dynamics were changing too. Kira was thinking of starting University, but not this year, as she didn't want to leave her partner who, being a year younger than she was, wouldn't be going until the following year. Steve's new partner was now the favoured 'mum,' being nearer to Kira in age she was a lot easier to get along with than I was, and she seemed to encourage it to be it that way. Kira's partner's mum was also always on the "better than you" group. Being best friends with Steve's partner. I seemed to be outweighed now by a double "favoured mummy" team. This was the beginning of a difficult and emotionally trying few years in our relationship. I chose not to get into any competition, but sometimes look back and wish I'd made my voice heard instead of avoiding the conflict I knew I could never win. It was certainly a lose-lose situation. I couldn't give Kira the reassurance she needed. Neither could I give her a job, as she wouldn't have wanted to work with me. She especially wouldn't have wanted to take the orders from this stressed and demanding boss. She did seem to harbour a little resentment over how well paid Daisy was though. Kira eventually got a job in a call centre. She didn't like the job much but it brought in a small income. I'm sure Kira would say this wasn't the best time in her life. Neither was it for Alan who became newly single and Alan has always functioned better, and is much more contented as part of a pair. On the other hand Dominic had met Katy the previous year. These two just seemed right together. I made jokes about being a Mother in Law. Very shortly those predictions came true when Dominic proposed to Katy while on holiday in America.

Taking the car to Spain

We couldn't put it off any longer. We had to decide which car to take to Spain and it was obvious. It had to be my little Fiesta. It still had a very low mileage at less than 50,000 miles, whereas Frank's car already had 140,000 miles on the clock. Although we'd looked after Frank's and serviced it regularly, it wouldn't go on forever. Also Frank was still using his car for his long trips to Wakefield and Leeds, whereas I could do without mine. So it was decided. This summer we were going to drive down to Plymouth, via my brother's house to take the Plymouth to Santander ferry. We decided to get our car freshly MOT-d and serviced for the journey. I planned to load up my car with all the valuables we weren't going to want to send by courier or transport company and which we couldn't take on the plane. So, that was particularly my guitars, some gardening equipment and quite a few of my miniatures tools. Frank took computer parts and electrical and computer leads. We also took a set of clothes, especially summer clothes which saw little use in England!

When we woke up on that morning in August I was horrified to find that once again someone had broken off both of our wing mirrors. This was not the first time it had happened. Frank would argue about how safe he felt living in that street as compared with Coltman street, but it was his childhood home. I personally had more problems and felt more threatened in the two years in Scalby Grove than I'd ever had in Coltman street. Especially from the kids across the road and their friends. There was also a guy up the road who took exception to our parking near his house so it could have been either of them. Or just some random third party. Whatever or whoever it was I was gutted and also worried about how on earth we were going to get to, and through Spain with broken wing mirrors. Autoafford (clever but cheeky name I thought), our favourite cheapo repair garage, had a drivers side mirror but not a nearside one. They agreed to fit that immediately. I suddenly had a brainwave. My brother Derek was very experienced in buying and fitting car and motorbike parts and I thought if there was any one who could find one for us he could. I set about bodgeing the nearside enough to get us down to Devon, calming my anger with the thought that whichever sad sap broke them off was not going on any of the adventures we were heading for.

I hoped Derek had fully forgiven me for the trick we'd played on him the last time we were passing through when I asked him if he'd like to come and see our new (second hand) car and he'd somewhat dismissively said " I've seen a Ford Escort before". I'm sure he had but this was my new car and I was mildly put out. When we got in the car to leave I saw his big boat-pulling Lada parked near us so I sneaked over and stuck a little note under his window wipers which said " Please remove your old heap. It's a disgrace to the village". We drove away giggling at the thought that I'd got a little mild and fitting revenge for his 'sneer'. Little did I know that far from working out instantly that it was a cheeky snipe by us, he'd actually been living with this sort of mentality for years and was absolutely fuming and knotted up trying to find out which snotty neighbour might have written the note! Oops. Maybe that was a little more revenge than I'd intended.

Derek really delivered. He'd phoned ahead to a company in Exeter and then raced out on his motorbike to get there and back before we arrived. When we got to his pretty little Devonshire village, Derek helped me fit it, showing me the magic hidden screw cover that made it all possible. That was going to be very useful knowledge in the years to come when our car was parked down the narrow streets off the Plaza and we needed new wing mirrors regularly.

The next day we took the ferry at noon. It took a little

over 24 hours to make the trip, certainly a more relaxed schedule than our trips to Holland. Frank remembers the trip as uncomfortable but I remember it as relaxed. We left the ship in Santander in the early afternoon. I guess we expected it to be sunny and bright, instead the weather was distinctly chilly and overcast with a little low cloud drizzle on the mountains. This was Asturias not Andalucía. For some reason we hadn't thought to fill the petrol tank in England either. I think maybe I was trying to be too clever and thought I'd get my fuel cheaper, which would have been smart, except that we were heading deep into Spanish countryside with very few petrol stations and our tank was nearly empty.

Our old sat-nav wasn't really a very good guide. As the tank got lower and lower we decided to take 'Jane's' advice and head off the motorway towards a little village down a vertiginous hillside. The village turned out to be very pretty and almost medieval looking. Unfortunately I forget its name. We got an ice cream and filled up and set off towards Villaviciosa. I didn't forget that name. It sounded a bit scary, but that was our next stop. If I'd known about it then, I'd have bought some of the cider the area is famous for to go with the local bread and cheese. I didn't realise how delicious Asturian cider was until a year or two later. I now rate Asturian cider way above anything you can get in England. Actually I'd given cider up after my first ever drinking 'session' at age 16 which ended in my getting home totally wasted. When I got home and found myself crawling along the side of the bath towards the toilet. I suddenly looked up to see my mother in the bath. I didn't enjoy the after effects much either especially having to get up early the next morning to have to clean the shop window below my bedroom. Cider was a definite no no from then on until I discovered Northern Spanish cider.

After "Vice town" we set off towards Salamanca which we bypassed and just kept on driving. I loved the journey, but then it was very easy for me because I wasn't driving. I have to recommend it as a trip though. There is dramatic scenery and some of the best road and over and underpass constructions I've ever seen.

Bypassing Salamanca and Plaesencia which sounded a lot more pleasant than Villaviciosa, we finally decided we'd had enough fairly late at night when we arrived at Cacares. Fortunately the Spanish late night meals worked in our favour and we ate at the restaurant next to the hotel. Funnily enough neither of us fancied the speciality maggoty cheese! Next day we completed the journey by way of Mérida. Stopping for a lunch break where we got talking with some English people in a bar in Monesterio. They were on their way down to Cadiz in a VW camper to take a ferry to the Canaries. In those days I didn't realise how very far away the Canaries are, and imagined it was just a hop over to their new lives. In reality it's two days sailing and the islands are pretty much equatorial.

Happily our car reached its destination with only a minor hiccup. A valve from the air conditioning system and the engine cooling system had started occasionally to get stuck back in England. As the temperature rose on our journey, so the valve decided to stick firmly blasting hot engine air directly at us. This had been and was going to be an intermittent fault which would come back to haunt us again and again over the next few years.

I had a great feeling of satisfaction parking my little car outside the rental house in las Cañadas and emptying our 'booty' into the house. We really did seem to have a foot in each country now and a full wardrobe, full work kit, all the necessities for a "normal" life in both countries.

The rules seemed to be that you could take your car to Spain and drive it on your UK insurance as a tourist for a certain period. I seem to remember that technically you can drive it until your UK insurance runs out or until it's been there 6 months whichever is the sooner. We weren't sure about the technicalities. We knew you could often get away with just 'blagging' it and if the worst came to the worst you could just take it across to Portugal. Faro was not the nearest airport, being two and a half hours away. It was however the cheapest for flights to England at that time. In the end we changed to Spanish plates a year later. Well, we were always backwards and forwards to the UK, often leaving the car for several months in Faro airport car park, for which we paid around 90 Euros a month on our concessionary card. Those were the days when we could make a decision like that. I wish we'd saved all those 90 Euros now!

Fire

Life, watched out of the back bedroom window of the rental house often brought a smile. Sometimes it's the odd menagerie of animals either ridden, driven or just seemingly wandering around which would keep me entertained.

The saga of the dead tree kept me glued to the window, transfixed for hours and reporting back all occurrences to Frank. It all started with a little bonfire, which I can only think was deliberately set, at the base of an old tree in the centre of a patch of scrub behind the nave (pronounced nah vey). Naves are the doubling up of the main houses by the odd collection of back outhouses, trasteros (junk rooms), sheds and garages built behind the terraced houses of which our rental was one. Separated by a patio, this doubling up of the house is a very common sight in Southern Spain raising their garden shed to the status of an integral part of the house. Sometimes it's just another living room, out at the back. The tree burned for half a day before the fire brigade came to put it out. Obviously they didn't make a very good job because it kept smouldering away for a couple of days after and finally someone came and chopped it down. Only a few years later, after we'd moved out, the remaining eucalyptus which had shaded the back of our rental, as well as trucks full of live animals over the years, came down in a storm on to the back of the rental house, completely destroying the garage roof.

At our own house, our neighbour Pepa was always chuntering on about the weeds in the garden before the demolition and rebuild of the wall between us. Just after we'd bought the house, when we weren't here, there was a bad fire between Riotinto and Campofrío. It even crawled half way up the hill immediately before the one which shelters the village. After that fire I began to understand her fear. I had brought a weed wand from England. I started to do a deliberate burn to any remaining weeds every April or May. By June the wand had to be put away and all I could use was a strimmer or a brush cutter. It's actually illegal to have garden fires out in the campo during summer months and I'm sure they'd also take a pretty dim view of any fires in the village in the heat of summer. In the local beauty spots there are often barbecue areas with brick-built barbecues. Woe betide anyone who uses one in the summer months though.

Once while driving home from Riotinto I saw a small fire in a place where we'd been scrumping wood for our greedy rental house fireplace. The fire was in the base of a tree. I drove on a little further and then felt guilty about trying to ignore the possible consequences and turned around so I could report it to the Guardia civil. The Guardia listened patiently while I reported it but didn't seem concerned. I hadn't noticed then that the fire brigade building was almost directly opposite. They must have wondered at the stupidity of the English.

The real con and the non-con

My stupidity that year didn't stop there. I got caught out by one of the gangs of con artists operating, all over Seville and Huelva provinces, knocking on doors and challenging homeowners about the legally mandated 'revision' of the gas appliances in the house. They had paperwork suggesting they were authorised by the Junta de Andalucía (The regional government). They flap their cards under your nose and tell you you have to have this revision done by law. I let these guys in because I was actually expecting someone to be sent by my landlord for a leaky pipe we could smell and which I'd reported. Of course I hadn't heard of this con before it happened to us. So we let them in to inspect the pipes.

They took our equipment apart while another of them distracted us by talking about the trees in our patio etc and then they filled in a load of forms and I realised half way through that I was being conned and I ran up the street and called on the local policeman who called in the Guardia Civil.

By the time I got back from calling Paqui, our gas installation was in bits all over the floor and they wouldn't put it together until we'd paid them 200 euros. They are very slick! I'm not a stupid woman but I got caught out.

When the Guardia first arrived they didn't know what was going on so they weren't sure who was doing what to whom. They took the gas guy's documents and went away and checked them they came back with a whole different attitude. Unfortunately for me, I'd already paid the money because I'd been told by my landlords to do so and they would sort it out with me later. They never did.

I did run (harrass) the culprits out of the pueblo a couple of days later. Apparently they were back yet again a year later while I was away, and a couple of old people got conned. I'm told you should be able to ask your Repsol supplier for the authorised agent's number and it should cost you less than 50 euros. They will change the rubber connecting tube to one with a new date on it and possibly the attachment depending on its age and wear. You only have to have it checked every 5 years.

When I went to do the denuncia (official report), the Guardia civil showed me that there was a string of denuncias against these guys.

They arrive at your door as one or two people, but once they get in a couple of others miraculously appear and they start talking to you while the others mess with your system. Also, when they're talking to the police they have a carefully rehearsed line that you invited them in and you asked them to test the system etc. all of which is only half true, but true enough to make you feel a fool, and make them look in the right. The problem is most people who get caught out feel too foolish or are too old to go and do the denuncia. The next year I got a call to go to court against these guys but it happened to fall on a very important date and I had to send an official letter to say I couldn't go.

I saw a report on Spanish TV news a year later that said a group of Gas con artists were jailed for a string of these cons. I'd like to think it was "our" con men.

Then a funny thing happened to us on the road from Portugal after one of our trips home. A car behind us started flashing just before we reached Valverde del Camino. It worried me and I said to Frank, "don't stop!"

I've heard about these methods of robbing foreigners using distraction techniques. They recognise tourists by their right hand drive or hired cars. Well, I didn't want to be a victim of modern day highway robbery, so we ignored them. Their flapping arms got more and more frantic. Then they pulled in front of us and tried to wave us down. We locked the doors and still ignored them. Then they started making rude signs putting two fingers of the right hand through an 'o' shape made with the left. This was pretty scary but we held our nerve. We were not going to be 'had' again! Eventually they gave up and sped off ahead.

When I felt safe I pulled the car up and took a look round it just in case, but saw nothing. I felt relieved but a bit shocked and confused.

The next morning when I went to the car I saw that the petrol cap was hanging open.

So that's what the rude signs were about.

New builders

I had been weathering the financial crisis until then with my business actually doing rather well and Frank getting enough contracts for a reasonably healthy wage. So, in 2008 we decided to look for builders again. Having made an expensive mistake the previous time we decided this time we were going to find 3 sets of builders and get 3 quotes and choose carefully from them. We made up a list of works we wanted done for a 'casa en bruto'. A simple build without any frills like windows, doors, electrics, or even rendering. This was so we didn't overstretch ourselves. We asked the boyfriend of our neighbour's daughter who was reputed to be a builder of high quality, a Portugese builder who had a reputation for being cheap, and, because our friend "El Mere" had a reputation for knowing everybody, we asked him to recommend some builders too.

"El Mere" brought us a guy called Jose Maria from a firm called Garcia Barrero. El Mere was always a bit cocky so when he brought Jose Maria in and introduced him as "your next builder" I wasn't at all surprised and I gave Jose the same specification as I'd given to the other two. Then we sat back and waited for the presupuestos to come in. Unsurprisingly the cheap guy was very cheap. Too cheap. I wasn't sure he'd included everything and when I asked him he was evasive. The kind of evasive we'd already experienced with our previous builder. The neighbours boyfriend's quote was very pricey and, I felt like Goldilocks tasting porridge when Garcia Barrero's quote came in at "just right". So we shook hands and the contract was sealed. Indeed the new builders did turn out to be approachable. Yeah! And quick. Really? And honest ... I know!

Builders on site

So we agreed with our new builders a fixed contract to build us the 'casa en bruto'. Our bill was going to be around 50 thousand Euros, which converted to around 35 thousand pounds at the time. This we felt sure we could manage with a back up plan of selling the English house to finish the Spanish one or if things got sticky, whichever was the sooner. Unfortunately they got even stickier than we could possibly have imagined.

9

One Wedding … And A Financial Meltdown

2009 year started with a huge reason for celebration. Any other year we wouldn't have been able to go. But this year after working like demons we started with money in our pockets and a very good reason to spend some of it. I was exhausted and in need of a proper holiday. Although we travel regularly, and get days off regularly, there is always a work element to any trip we make. Our first trip of the year this year however was purely for pleasure.

These days many couples spend the price of the deposit on a house on their wedding just for the bride to be the star of the show. I can't understand this and never could. After my son Dominic and his wife's wedding I know that there's a better way. Their February wedding cost them, in total, including their travel and honeymoon something around 5 thousand pounds. A quarter of the average wedding and for such a memorable time! The drawback? Each guest had to find the price of a flight to Thailand and accommodation ranging in price from dirt cheap to not bad. The benefit? Keeping away everyone who didn't really want to make the effort to be there. For those who did it was the trip of a lifetime and not one of them would ever forget the experience. For Dom and Katy a very special wedding that would mean more to them than any fuss and froufrou ever could. Of course they didn't end up with the extra toasters either! Most of us couldn't afford a big wedding present as well as the trip. We did get them one of the new Eepcs (A tiny laptop, pre-Ipads and tablets) I had one and I loved mine. They were a little sceptical that they would manage to find internet connections in south east Asia but in fact they did and called us, and Katy's parents several times and managed to keep most of their booking information and photos on it.

Dom and Katy were going to do an upside down honeymoon then wedding trip around Vietnam Cambodia and Laos. finishing in February that year with meeting up with the family for their dream wedding on Koh Samui. A pretty little Thai island. Dom was a bit worried because he'd opted for a club style accommodation on the top of a big and steep hill, only accessible by a hair raising drive by hotel Jeep. When I told my sister he was getting married on Koh Samui she told me a friend of hers had recommended a place. It was called the Jungle club. The same one as Dominic had just booked!

Dom hadn't expected us all to be able to come but both his brother Alan and sister Kira were there as well. Kira was having serious misgivings about going to University again. It all seemed too much for her so I said "well great! No problem. You can go to Dom and Katy's wedding now!" That was a good enough excuse and she and James just wangled it. It wasn't easy to find that much money of course but they managed. Even my sister came from Australia. Most surprisingly Katy's mum got over her fear of flying to be at her daughter's wedding too, along with her step dad and brothers. Several other relatives and friends completed the party which was around 19 or 20 in total. We booked the whole of the Jungle Club which was like a private family hotel for the week. It had several different levels of accommodation which really suited our different budgets and the central bar/restaurant was beautiful. There were several different places to hang out, including a small infinity pool and open cabins perched sticking out from the hillside with Thai cushions all over the floor. The whole place exuded tranquillity and beauty. It was high up enough to have beautiful views of the whole of that side of the island.

It turned out to be an incredibly memorable and moving experience from start to end. A dream wedding with dancing girls, a baby elephant and three separate but connected ceremonies. It all started with a Buddhist ceremony where they were bound together in this world and in past and future lives too, signified by three white dots on their foreheads. I'm atheist, but even I had no problem putting my hands together and wishing them all these lives in each other's company. Then there was a water ceremony where everyone poured water over the couple's hands and made a wish for their futures together. Finally a western style ceremony on the beach where they made their vows under an arch of thousands of fresh orchids. There was not a dry eye to be seen. The newly-weds wandered off along the beach to have their photographs taken by a talented amateur photographer friend, as the sun set. After dark we retired to a special private bar area set into the beach. We lit paper balloons and set them off making our wishes for the future and then Dominic and Katy's favourite music was play-listed for the rest of the evening. At one point the barman came out from behind the bar to do some cocktail shaker moves and juggling. What he didn't realise was that both Dominic and his best man had trained in cocktail bars when they were younger and they hadn't forgotten their tricks. They gave a performance too which had the guests whooping and hollering. The atmosphere was lovely, light hearted and celebratory.

A couple of days later after some of the guests had drifted off home, the rest of the party hopped off to spend a few extra days on Koh Tao, a slightly quieter but more expensive location where we booked the honeymoon suite and then swapped with Dom and Katy as an extra surprise. I got to go snorkelling. The first day the water was really clear and lovely but the second and third days the water seemed cloudy and churned up and there weren't so many fish to be seen. It was only later we found that was peak shark season! Kira stepped on a purple caterpillar in her cabin and ended up in A&E to be on the safe side. We still don't know if it was poisonous but she was given some tablets to take and suffered no ill effects.

I bought a stack of beautiful cotton sarongs for around 3 pounds each. More than I can ever use but I just couldn't resist. Maybe they'll make very appropriate little dresses for future granddaughters.

This was to be our last 'splurge' paid for by the nail art business before things took a distinctly financially rocky turn.

My nemesis vanquished

When we got home I decided it was time to start again investigating the damp problem in our English house. The idea to do it then was precipitated by Eileen being away for a few days. Frank was sure he heard water running but we didn't have any taps on and after investigating, none was on in Eileen's house either. We had previously taken the floorboards up so we knew that under the floorboards it wasn't just damp; there were still distinct pools. This was clearly nothing to do with the 2007 floods. I remembered a trick the water men had used at the church building and we went around the house with a long stick touching various parts of the walls and the other end pressed to our ears.

We were sure the sound was coming from either under our back kitchen or under my mother-in-law's next door. So we called the council in to check Eileen's house as she'd suffered for years and years from really serious rising damp in her living room. Along came the council water man and he checked all around Eileen's house and pronounced that, as we thought, the water was coming from somewhere between her back kitchen and ours. Most probably under or in a wall. So he trotted round to ours and identified the spot where there was a definite running water sound where there shouldn't have been. Our house was private, sold off by the council to the then tenants under Margaret Thatchers right-to-buy scheme. Eileen's house was still council owned.

Still the man agreed to dig up our floor to find the source of the running water as, he said, often council workers had simply bent old lead pipes over to cut them off and over the years the force of the resulting trickle of water had become greater and greater and simply blown out the old seal. This, it turned out, is exactly what had happened to ours. In spite of our house being private and because the fix was so quick, it was easier for the council man to fix our leak permanently than for us to argue over responsibility. So, another water demon slain at the cost of replacing a couple of broken tiles. No problem. Anne had already sourced and stored extra tiles in the same colour. So I simply filled in the hole after the man and tamped it down hard. Cemented it over and patched the tiling. Finally we could contract a company to dry line and plaster the walls and the house looked a little less like a building site. One more step towards selling. At that point the houses were still at a fairly buoyant price but I could smell the fear in the housing market. Unfortunately there was nothing I could do. The house wasn't quite finished and we hadn't been living there for quite long enough. In a few more months our regulation two years would be up.

However those 'few more months' were going to see quite a lot of changes.

This was a good excuse to take a trip to Spain and see how the building was getting along. Our friend Quique had sent us some photos of the main structure which seemed to be a sea of Acrow props. It was intriguing! We had to see for ourselves.

I could hardly contain my excitement when we arrived in Plaza de Andalucía. The props had gone and you could scramble right up the sloping stairway (no stairs yet) and get to the first floor. It was vast! "What the hell are we building Ange?" Frank asked me. "Our dream house?" was my insecure reply. The view from the first floor was every bit as beautiful as we thought it would be and I started imagining us sitting out and having breakfast on the back patio next to our upstairs kitchen. Of course it wasn't a house yet, it was just cement pillars and slabs. All the same we were in awe of what "we" had built already.

Registering the car

Once the UK MOT ran out, we couldn't get UK insurance so that was that. It was time to take our biggest foray yet into the impenetrable nightmare of Spanish red tape. We had to get the car sorted out.

You know really, you can skip the next eight paragraphs as its boring as hell unless you're really interested in the complexities of Spanish paperwork. There's a video going around the internet in Spanish that sums this tangle of bureaucracy up perfectly. Watch that instead, especially the end bit with the stapler. Its much shorter than the real thing. After this experience I have very little time for, or interest in it.

First we needed to change the headlamps to point in the right direction for the Spanish roads. No problem. We were happy to have some shiny new undamaged lights anyway. Then we needed to travel to Huelva, around 100 Km away, to get a technical specification in Spanish made up. We had a terrible time looking for what we thought would be an important government building. It wasn't. It was a tiny little office that could have belonged to a part time Private Investigator. Actually that could easily have been his other 'pluriempleo' job. Pretty much all he did was check the chassis number, ask us if there had been any modifications, and photocopy the V8 document. Then we're guessing he simply picked up a similar enough translation off the internet. In any case it was a well paid job. I think that cost us over 300 Euros and wasn't going to be be ready for a week.

So a week later we picked those papers up, and then we had to take that document all the way back and get an appointment at the ITV (MOT) inspection centre. This was just a 20 minute drive from Campofrío. They charged us for the MOT of course. Extra, because it was a foreign car and the first time they'd inspected it. It was very strange. Like no MOT we'd ever experienced. We stayed in the car and drove over several testing runners and a pit while they checked the brakes and chassis. Hooray! They gave us the coveted yearly sticker and then it was time to go back to Huelva Ministry of Traffic offices. Of course we couldn't do that the same day. You can never expect to do any of these paperwork tasks in one day or even one week.

Back in Huelva the woman at the information desk told us to queue (for an hour) for counter 8, 9 or 11. Definitely not counter 10, because that was for some other purpose. When we got to the front of the queue they just told us to go to the information desk across the room for a form. The person at the information desk gave us a bill for another few euros, then sent us to the payment counter where we were told us about two other places to go to pay two other things. The import tax and the annual road tax. Without that the car had no permission to drive on the roads. These offices were back near home of course.

At the first of the other places was the Hacienda (tax) offices in Aracena. The man looked through several well thumbed books and this seemed to take ages, because our car had a different name to the Spanish version of the same year. We were glad we'd kept the old V8 to show that. An official in a bad mood can cost weeks of frustration and hundreds of Euros. Some just choose give you a flat "no". Eventually he gave up and fortunately was in a good enough mood to choose the nearest model to the one we had. This decided which payment band we were in. Three hundred Euros more to pay in import duty. Well, It was an eight year old car even then. Then he sent us away to the bank to pay. We had to come back to get the payment form stamped before we could proceed any further.

When we commented on the complexity of the paperwork, the guy assured us it would be harder to re-register a Spanish car in England. Actually, our previous car had somehow been registered as German even though it was a right hand drive car and clearly English when we bought it. It had been registered as second hand but had low mileage on the clock and so cost several thousand pounds less than a brand new car would have. We imagine there was some tax avoiding scheme involved. Anyway one 2 minute trip to the DVLA sorted the lot, no payment to be made and all in the one place.

When we got back to it the next task of paying the road tax it was surprisingly near, surprisingly easy, and surprisingly cheap, something like 39 euros for a years tax at our local(ish) town hall in Nerva The next mining town along from Riotinto.

So then the second part of the process began. We went all the way back to the main office, in Huelva. To another long queue, this time different counter numbers where they took all our details (all those hard won pieces of paper) and also our English V8. We made sure we had a copies in case an earlier stage failed. Oh yes we'd seen the video circulating the internet about someone needing some piece of paper in Spain; consisting of two people staring each other down while the official requested, and received a dozen different pieces of paper, some in triplicate which eventually climaxed in a battle of staplers.

Finally, they gave us our new registration number. After all that I was pleased and amused to be assigned a number which ended in 00 GRR! Of course we then had to go hunting for somewhere nearby to make the plates. Only to find that they attach a slightly different way here than the ones on our car. Victory was ours! At a cost of a little over a thousand Euros. Much cheaper than a wreck of a second hand car. And my car had a young Zetec engine having only done about 45 thousand miles.

Franks advice would be different:- "Get yourself a real bargain runabout from some dodgy garage in a back street near the coast instead". I'm not sure that's such good advice given our experiences.

It would probably have been safest to get a new car really. And at that time we possibly could have got the finance. It would have had guarantees at least. Frank said on our new self build website "Choose the colour you like. Then, to save upset when you get it home, specify a Seville Paint Job … This means get them to hammer the crap out of it in random hard to reach places and scratch it all down one side. This really is compulsory in Andalucía, so if you don't get it done at the show room it will only cost you time and money later". Frank also has some advice on drainage. I wouldn't take that seriously though. Franks sense of humour can sometimes be a little sarcastic.

We had cut our fairs and workshop schedule massively, partly due to the nail art canes having taken up all of my time for the past year and partly because Fimo had once again changed their formulas in the middle of a book publication. The new formula was so fresh and unpredictable that I couldn't guarantee results in classes so I'd given up teaching completely. My new book was out but I couldn't teach it live and I wasn't going to see much income from it that year at least. We had done Miniatura in spring although we had very little stock. It seemed to me to be a poor turnout too. For us, Miniatura was dying.

By May I'd recovered enough stocks to do the new Spring Madrid fair. That wasn't a huge success either. People were nervous and such luxuries as miniatures started to be lower down many peoples lists. This seemed to be the year when people stayed at home and consolidated. It looked more and more like we had nothing to consolidate.

Oh well at least there was Soest and then Paris both of which fairs I really enjoyed. And we had a new book to push, but otherwise it was a poor year for us just because there really wasn't enough stock to sell.

A nice reprieve from the worries came in August though, when we took another trip to Sweden. This time it was organised by Agneta of Skala Minimal. Agneta generously lent us her flat as she had moved recently. It was a lovely Scandinavian style flat, all wooden floors and very light and airy and only 200 metres from Skala Minimal where two of the classes were held. Before the fair at the next weekend we walked and walked and walked. One day through the parkland down to a lake where I, bravely I thought, took a dip in the very cold water. We took a photograph of me swishing my hair with the droplets flying into the air in an arc. It would have been an attractive photo of a younger girl but I was just a brown blob in an ill fitting bathing suit! It was very fortunate that Agneta had plenty of class members for 3 different classes during the week before the Stockholm miniature fair because the fair itself was a washout. It had moved venues and was in a little schoolroom with poor public transport access on a day when there was a marathon closing many streets. Visitor numbers were what I'd call "a handful". We took time to take Agneta and her new boyfriend (who is now her husband) out for a meal to thank them for all Agneta's help and the use of her flat. They chose the very posh restaurant over the harbour called Gondolen. To be honest though, in my opinion neither the venue nor the menu warranted the fame, or the fortune it cost to eat there.

We knew we were going to need a serious wedge of cash, and soon, so we got busy and rather tied up renovating our English house after finally putting in the damp proof course in. However, every hour I spent on the house was an hour I couldn't spend making miniatures. I asked Dave to come back and put the second upstairs dividing wall back in which I then plaster boarded myself. I didn't plaster over the boarding, I simply filled the joints and put lining paper over to prepare for painting. I knew we'd be selling the house that year and I knew that the profit would be much lower than we'd previously expected so I did do a changing rooms job on it, just decorating simply with a feature wall in each room and a few co-ordinating cushions to give it a bit of a cosy look. I did a similar plasterboard job to the stairs into the loft room effectively making it back to the 3-plus-1 bedroom house that it was before Anne took all the internal walls out. I stood back and assessed the job. It looked nice! Anne's hardwood door and window frames gave it a quality look and my simple finish didn't detract from that.

The transformation into a 'normal' house was completed by the addition of a thick Berber carpet to the living room and hall. I jazzed up the back garden with another layer of red chippings. It was finally ready to sell just over 2 years after we had taken possession of it ourselves. We put the house on the market immediately it was ready as I was already receiving bills for the stages of work from The builders in Spain. We knew that the house values had already dropped a little from their peak, but we were still hopeful. We knew we'd have to take things a bit steady though.

The pound crashes

I blame Lawrence Llewellyn Bowen for the financial crisis and the housing crash. Well maybe that's a little unfair. On the other hand I, along with millions of others used to watch programmes like Changing Rooms and Grand Designs and Place In The Sun and I followed them avidly. I too wanted these dreams. To be honest I didn't covet the purple and black trashy room-in-a-weekend type places but I was doing the buying a house, doing it up and enjoying a greater sense of achievement because of it thing. And so were we all, it seemed. We all knew that our houses would be worth more, we'd have more freedom to choose the sort of life we wanted to live. I knew even then that it was all getting a bit overblown and I knew with certainty that once mortgage payments cost more than 1/3rd of an average family's income something was bound to give.

As the value of the £ started to fall we gritted our teeth and started to make adjustments to our expectations. The original plan for our Spanish build which had finally got under way, was to have a house which was unfinished but was still definitely a house. This was to be paid for by a small mortgage, or, if that couldn't be achieved, the value of the sale of our house in England would cover both the builders and our remaining credit cards etc. Until now we thought it would be fairly simple get the mortgage to finish the job. Up until that point my business had been doing really well for a year or two. Bucking the trend actually.

Even before the fall in the value of the pound things started to go wrong. Firstly a couple of Franks customers went bust without paying him. New clients were getting difficult to find and those possibilities that there were, were looking like committing him to long travelling hours for little reward. Never mind, we thought, my business was still buoyant even though the long hours were wearing me out.

Then the crisis suddenly deepened for us as the pound started to fall dramatically against the Euro. Of course this meant our Spanish bills were rising in comparison. We started trimming things off the build to try to bring the costs down. Keeping our spirits up and just 'digging deeper'. First the fireplaces went, then one by one the internal walls were knocked off the contract. All this seemed to do was to keep the contract at the same price as the builders found more work which needed doing to keep the neighbours happy. Then the pound started to drop faster. We watched in horror as the exchange rate dropped from 1. 47 Euros to the pound lower and lower. Suddenly it was at 1:1! This meant our expected 35 thousand pound bill was suddenly 55 thousand Euros which of course was now the same as 55 thousand pounds. We tried to stay positive throughout, but it was difficult. It was already too late to stop now. The builders already on site and throwing up the house more quickly than we thought possible.

Although we hoped that the pound would rally, we knew it was hopeless. OK, we thought. We'll put the English house on the market and get a smallish bridging loan to keep the builders happy. We got the loan but it was touch and go and they squeezed us as hard as they could. It was almost as if they could smell desperation. No. It wasn't "almost." They sure as hell could tell they could get away with it. It was this single experience which led me to lose all respect for bankers. When the lending rate was at a historic half a percent Lloyds TSB were asking us 18. We'd sell the house soon. Wouldn't we? That would do it. After all, our house was worth a lot more than we paid for it two years before. But, of course, house values also suddenly dropped dramatically because of the difficulty finding mortgages. Even on our little house it wiped 20 to 25 thousand off our possible asking price, meaning the amount we could make, though it could finish paying the builders, was suddenly no longer enough to cover our loans and bills. We were getting into choppy waters and as my mother would have said "sailing very close to the wind." Of course this new loan was only to part pay the builders, and was supposed only to be a bridge to selling the house.

We suddenly realised just how precarious a position we were in. Then, the final straw. The cheapness of the Chinese copies was bad enough. Along with the fact that nail art customers are not as perfectionist as miniaturists when it comes to colour and scale, and, given the fact that I couldn't keep up with the orders with my one helper choosing to work only part time, it wasn't surprising that in early 2009 Bjorn cancelled a large order and went with the Chinese. OK I got him and other companies back for certain of my products which the Chinese couldn't keep up the quality of, but not before my business was thoroughly damaged. Although this few thousand was peanuts in the scheme of things it smashed my cash flow to bits. I'd just ordered huge amount of clay up front too. Our choice was suddenly very stark indeed. Sell the house for what we could get as fast as we could and pay the builders ... or stay in England leaving the builders unpaid and the house open to the elements and vandalism.

On a moral level there was no option. The builders had to be paid. Also leaving a dangerous building unoccupied and uncared for could have caused us even more problems, legal as well as financial.

There was no other solution. We had to move all our goods and chattels to Spain and get ourselves into the house as quickly as possible even though it was totally unfinished. Fortunately the English house sold quickly, though cheaply. In the end we accepted 85 thousand. We paid the builders off, packed everything we could get into 3 of Britannia's box trailers and arrived in Spain with only just enough money to put the windows and doors into the house to make it waterproof. Nothing to pay our debts in England. It had been the perfect storm financially and we were washed up!

... and washed out.

We moved to Spain on the 18th December 2009. Our removals van arrived on the19th. Of course, predictably, as they were unloading it started to rain. The rain never stopped from that day until April the next year. It felt apocalyptic. Some of our goods and chattels never arrived and I'm sure some more disappeared in the few hours we left them unattended in the front of the house before we had energy to move them. We had no real security at all. Just builders fencing which was easy to pop out from its supporting blocks. My ladders didn't arrive. One of my rugs. My garden pots. A wheelie bin full of garden equipment and most of my Minicraft tools were missing. Though strangely I did get all of the transformers. We grabbed a coffee to perk us up and then moved everything from the front into one of the two offices which were the only rooms with doors. They didn't have windows yet. They were semi bricked up in the temporary style common here. Everything was going to get irretrievably damp. We still had no front doors or any windows at all. The doors which came in the removal van and were 2 old stable doors I'd bought from an architectural salvage yard and had dipped for 150 pounds in total. There was no way we could afford the 2 thousand Euros we'd been quoted for a Spanish front door, So I was going to have to learn to handle a router.

We were exhausted and more than a little depressed. But we were here and we were going to get ourselves ready for the challenges to come. We really did have to give ourselves several talkings-to. We kept on believing that my business could keep us afloat. Of course we hadn't calculated on how heavy the tax burden is on honest small businesses in Spain. If I'd known then what I know now I would certainly have done things 'the Spanish way' right from the beginning. But I didn't.

Our first Christmas as new Andalucíans was spent in the rental house. Our one Xmas present to ourselves was a lovely big orange cement mixer. We were going to need it!

10

Family Matters

In 2010 we did eight fairs, which was a definite improvement on previous years, but still too many and one of them was a ridiculous thing to do. We decided to do Miniatura and Hobbycraft, both in the NEC on the same weekend. I shared the Hobbycraft stand with my friend Nicola Croad who also decided to do both at once with the help of her sister. I was poorly the whole weekend and it half killed me, especially the distance between the two halls. Far from being a double success for us it was much nearer a double failure.

This was the last year I did Miniatura. It had moved halls and I didn't like the new hall. Plus the stands were just too expensive and we weren't taking enough money to justify the travelling. One by one we were dropping fairs which had run their course and taking up fairs which were more interesting and hopefully profitable. I must admit when it came to it, location had a lot to do with our decision. When you were taking a risk on making a profit at least the place should be worth visiting in itself. More and more we wanted to stay at home and build on what we had. Besides we had a family visit coming up.

My sister Stephanie had rung me up one day during the previous Xmas and new year holidays. She had decided to make a rare visit to Europe this year as she wanted to touch base with her family. Since all the brothers and sisters and their families lived in diverse places and diverse countries, it was decided that a central location in Europe and an interesting holiday location for everyone else to get to would be our place.

Of course in our old plan the place would have been ready or at least nearly ready, but since the perfect storm of the fall in the pound etc. we still only had our "casa en bruto" and rather more bruto than we'd planned. We had to get the house "campable" at least. We needed to have downstairs internal walls enough for rooms for each visitor, we needed plumbing for loos and hot water for a shower or bath as an absolute minimum. It was also the absolute minimum for our own needs. So our plans for next year were set. We were to get ready to have the family over 'camping' in the unfinished house and then when they had gone we would move in ourselves. This was quite a tall order since at that point we had none of the above. We still didn't even have doors or windows.

Just before we'd realised quite how dire our situation was getting Juan Manuel had convinced us that it was a good idea to lay plastic underfloor central heating pipes. He said he could bring some and lay them next time he came to Campofrío and all we had to do was lay the first course of bricks to mark out where the rooms were going.

I'd ordered a 'gizmo' from England called a Brickie which was a plastic shape you put over your walls to help you lay bricks easier. It did help with levelling and not using too much mortar. The trouble was it was English brick size so I couldn't really use it exactly as intended.

Frank became the cement mixer master and I laid the first two layers of bricks round the upstairs rooms. We had to make some fast decisions and measurements and knock up the divisions really quickly. On the Saturday Juan Manuel came over in a van, laden with insulation and pipes. He offloaded everything and showed us how to lay the insulation and left us to it. We worked for the rest of the day cutting and sticking together the big boards of black plastic-coated polystyrene and laid the edge strips which were meant to stop any heat escaping into the walls. It was a long job and we were exhausted after it.

First we started to build the downstairs internal walls ourselves in the wettest winter I've ever experienced with whatever money we could scrape together for building. We were struggling with bills that we still had in England, trying not to, but sometimes being forced to dip into credit cards to keep going and to buy essential materials. We were already learning to live a much more frugal life than we had previously done. Of course my business was still earning, but a little less than before. It was still an English business at that time. I planned to change over at the end of my tax year. For now we were going to spend our first Xmas as Spanish residents in the cold rental. Water was pouring into the light well and through all the big window holes, running off the first floor onto the ground and out of both the front and back doors. Every day we went to sweep it out and do as much work as we could bolstered by a coffee and Kit Kat break in the middle of the morning. We soon added up how much the 4 euros for two coffees and two Kit-Kats was adding up to each week and realised that was one of the first things that had to go. That many euros bought enough cement and sand for the day's work.

After warning everyone that our house would, by summer the following year, still only be fit to be considered a "camp site with a roof" I realised the first thing we needed to do was to get some windows and doors in. I'd made a front door from the two old stable doors brought over from England. I'd got a router and I was not afraid to use it. Well, if truth be told I was afraid to use it but I had no option. I was going to have to learn some new skills, and fast.

We'd come out of the house sale and paying the builders with just over 10 thousand pounds or thereabouts. We would have loved to have been able to pay off some of our cards and loans but that really wasn't an option by this time. We were now thoroughly stuck between a rock and a hard place. Even if self build mortgages had been available at that point we had been so choked by the whole situation from being really good credit risks we'd dropped like a stone to "wouldn't touch with a barge pole" status. The original estimate from Jesus was around 8 thousand just for the light well cover. And we had adjusted the design of the roof to make the risers brick built which would reduce that figure considerably, but still, we didn't think we were going to get away with anything less than 4 thousand Euros and that was just going to be too much. We didn't have a back door or any windows at all in the house. All the front openings were temporarily bricked up in the style they do in Spain for security, which is a honeycomb effect where every other brick, more or less is left out. It's bodged in with yeso, (plaster) to make it easier to replace later.

Juan Manuel came to the rescue again. He knew a metalworker and he came himself to measure everything up for all the main house windows, except one which we'd managed to buy from Leroy Merlin. Two patio doors and a back door. As well as designing and quoting for two tilting windows in the walls of the light well and the front rejas (the bars on the front of every Andalucían house) and balcony rails. It was a big shopping list but didn't include any of the office windows or the laundry room door. We also decided the temporary builder's doors we had had put on the offices were going to be at least semi permanent. They just weren't ever going on the high priority list. Juan Manuel 'monkeyed' around on the roof like a natural. Naturally I was up there with him which seems strange looking back just a decade later. He measured everything twice and it's a testament to his accurate measuring that when the roof came it fitted perfectly. A week or so later he was back with the 'presupuesto' (the quotation) and the whole lot came in at around 11 thousand Euros. With recent income we had just enough. The quotation for the light well roof was just a bit over 2 thousand. Way better than we'd feared.

Nasal hair

Juan Manuel's friend David turned out to be a 'silver fox'. Well, I can't help it. I said something because if I didn't Frank would notice anyway. Blushes give me away as do tears and tantrums. I'm just over emotional. So I said "I quite fancy grey haired men". Well, Frank usually isn't at all jealous. He knows he's "young hubby" and the second and final love of my life. This time I think he knew I meant it. Well I do. I'm just waiting for Frank to go grey.

He hurrumphed and said. "but he's got nasal hair!". Well that did it, as he knew it would.

Unfortunately for him that has given me rights to demand the removal of, or to remove myself any offending facial or body hair that he develops forever into the future. Well he tries, bless him, but those tusks keep on appearing. Of course I now have carte blanche to demand their removal on pains of stopping fancying him wherever and whenever they appear. Like the time, on a particularly bendy bit of Sierra road. Yes, while he was driving. No I didn't remove it myself. A pathetic plunge into a tepid reservoir just isn't my idea of a dramatic enough end to this little old lady. I did make him remove it himself. "ooh Ooohh OOOOHHHH." Was that a full on brain itch then? I asked him. Aargh yes.

Fully eyeball to the back of the head. Well now Frank knows he shouldn't ever have used that tactic to put me off of that sexy silver fox. It's now used against him and he knows it always will be. He'll be a bit more careful how he quashes my fantasies in future.

The roof went up with 'Silver Fox' welding and the showers of welding sparks falling into the light well were quite dramatic. I remembered at the last minute to ask him to weld me a hook into the centre for hanging a light from in the future.

The rest of the doors and windows were put in. The front window only after Frank and I had taken a lump hammer to the temporary bricks. It really did start to look like a house. The rejas were left for us to put in and I wasn't at all sure how I was going to do that. I decided that was a worry for another day

Am I going to dye?

On the subject of silver hair. I had to decide. Should I dye my rapidly greying hair? This is an easy answer for a blonde. No, don't bother. You'll look gorgeous whatever your height, weight, age. Oh yes you will. Don't worry about that. And slim women with short grey hair look serene and lovely. Also, if your life partner is the same age as you, well you can both go grey together. All say ahhhhh. Unfortunately me, I'm not blonde, and I'm 'dumpy'. I've been dyeing for a good few years now. Frank is blonde and when he has a short beard he looks much younger and the age gap starts to look much more apparent. On a bad hair day, even more so. And I look more and more like my mum every day.

According to Frank my mum looks like Mrs Doubtfire in her photos. Good grief! At least I'd kept the long hair against an onslaught of Spanish 'ladies of a certain age' who ask me matter-of-factly when I'm going to cut it. Probably they think it's way past time I conformed and got the shapeless summer dress and the short permed and regularly tinted hair.

So, for the second year running, I was looking at 'summer-swimming-pool grey grow-through' and ginger straw ends. As another glorious summer drew to an end, it was decision time. The previous year I chickened out and went a bit experimental. A couple of flashes of bleach, a deep blue temporary dye and then purple. but that's all such a hassle. The local shops only sell the standard black through brown to blonde range, and it's expensive when we're living on a tighter-than-tight budget. Is there enough time in my life for all that 'faff'? So should this little old lady dye, or live grey?

The maverick side of me thought that as none of my peers round here had long grey hair … That's my natural place. That said there's clearly a three year transition. Plus the sudden pulling away from my husband in apparent age. Fortunately Frank was already going grey, in his beard at least. So I decided I'd have to make sure he kept the beard on the longer side. There's nothing worse than going into a shop and leaving your husband outside only to have the squinting assistant ask you if you're buying something for your son. Grrr! So I decided to grow out the colour and just bleach a little in the centre front to link the greyer sides in with the rest. I really did start to look suddenly older though. Sigh.

My family and other animals

The family visit was getting closer and the time I had between fairs was extremely short. Because the house was so unfinished and I knew wouldn't be nice to sit in, I splashed out. (I knew I shouldn't) on a pergola and several garden chairs. They were cheap for what they were as Chinese goods were now flooding into Spain The pergola even had an integral mosquito screen and seemed good value. The next year it was destroyed by a freak 'tormenta' while we were out of town. Still it had been a pleasant place for us to sit and eat and chatter.

We didn't have any plumbing yet though. And really no money left to buy any unless we abused our credit cards again and we were already starting to wonder how the hell we were ever going to pay them. Just the minimum monthly payment was getting to be difficult to find.

We were at least going to a few fairs and we went to Soest just before the family visit was due. While we were away Wamma stepped in again and put us in a 50 litre water tank and piped round the house to the kitchen and then down to the bathroom. Of course there were no kitchen units and there was no bathroom as such but when we got back there were taps and there was hot water. The big bath that we'd ordered and stored in the light well was still sitting there upside down and covered in cloths. The toilet was still in its box and the family visit was less than a week away.

My anxiety levels were ramping up extremely high and I worried I was going to get myself back into full on panic mode. I realised I needed to build supporting walls for the bath and then add a wooden frame on top to sit between the bath edge and the brick walls. We'd ordered a rather expensive bath because we wanted it to double as a shower so it was fairly flat bottomed and nearly a metre wide. Rather expensive, but very fitting for the house and so I've never regretted it.

Somehow, at the last minute we managed to get enough plumbing in for toilet and showers to be fed with fresh water and with the early arrival of Alan (my son) who we called 'Polish Al' from time to time from then on for his ability with plumbing, we also got the waste water pipes fitted just in time. Looking back it seems to me he did a hell of a lot of plumbing. He generously reminds me that it always looks that way when someone takes a job off your hands.

There was no time to get a sink in for washing up so we arranged a sort of washing station outside the back door with a washing up bowl on a small scaffold. Water was to be got from the bathroom and disposed of either down the toilet or in the garden. One by one bedrooms were made up for arriving guests. Alan had a fold-out bed in Franks office. Steph, who Frank had picked up from the airport without me, as I was just too busy, was to have the newly built brick box that was the guest bedroom. Still fairly recently married Dominic and Katy had the not-quite-built master bedroom. When Derek and Sue brought their son Damien, a bed was hastily made up on the floor of the training room with a screen to provide him with just a little privacy. Derek and Sue had sensibly opted to stay in a local Hostal.

I was also hoping the donkey who seemed to have moved into the field at the back wouldn't bother the visitors. He was either angry or randy whichever it was, he didn't shut up "EEEh Awwww EEEh Awww." And then there was the stork family on the building crane up on Campo Alto. "Yak Yak Yak". Pepa had clearly just had a new air conditioning unit installed. That was making a drill like racket, "BabababaBabababa" on hot evenings. On top of all this the hunt dogs and the cockerels were also piping up and their calls carrying further than usual through the unusually still night air. Between them the 'campo' was not so peaceful anymore.

We were going to stay in the rental house and I came to be very glad we had. The whole visit became what Frank rather aptly described as a 'circus'. Steffie, had spent the previous few days unreachable in Amsterdam, having bought and consumed quite a lot of of the greeny-brown stuff. After her arrival she had ignored my sage advice to avoid drinking too many sugary drinks and tintos and to get plenty of water into her. Both my sister and I are confirmed water-dodgers but I've had to learn from my mistakes. Steffie then got a terrible neck-based migraine overnight and the next morning had to be taken to the local doctor for a shot in her rear end. I was summoned the following day to take her to the doctors again. To be honest I'd "had it up to here" by then and told her I was too busy, and my mean streak came out when she asked me to write a note for the doctor since she didn't speak a word of Spanish. I wrote one that said something along the lines of "my sister, having spent the last few days stoned in Amsterdam and having come down off yesterdays opiates now finds herself in need of another score". I altered it of course and this story is exaggerated (I'm told), but the tears of laughter while I wrote it did do something to alleviate the stress.

My sister is rather, what would be called here in Spain, "mandona" although in her defence I'm very similar and that's probably why we knock heads, the difference being that Steffie also smokes and drinks coffee. There's something about those two drugs that seems to me to make people extra difficult and demanding. I do know how painful that type of migraine can be though and appreciate that Steffie, whatever the rights and wrongs were, was in great pain and I was a bit mean.

We are an odd family. Probably because we have spent so little adult time together we've never really got past our childhood roles. Even though our childhoods were all mostly happy there were family 'chips on shoulders' which were passed on to each one of us. Our childhoods never quite leave us and I still needed to get over the feeling that I was often scapegoated for anything the girls of the family did wrong. I had never conformed and I was the apple who didn't fall far from the tree. As adults we were never close enough to learn to be diplomatic with our siblings so we always say what we think and often do have arguments rather than seething inside. As a result family get-togethers can be both great fun and occasionally a bit fiery. I was certainly not at my best and wasn't about to take any extra stress so I spent most of the time avoiding being part of the "circus". Howard, because of a medical problem had rather sensibly decided not to come and though Steph was disappointed, maybe a little annoyed, I think he made the right choice; there were enough egos on site already and Howie may have been even more blunt than I.

Derek and Damien's arrival was also quite spectacular as they were having a fiery father and son argument about directions as they screeched around the entrance to the village. I can just imagine what it was about as our Sat Nav coordinates have, or had, a great big error on them. The rest of us had a bird's eye view of the comedy as we were sitting outside Cecelias Bar waiting for them and enjoying an early evening Tinto de Verano. They soon calmed it down with the good company and great food. We took everyone back to the house where Damien did a spectacular 'dive' over the threshold, badly spraining his ankle. I soon realised that Damien and Steph were very much out of the same mould and Steph had to hand her diva crown over to him as Damie (who hates that name and told me so in no uncertain terms) took on the mantle of impatient patient.

Derek's wife Sue was, and always is the calming force over everyone. It seems we all needed that. People left in a trickle just as they had arrived. Alan first and then Dom and Katy. After a couple of days we nipped off to a small fair in southern Andalucía which thankfully saved the frayed family nerves even though it was successful in no other respect.

I adore all my siblings and am immensely proud of each one of them. However I handled them better in those days one at a time and I'm not sure if that's a symptom of the tail end of my own social phobia or just that there are too many entertainers in our family, all of us are in turns quite witty but there isn't enough oxygen in a room for more than one at a time. I find those social situations exhausting.

I pretty much vowed never to have such a family get together again. At least not in "my" space. In future, if there were any family dos we were definitely always going to be away from home and have our own space as we did at Dom and Kate's wedding. I think Derek and Sue had the right idea. In fact various combinations of us have got together a few times in the last few years and each time relations have improved. Absence doesn't make the heart grow fonder. Familiarity does.

Family Support

Where families can be difficult they can also be our salvation. At some point in the week I found time for a one-to one chat with Dom when I pretty much broke down and told him how difficult things had got for us. We realised we had crashed right into the financial wall and the house of cards was falling down around us. We'd spent our last few Euros preparing for the family visit and we were definitely in the brown stuff … The British tax office was demanding, with menaces, that I paid a rather large tax bill. We were unable to pay our credit card bills that month. This was not the last of such crises we came upon. Dom had been offering to organise a loan to complete the build but I said I had no idea when we were going to pay anyone back and just didn't have any confidence in doing so. Our house was at its point of least equity looking as it did more like a building site than a house and we faced a stark choice. Selling the project for a fraction of what it was worth to pay back the banks and returning to England with absolutely nothing. Or pressing on and living in the house like squatters. In reality there was no contest. We were staying somehow. And the somehow was, not for the last time, with Dom and Katy's help.

Dom rang me up a week or so later and told me I didn't have to ask for a loan. They were going to pay my Tax payment scheme for 6 months. And our Seguridad social. We promised to pay back 'one day' but Dom insisted there was no rush and I rather suspect it could be from my estate since things have never been easy since then and when there is money Dom agrees it's best spent on the next small step of the build. This is because the house can't be classified as fit for habitation until the architect signs it off. He's already told us he'll never sign it off until it's fully built down to the last tile and largely to his specifications. However, If one day Dom and Katy find themselves in real difficulties, then we would of course have to sell the house or rather "the project" as is, and it would I'm sure be worth more than if we'd sold it right at the beginning, Though maybe not much. You don't get much for an unfinished palace these days.

First days in the Spanish house

So we'd moved into the box of bricks we'd just staked everything on. Well it wasn't much but it was ours. Ours in the sense that it was paid for even if the debts we'd left beihind in the UK amounted to more than we could probably sell it for at this stage of construction in these financial times. So we had to make the best of it, content in the knowledge that at least we'd paid the builders who weren't at fault for 'crisis' or the fall in the pound rather than the banks who certainly were. Yes we'd sailed close to the wind financially but we hadn't expected the perfect storm.

My feeling of foreboding getting up in the early hours of the morning on that first day was intense and that feeling was to revisit me many times over the next few years. In many cases around this time it was Frank who asked me to dig deeper and not the other way round. And dig deep we did. Not financially as there was nothing to dig into but physically and mentally. We couldn't give up now. It was a choice of work hard for everything or 'wimp out' and end up with nothing which was certainly a depressing vision. After all, we lived in paradise. A very unfinished palace in paradise but nonetheless you could see where we were going.

Thanks to Juan Manuel we did have running water and thanks to the builders we still had builders' electricity. How we were living then would also have made up a catalogue of health and safety breaches, I was told any one of which could cost us 2,000 Euros which, of course we could never find and so we heeded the dire warnings never to open the door to anyone with a clipboard, and if we accidentally did, to "know nothing". One by one we made everything safe and each time something else was done we breathed a sigh of relief. We'd lived for the first six months for instance without a balcony railing on the upper floor leaving a perilous drop to the ground.

First Alan and then Dom came back for a few days each that year to give us a leg up with the awful job of screeding over the upstairs underfloor water pipes. This consisted of ramming a fairly dry cement and sand mix between the pipes and then to a depth of a couple of centimetres more. It was back and arm breaking work and dreadfully slow and I began to wish we'd never started it. Especially as to this day we've never been able to afford to connect the system to anything. It was impossible to get the work perfectly straight either which caused me no end of problems tiling over later and we had to leave big gaps round the edges for future pipe works. The boys gave us the impetus to get going and Dom was also there to help us get the upstairs balcony rails fitted. We were very happy to have the extra hands as those things were heavy. We built our scaffolding and painted the front of the house and dug out slots for the ends of the rails to be cemented into. This was quite a bodge job and we never have got it tidied up. It's on the "one day" list. As soon as the screeding was done we were able to put the railings round the light well. This was a hell of a job in itself and I remember poor Dom trying to help us drill just one hole through the Gresmanc tiles. Eventually we realised that we had to take the bit out of the middle of the diamond hole cutter but it was another of those tortuous jobs.

We managed to get most of the upstairs walls built by the next Xmas and decided to put up our Xmas tree for the first time in Spain. In spite of still living in a box of bricks this brought a rosy glow to my cheeks along with the output from the tiny and very ugly barrel stove which I think we changed that year for the bigger brother version. Still ugly but we couldn't afford a proper wood burning stove which, in those days were going for more than a thousand Euros for even the most basic version.

These were difficult years, but in case I'm giving the impression that the dream had gone sour it's important to point out the simple pleasures along the way. We loved the weather, whether it was hot or cold. OK, to be honest we preferred it warm although hot was pretty good too. The rain could bucket it down and did for the first quarter of 2010 but for most of the rest of the year the skies were entirely or almost entirely blue. From the upstairs front window we could see the sunrise over the hill leading out of the east side of the village. From the back kitchen (also upstairs) we could see the whole sweep from the big hill under which Campofrío is nestled to the mountains to the west where we watched spectacular sunsets most nights and over the village to Alajar in the north west. Our view of Aracena was only obscured by our own patio wall between our neighbours and ourselves. I'd have loved to have put a viewing window in that. We had brought my wooden swing seat all the way from England and after some minor repairs which involved some cutting out and replacement of some rotten wood on a very precise angle (I was proud of that work) we placed it on the upper patio pointing in the direction of Alajar. It was a beautiful place to sit and contemplate the world in the evenings and not a bad place to eat my cornflakes in the morning. I had put a cover over it which hung down the back to protect me from the afternoon sun but when Pepa complained I had to admit she was right. It blocked her favourite view of Alajar, something of a spiritual link for her as there is a religious procession from the village to a church and hermitage there every year. So, of course, I removed the cover.

German shopping

The views were so beautiful in the sierra, and so changeable with the seasons that the trip to the newly opened twin supermarkets of Mercadona and Lidl on the road towards Portugal was the only spiritual procession we needed and we tended to take that drive at least once a week. It was like coming into this century.

Even so it was one of the stop offs for the woman with a donkey with two panniers which was straight out of 1900s Spain. Joy of joys. We could finally get pasteurised milk from Lidl to replace the horrible UHT we'd been putting up with. Even Mercadona sold an acceptable "Alta Pasturizacion" (high temperature pasteurised) which tasted nearly as good and was kept in the fridge but lasted a week or so longer. These two supermarkets were so popular the also recently built El Jamon supermarket stood pathetic and unloved from the day it opened.

Lidl was a treasure trove for us. We eagerly scanned their publicity for the tools weeks when you could buy German quality tools at Chinese prices. You had to queue for any large items because in spite of the big advertising they were loss-leaders and there were only a handful of each item available. One of our earliest purchases was a large generator which we put under the stairs and never looked at again. It's there for the day when the electricity is cut off and we can't wangle getting it back on again. The best buy ever was the winch. After dragging so much mixed cement up the stairs for the floors we were excited when we saw Lidl had a special offer on winches and we were there in the car park that freezing cold winter morning to make sure we were first through the doors and running down the aisle. We were used to Lidl's extra special offers being thin on the ground and I wasn't going to miss out, shamelessly blocking the door from all the other contenders and running down the aisle as soon as the doors opened. Surely nobody in the world had more need of that winch than we did. Our winch only cost around 75 euros. It was very good quality and worked really well attached to an Akro prop which cost us an extra 20 euros. Whenever we needed to use it we simply took out the bars on the safety rail round the landing so we could swing bags of bricks or later tiles and buckets of mortar through the gap. I was the winch operator, known by Frank as the "Winch Wench". The winch stayed there for 6 years. It carried all the cement for all our upper walls and all the bricks and tiles. Frank mixed the cement, filling the big black dual handled flexible plastic buckets which all builders here use. He would wheel it into the house on a wheelbarrow and shout "Wench … winch!" for me to haul it up and swing it onto the upper floor. After 6 years I was keen to get rid of it. I had loved it but become bored of its unsightly presence. Frank would have preferred to keep it. The fact we got nearly as much for it second hand as we had paid softened the blow for him.

The tile cutter was another of our expensive but ultimately invaluable purchases. Fortunately I had bought that back when we first moved to the house. When we still had credit available and before we realised we really couldn't afford it. At that time our maths were; if the tool is cheaper than one of the jobs we would do with it would cost if we paid a builder, it was in. The tile cutter certainly filled that brief. It was a table cutter with its own water bath and it lived outside our house in the yard for years. We had nowhere to store the cement mixer or the tile cutter so that was that. They lived outside. It seemed were none the worse for it except having to clean out the water bath every year to remove the grape vine leaves that filled it each autumn. Because we chose really heavy quality Gresmanc tiles throughout the house a smaller cutter just wouldn't have done the job especially when it came to the edge tiles for the window ledges and the even heavier ones for the stairs.

Lidl also sold mosquito netting in self assembly kits. Although several of the outside windows and the front balcony doors were made with integral mosquito nets, they are so vital here especially in the warm but damp seasons of late spring and the end of summer, we needed more for the internal windows and the back doors. Each year we bought another window or door net and we really didn't suffer as much as our neighbours from "mozzies" because of them.

11

Getting On With It

After a very tough year in 2010 things started to look up in 2011. With some financial and physical help from family members we really felt we were starting to get somewhere. We managed to finish building the partition walls upstairs and then it was time to choose which of the next jobs was the most important according to our finances and the materials we already had around us. Of course, electricity had to be high up the list. Mostly because you cant think about rendering walls until that's in place. We were still living with long extensions all round the house but we managed to get all the lights connected using the builders supply.

You aren't allowed to do your own electrics. Any work done must be finalised by a qualified electrician. Fortunately we had a qualified electrician to oversee and so Frank got on with the very messy job of cutting out all the channels in our newly built walls, using an angle grinder which he hated because the dust gets everywhere and you can't see what you're doing after just a couple of minutes. Then using a hammer and chisel which is cleaner but slower and more difficult he finished each job. Wherever the builders had erected internal tabiques (partitions) the job was off the scale more difficult as the tabiques were extremely thin and very fragile. Our bricks were harder to break through but less likely to come crumbling down around your ears. We erected curtains around the space Frank was working in for the angle grinder bits but that made the pea soup around him even more dense. Everything tasted of brick dust.

I'm sure all my miniatures were full of it. Bit by bit Frank became a trainee electrician and at every stage we found out he'd done it right as he was very thorough placing the wires and doing everything step by step When Juan Manuel came to test it all it was all done correctly.

Pantry

As we got the walls built towards the kitchen I decided that I'd always wanted a cool little pantry. In my mind I was imagining a time when we might be off grid and need extra support for keeping our food cool. We picked a spot on the north wall and built in a pantry, with its own little roof, leaving a corner in front of it to fit a big fridge freezer in if we ever found we could afford one. I built the shelves into the walls using what we called "razzas" short for rasillones which are like very long lightweight bricks, normally used to fill in between roof lintels. They are ideal to provide a support for a more solid surface made by either tiling, or in this case shuttering and pouring cement on. I wanted deep cool cement shelves so I poured approximately 3 inches onto each shelf. This made them super solid and thermally the very best way to keep my provisions cool for as long as possible. Then I put a little sloping roof on it. There is a very old fashioned way of keeping spaces cool which is simply to wet the top and let evaporation cool the surface. This was the basic idea behind my pantry and although I've only felt the need to damp it once or twice it does seem to work. The "razza" shelf building method has been used over and over again in our build ever since. It's the very cheapest way to build fitted furniture.

This year it was still common to hear the strangest conversations in the street or the doctors surgery. "Have you killed yet" "No, have you ?" "Oh yes I killed last weekend".

The very cheapest way to fill your pantry or dispensario of course is to have a pig or three and slaughter one each year as was very customary here during our first few years as residents. A few years later though this was outlawed and so the sound of a squealing pig that's just realised it's not going to have a fun new year was still a common and slightly unnerving experience. I was invited a couple of years running to the matanza at Amador and Angeles' house. The men, including Amador and Miguel (Loli-the-shopkeeper's husband), would go and drag out two or three of their pigs. One for each family and the pigs would be dispatched, actually fairly quickly and humanely although I never had the stomach to watch the slaughter. I did go just a few minutes later and see Amador burning off the pigs hair and cutting the biggest one's belly open. All the insides just fell out and it was remarkably un-bloody; the blood having been collected in big pails from the slashed neck immediately and carried still warm into the kitchen. No sir I was not interested in that either, nor the women's work of washing out the intestines. This Englishwoman scuttled into the back of the nave (outhouse) and found herself a corner to pick and chop huge bunches of hierbabuena (mint) and coriander for the morcilla tonta (crazy black pudding) which was and is my favourite. Yes I'm a carnivore and I shouldn't be squeamish since I'm prepared happily to eat fresh killed pork as I did that very day. Thrown straight on to a metal plate on a big log fire. Big crunchy grains of salt were thrown on top and delicious it was too.

In the middle of the day work stopped and hands were washed, tables were cleared and big bowls of stew were put in the middle of the table, along with big glasses of white wine. I suspect the stew was puchero which I'd already eaten in England made by the Spanish sister in law of my cousin. This puchero was truly a peasant dish though, it had great big lumps of fat in it. At this time I was only just getting used to the fact that pig fat here is one of the most delicious homegrown foods you can eat and is actually pretty healthy coming from acorn fed free range 'pata negra' pigs. I hadn't quite got used to it in this form yet and neither was I used to the communal eating from the same bowl. This was real rural Spain and I was honoured to be accepted in and grateful that they understood my English reserve when it came to the 'dirty jobs'. I watched the saussages being stuffed into the now perfectly cleaned intestines and I helped hang them up using a hook on a pole before excusing myself from the rest of the hard work and very possibly the singing. I had a knock at my door a few days later with the gift of a couple of morcilla tonta. It didn't go in my new brick dispensario though. It went in my fridge for a short while on its way to my frying pan without going anywhere near my vegetarian husband who'd stayed home behind the computer while I was playing campesina.

Old fairs and new

In May we attended the 1st International Portugal Miniatures fair. This was a strange little fair which was designed to last a long weekend from Friday afternoon to Sunday afternoon. We didn't realise that Friday wasn't just for set up so we turned up late. Fatima was a bit irritated with us and we were a bit irritated too as we hadn't understood the strange timetable. The fair was already in full swing when we were setting up but it didn't seem to do us any harm as everyone was interested in what was going on. The building was small but prettily historic, but the parts of Lisbon that we saw were a bit run down. The fair was OK, though not what I'd call a good fair, that couldn't be expected from a first fair. So we decided we'd give Fatima's fair another chance the following year. Besides, there was cake.

Then it was the spring Madrid Fair. There seem to be several kinds of stallholders at the international miniature fairs. The makers, the merchants and the dealers. I rather appreciate the dealers of which our friend Karon Cunningham is one. They're the enthusiasts who are prepared to buy the best of the best of the makers work and carry them to other fairs which those makers don't attend. Of course there has to be a significant mark-up on the price at the other end of the chain.

They are prepared to invest, like an art dealer and then do the significant amount of work it takes to unite that special piece with that certain person. A skill in itself. Often that maker will only make one piece like it. Or a very limited edition and may not sell online so these dealers offer a real service to both sides. When Carol took an extended break from miniature pottery Karon (from England) bought up Carol's remaining stocks. This must have been a significant investment for her and I would urge anyone to get hold of a piece or several of Carol's extremely fine work.

From Canada, The Little Dollshouse Company do a similar but less exclusive job, travelling all over Europe taking European miniatures to North America and North American Miniatures to Europe. They also have some of the far eastern products but do choose carefully for quality. It's good to see arts and crafts getting a viewing on other sides of the 'pond'. I had to give Frank a sharp telling off for refusing to sell some of my work to one of these dealers because I only had four examples and three more fairs in 4 weeks. I had to explain to him that having my work seen at fairs where it wouldn't normally be seen was worth more than the discount and loss of the stock. Bless him. He was trying to protect me from the overwork he knew was coming.

This year at Madrid Karon discovered "Muffas Miniatures" owned by an Italian girl who crochets really tiny and very sweet toys. She even makes a teeny potted cactus. Her pieces at the time were really unusual and had to be seen to be believed. Sadly she too fell victim to copyists from the far east.

One girl who makes ceramics (I don't remember her name) came into the wash room while I was there washing my hands and while I was trying to get the stupid hand dryer to work she flicked water at me affectionately. I sometimes enjoy practising my Spanish, so I said "No tratas a empezar una guerra que no puedes vencer" I really can't say if my Spanish was correct, but I think she caught my drift … "don't start a war you can't win". I chucked a handful back but carefully enough that she could duck and miss most of it. These kind of humorous and affectionate encounters between the "big kids" that most miniaturists are, do give me real pleasure to remember.

On the way back home from this fair, crossing Extremadura at dusk we had to stop every 15 to 20 minutes to remove the suicide bugs from the windscreen. I had wondered when we stopped to fill up, just before dark, why the Repsol garage provided a big bucket full of soapy water with a mop and squeegee in it. Now I knew.

Soest used to be my favourite fair of the year as all of the stallholders, students and quite a few of the visitors stayed together at the little hotel just across the car park from the venue. Unfortunately the organisers were put in the difficult position of having to choose to stay there with half the exhibitors complaining about being in a tent, and after much soul searching they chose the

A2 forum at Rheda Weidenbruck. What it gained in space and ease of organisation, it lost, for me, in ambience. It was much more difficult to get to. This was further complicated for me because I had chosen to take a Spanish friend Angeles with me instead of Frank. I wasn't sure how I was going to get there and Angeles had to work until the day before. This became a nightmare,. We thought it would be easy, Ryanair had just started a flight from Sevlle to Weeze, which Ryanair calls Dusseldorf-Weeze but which is nowhere near Dusseldorf, nor anywhere else for that matter but we booked a Hotel in Dusseldorf from where we could make the onward journey the next morning early.

Unfortunately Ryanair's flight was badly delayed and when we arrived in Weeze there were no more trains or buses to be had to Dusseldorf. We jumped on the last bus out of 'Dodge' and there followed a frantic series of phone calls after midnight to Frank who had to cancel our Ibis hotel and try to re-book a hotel for us in the town the bus was going to. Unfortunately there was both a cycling and a rowing championship on at the same weekend in that town and every bed seemed to have been taken. Finally we managed to secure a single room at a ridiculously inflated price and get a put-u-up bed put in for Angeles. I was not feeling self sacrificing that night. We travelled on the next day and got to our room at the Sport Hotel with relief. Unfortunately Angeles, who was still a smoker at the time thought it was OK to smoke out of the window while I was in the loo, and stank the room out.

The A2 Forum was impressive but difficult enough to get to without the bus which was laid on in the mornings for the visitors. We managed to get a lift on the first bus of the day.

We didn't really like the new venue for the former

Soest fair. It was another of those places that seemed to be in the middle of nowhere and looked like an aircraft hanger. Yes there was plenty of room but the customers didn't pass by in the numbers they used to. Perhaps Barbara had upped the number of stallholders because there was extra space. Rheda went from being one of our most successful and enjoyable fairs to one of our least successful. Whereas Soest had been one of favourite fairs of the year, Rheda was just another fair to me. I understood that they had to move but I was disappointed that they didn't ever move back. For me it was never the same again. Proving once again you should never change a winning formula for the whingers unless you're going to keep your happy customers happy too. I loved Barbara and her kids, who always mucked in and helped out along with their friends. I didn't love Rheda though and I went once or maybe twice more but that was it. It bothered me that Barbara had bowed to pressure from the very few unhappy people from Rheda and in doing so, to my mind lost the essence of the Soest fair. The complainers continued to complain anyway.

I chose that year to join in the communal meal which I usually miss because of Frank's vegetarianism. That year there was a young girl who sort of attached herself to me at the meal. She chattered away at me which I found a bit distracting as I had my friend Angeles from the village with me chatting on the other side in Spanish. I'm a bit of a social phobic at the best of times. The young girl was Steph Kilgast who after spending her younger years in art college was now making fruit and veg and also some very pretty cakes, and wonderful French bread based on Betsy Niederer's tutorials but with a very crusty French looking finish. In the subsequent years Stephanie has developed a different style, drawing influence from many other arts into her own incredible work.

Another of the German artists I met who excited me that year was Georgia Marfels. A shy girl who had a full time job in ... was it medicine? Anyway Georgia had her own style right from the word go I loved her quirky and macarbre sense of humour. For instance she did a nice line in mice in sandwiches with a fork through them. This really tickled me. Georgia was quick to thank me for my inspiration which was very kind of her, but it looked like she had plenty of her own.

Of course we did Paris again, How could we not. There were some exhibitors I just didn't meet anywhere else. Julien Martinez is an amazing and quirky artist whose style owes nothing to anyone else except the weird world of films like Edward Scissorhands. Julien is a quietly spoken and utterly polite Frenchman and I adore him. His work is fascinating and disquieting at the same time. Of course partly I adore him because he always sees what I am trying to do and he comes early to my stand and, blast him, takes away half of my best work. He introduced another quietly spoken man. I had no idea who he was when Julien brought him to my stand but there was something unusual about him. He was very focused and serious and also very charming. Only later I realised he was always followed by one or two 'minders'. He also became a very good customer. It was only after the show that I was told that he was an Arab Prince who had become fascinated with miniatures. He told me later, when I was asking him questions about lighting and potential fading for my colour book, that Kristin Baybars' famous old shop in London was one of his early inspirations. I'm sure that many many collectors would say that but I was particularly impressed with his relaxed attitude to ageing, fading and scale. He didn't go around with his nose in the air and a tape measure in his hand, and I saw his appreciation was for the art and imagery and 'mood' that miniatures evoked.

Tokyo

In spite of all my international travelling and the places I'd been invited to and hadn't taken up, places like China and Indonesia where I just felt out of my depth even negotiating a visit, I'd always had a yen to visit Japan (pun intended).

I had been receiving trade orders for a few years from a company called Folks inc and Mike (that was his English name) who was the proprietor, had invited me to his Fair in Tokyo once or twice during this time. So, this year I decided to take the plunge if I could ensure that we could actually afford to get there. I let Mike know this and Mike came back with an offer I couldn't refuse. He was going to pay all my expenses but he expected me to bring lots of miniatures at trade price and he was going to earn the money back through my sales. In effect I would earn money for my classes plus half my retail price on anything I sold on top of having a guaranteed airfare and hotel bill paid.

Mike spoke no English but had a secret weapon. Mr Hiro (our Hero). Hiro did his best to interpret and broker the deal and I was really grateful that we had his help. Mike left it to Hiro to explain the offer which resulted in a comical stream of communications in barely understandable jinglish. The offer basically consisted of them guaranteeing that our expenses would be paid by agreeing to buy stock from us that they would then sell at the fair at a profit. It seemed like a reasonable plan. We weren't going to make a lot of money but we were going to be covered against losses.

Our trip to Tokyo wasn't exactly hassle-free though. In fact it was quite the opposite. Our Emirates flight arrived in Dubai after the first leg of the journey just in time to see our next flight close its doors leaving us behind. I was distraught. The next plane was the next day. We, as usual, had very little money and certainly couldn't afford an overnight stay in Dubai. Too often, for lack of funds we were having to book our travel at the last minute and having to take the risk of going away without even enough money in our pockets to pay the hotel fees. These were dangerous situations and I found them very stressful. We only needed one of us to be seriously ill or an event to be cancelled for some unforeseen reason to be in the deep "doo".

So it was on this trip. We couldn't afford to miss the evening class which was scheduled the next day. We explained this to Emirates who agreed to put us on a flight to Singapore which had a connection to Tokyo that would get us in just in time to get to my class. Of course we accepted. We spent a few uncomfortable overnight hours in Dubai airport. I had no idea what time of day or night it was and we'd been given yet another meal so my stomach wasn't sure either. I remember very little about our Singapore flight except that in the Airport there was a showering facility which we really needed by this time. We weren't allowed to go in together so we separated with one hand luggage each and refreshed ourselves. By this time I was shattered already. Then on a plane to Tokyo. We arrived in Tokyo airport with four hours to spare before my first class and by the time we'd collected our luggage and taken the train into Tokyo and found our Hotel I had just two hours left. We found that our phones wouldn't work either in Dubai or Singapore and we hadn't been able to contact Chris, who was an old friend of ours from back in the Computer Club days, to let him know we wouldn't be meeting him the day before. He'd waited for hours for us but finally taken his last train home. So we didn't have any of the maps or information he'd printed out for us.

Fortunately Hiro came to our rescue and explained exactly how to get to the venue. We were dazed and culture shocked but finally arrived at the World Trade Centre which was confusingly one of two buildings with the same name, a mile apart. Chris met up with us there and helped Frank to set up the stand while I gave the class. Fortunately I'd chosen to give some of my easier classes, so I won't say I sailed through it, but I managed. What I did find was that even the simplest of classes took twice as long to give to a group of Japanese students because at every point the whole class would stand up and in turn take photographs of the process on their cameras. And there was no way of getting out of this especially as I spoke no Japanese and most of the class spoke no English. I soon learned the Japanese 'aww' sound which, though it sounded like disappointment, actually meant acknowledgement and, in most cases understanding.

After the class we went on the search for something Frank could eat and some more interesting stuff for me. Chris took me for some interesting and challenging foods (Like tapas but Japanese) We decided not to go for the interestingly branded soft drink Pokari Sweat. It seemed to us we didn't need it. Water seemed to be adequate to do that job in June in Tokyo where the humidity was around 90%. Then we dragged ourselves back to the smallest bedroom in the world where I went to the loo as a first priority. Frank was very amused at my screech when instead of the flush I hit the integral bidet button and got an eyeful of hot water.

The next day was a very busy one again but somehow I had managed to get enough of a second wind to give my classes, Chris' help was invaluable with the translations. We'd worked out the night before that Hiro just wasn't up to the job, neither being interested nor capable enough to translate the technical terminology. He did go off and find me a Bento box which is like a small picnic consisting of a whole meal in a little card container with several different compartments for different items all beautifully presented. It looked like a box of chocolates but to be honest the contents were uninspiring. One thing I did take to were the tiny, red, pickled plum-type fruits.

During the weekend I had no time to speak to any customers or other miniaturists, because I was totally taken up with my classes. So it was quite nice that after the first full day there was a party for the traders. It consisted of a canapé type of buffet with, surprisingly, beer and wine and even fruit. We had already learned that fruit was something of a luxury in Japan- an apple could cost the equivalent of five pounds, so fruit is often given as a luxury gift there. Packaged beautifully and handed over in the customary style. Two handed and with a deep bow. Of course we didn't buy any and by the time we were on our way back to Spain we were craving a piece of fruit or some non-pickled vegetables. The only vegetables I remember getting there was a bowl of roughly cut ball cabbage lightly blanched and totally uninteresting.

Before the visit Mike, the organiser had asked me if I was interested in going to see a Kabuki show. I'm sorry to say in this respect I'm a complete philistine. I'm not fond of the theatre anyway and the idea of sitting still through hours of Japanese mime horrified me to the core. I was intrigued when he told me we would be having bingo instead. I'd heard that bingo was actually illegal in Japan. Things had either changed or we were going to the equivalent of a crack den. In the end after the party we had a game of 'silly' bingo. Apparently bingo was so newly legalised it became something of an adult party game. It was hilarious because as each person's card won (and we had two cards each) we were to take a carefully wrapped present. The presents were anything from a pair of tea towels to some rather childish 'naughty outfits'. I think I ended up dressed over my clothes in a maid's outfit while one of the other guys was dressed in Pink Panther ears with his tail tucked back between his legs. It was infantile ... We really enjoyed it.

The next day we were back to the more serious matter of earning a living. The problem was our best salesperson (me) was otherwise engaged, so I'm not sure we made the best of our sales potential but still, there was a steady stream of interested customers though I seriously doubted that Mike was going to make his money back on booking me. I realised I was there for the kudos of having a well known European artist and it did seem that the fair grew by a couple more prestige artists the next year including Ichiyoh Haga.

After the fair closed I was pretty nervous. We hadn't received any pay for any of the classes or for the stock. We were waiting for the addition to be done by Tomi, Michael's colleague. We didn't know if we could trust them and when Hiro took us away from the building for a coffee after packing up, I must admit for a short time I was suspicious and worried that we wouldn't get paid at all. We'd been living off income from books and videos as those were the only things that weren't going through Mike's system. Eventually though Mike, Chris, Frank and I piled into the smallest bedroom in the world and Mike handed over a large wad of Yen and Chris went through the maths with him. All apparently was good. Mike had just about made his investment in bringing me to Tokyo and back and we had done rather well on the deal. Considering I'd had my dream trip to Japan … well nearly.

On our last day we had planned some tourism before catching a late flight but we didn't think to set the alarm and when I woke up it was already eleven o'clock. Way past checkout time. We'd slept for 12 hours. We rang reception to apologise and raced to get out of bed and dressed. Of course it was too late for breakfast. We had only three hours to spare and were determined to see at least something of Tokyo. So we opted for Asakusa which is an old market area. It was pretty and busy and we found a nice café and ate late breakfast/early lunch upstairs. Afterwards we mooched around for an hour. I spent most of the time eyeing up Japanese fabrics and even buying Japanese paper offcuts, socks with toes and a small paper fan to remember Asakusa.

The next fair was Paris and I was pleased to find we could get reasonably priced fares from Seville. Many of our fair choices from now on were going to have to take airfares into account.

"Eso es mi madre"

When Alan came over in summer for the fiesta I was a bit concerned that we old fogies, and by that I particularly meant my younger and even fogey-er husband, wouldn't be able to stay up or keep him entertained long enough for him really to enjoy Spanish fiesta hours, which don't start until well after midnight and continue through the next day. We needn't have worried though; our friend Amador had it covered. He instructed one of his nephews to take Alan off and make sure he always had a drink and he, Amador, was paying. I'm sure Alan paid his own way and no doubt that of his new friends. I encountered him when I got up the next morning just before the Alegre Diana. (The happy dawn) a procession of those who'd stayed up all night and those who were woken by the noise. Alan had gathered around him a bunch of happy Campofrieños who were all keen to try out their elementary English on him and Al in his turn also quite 'happy' was keen to tell them "Eso es mi madre!" Not a bad attempt at communication on his part though of course they all knew who I was already, several of them being next door neighbours.

I was carrying a cup of tea. It had actually been for me but Albo took it from me and thanked me for it. I didn't protest. I felt maybe his need was greater than mine. The band lead the villagers singing and dancing all the way round the village to well known songs such as "La cucaracha" where the whole group lie on their backs kicking their legs and waving their arms. "La cucaracha la cucaracha, ya no puede caminar" (The cockroach can't walk any more) and another song which seems largely to consist of the one word alcohol where they, with their arms in the air, bow down over and over again increasingly rapidly. It looks totally crazy but a lot of fun. It seems to be a tradition to pass around big bottles of aguardiente (aniseed liquor) with water in a lemonade bottle with a hole in the top so you can pour it into your mouth without touching the bottle. From this year on I made a point of getting up for the Alegre Diana whatever else I missed.

The procession ends with the middle aged ladies of the village giving everyone cakes and coffee or hot chocolate. That year there followed a foam fiesta which Alan also got involved in. The second time he dropped his new iPhone into the foam I took it home for him. A good job too because it was already cracked. I'd had a go in the foam myself and I didn't much like it. In fact it made me panic.

Alan hadn't been feeling well for a while. He'd had

a really bad back and was on almost constant paracetamol and ibruprofen and after the fiesta seemed to go downhill even more. I was worried about him. It turned out he had a liver problem on top of the bad back he'd got snowboarding the year before and I don't suppose our encouraging him to party down with "da yoof" had actually helped even though he seemed to enjoy it at the time. His illness had also made him a bit depressed. Fortunately over the next year or two he sorted all his health problems out and started running in park runs and marathons. He got really well again, but he didn't come back to Campofrío for several years and I hoped he didn't associate it with a bad time in his life.

Nil carburundum illigitimae (as my dad used to say)

Sadly our little English car didn't pass its ITV (Spanish MOT) that year. The rear right hand brake just wasn't achieving the correct pressure. They slapped the papers down in front of us, told us we had up to 60 days to remedy the problem and gave us a little slip of yellow paper to prove it, and the dreaded stamp on the green booklet.

Certain that this was something relatively simple we opted to take it to a guy in the village.

"The little guy in the village" said the brakes looked perfect … new in fact. Just a bit rusty from living in England. Just to be on the safe side he gave them a sand, a clean and a grease.

Sadly the brakes weren't perfect. Something had obviously passed him by. Well, he was getting on a bit and looked like he liked a beer or three of a lunchtime … if he hadn't already had aguardiente for breakfast. The car still didn't pass.

So we went instead to "a very well known garage in

Aracena" to see if they could find the problem. An hour or two later they called me up to tell me they would have to replace the whole brake drum at a cost of 335 euros, sadly way beyond our abilities and we told them so. Out of desperation we asked a retired mechanic who we trusted just round the corner, to give us some advice, and he said the results can be affected by different wheels or tyres at a different pressure, and that if we changed the wheels over it might just make enough difference to pass the ITV and that he would test them for us if we got the wheels swapped over.

So we went back to "little old guy in the village" and asked him to swap them over, and give the other one a clean up for good measure.

We stood and watched as he took our little car's wheels apart and sat among a mess of spanners and wheel parts looking confused at times … and at times back in the room.

Just as he was going to put the left wheel on the right (and vice versa) he told me it would be worth checking if there was any brake fluid in the system which he said might cause the problem. Lo and behold. The little valve (bombin) on the right hand side was broken. The one on the left was also very short of thread when he took it off to check whether we could be lucky enough to find one in the garage which looked the same.

Looking up the translations of the word 'bombin' we got 'bowler hat'. However it seems the correct translation in this case would be nipple … as in "bleed nipple". There were plenty of nipples to be seen on the calendars in the garage … I felt sure none of them were going to help lecherous little tired old shaky guy in the village's concentration any.

So then we had our car chocked up in the old grease pit with its wheels off, slowly leaking brake fluid and

"Little old shaky guy in the village" was about to collect a couple of the "little bleeders" from Riotinto. Whilst I was delighted and impressed that he'd found the problem I must admit I was a little concerned that he looked like he might lose bits of the car or of himself in the process, and I was worried that our car might end up chocked up on bricks forever like a couple of other neighbours vehicles outside his workshop.

In the end it took 2 days to fix. It turned out it was only the bleed nipple. The parts cost just 36 euros, the brake fluid another 6 and the labour took it up to a total of 94 euros. Still a chunk for us to find but not as scary and impossible as the 335 for something which wasn't needed. Mechanics eh? Just the same in Spain as in England. As for "little tired, possibly drunk and very shaky old guy in the village", we became rather fond of him even though he was clearly an alcoholic and he would drag us to his table in the bar whenever he saw us to tell us tales of his time in Germany and other far flung lands. There was the sorry tale of his wife leaving him. Later Maria Luisa told me he'd had just one child, a daughter, who died when she was young. So the drinking was understandable. His speech however pretty much wasn't. But he could fix a car and he did so for us a couple of times more before he retired a few years later. We finally found out his name was Laddio. Once again we had no idea why. It was an easier name to remember though.

'Jose Muckyflicker'

As soon as we could afford it we employed a local guy to do our rendering. I just didn't feel up to it. All that flinging huge globs of cement from three feet away with the inevitable splash back. I knew how to do it in theory, I'd even successfully built a fully rendered raised bed in the garden and rendered the base of the greenhouse and even had a bit of a trial in the under stairs bathroom which was at this time still serving as a shed. When I looked at the huge expanse of house and felt my fifty-something back, my family heart and my just starting to ache knees. I knew that my "albanil" (brickie) days, if not over, were beginning to be reduced. So. Angeles' brother was called in.

Whenever we tried to explain who had done our rendering people looked blankly at us until they worked out we were talking about 'El Pollo'. No idea why Jose has this nickname but it seemed also to have attached itself to the bar he ran at one time. Or vice-versa.

On the first day, when Frank realised that Jose was a smoker he said "we aren't having him smoking in the house". I tried to explain this to Jose, with little success. I told Frank that he would have to cope with Jose's unintelligible Campurriano. Either because Frank had even less success than I did understanding, or making himself understood, or because Jose was a chain smoker who didn't seem to be able to work without a fag hanging out of his mouth, that was the last ever said on the matter. Frank filled in as Jose's sidekick and mixed buckets of cement on Jose's command of "meha!" which double translated as mezcla … or mix. It was all but impossible to discern what Jose was asking for at any one time but first and fairest guess was always "mezcla". Just occasionally Frank turned up sweating and panting with a tub of freshly mixed cement to be greeted by a look of incomprehension, waving hands and a stream of consonant-free invective. Why could he not understand the difference between cubo pronounced cu-o and cubito pronounced cu-o. The difference was of course whether Frank was to make a full or a half mix. Frank always made a full mix. Our name for Jose arrived very rapidly as the flinging of cement on to one wall invariably ended in the splattering of the opposite wall, the ceilings, and of course the floor where it became mixed in what appeared to be a 1:10 ratio with cigarette butts. We dutifully swept up the mounds of fag-filled cement splatter at the end of each of his work days.

I thoroughly enjoyed watching, listening and for once in my life standing back while the guys got on with it. This formed a turning point in my life. From then on I restricted myself to tiling, painting and plaster boarding. I had by now handed over a good fifty percent of the DIY to Frank, who turned out to be much more able than I, or he for that matter, ever thought possible. Jose seemed to be able to do a small room in three days, a bigger one would take five.

We asked him if he could do ceilings as well as I was really keen to get the guest room finished. Jose set to work. I wasn't very surprised that the level of 'chuntering' and swearing ramped up significantly on the ceiling jobs, so I just ignored it. After two days Jose declared the guest room ceiling finished and he sloped off, looking a little less jolly and more sheepish than usual. We took one look at the results and decided on plasterboard. The best you could say about the texture was that it was 'a bit rural'. Less kindly but perfectly fair, would be that it looked like a homage to the local gruta (cave) but somewhat less of a 'maravilla'.

Still, we were bit by bit turning the brick box into something that started to look like a house and it began to feel like we were turning a corner. I was particularly pleased when the bedroom was rendered. No more gaps to the outside which I had been convinced were night time motorways for rodents and all manner of six and eight or more legged critters. After one well timed trip out of the country we came back to the bedroom rendered, dry and ready to paint. What a rewarding day's work that felt. We didn't get every wall rendered. We just couldn't afford to and eight years later we're still no closer to getting the the upstairs bathroom and junk room finished. Jose is more than likely retired by now but I'm sure when the time comes the village will still be full of similarly mucky-workers.

At the next Arnhem in October I did a very special William Hamer painting themed workshop. We had a large space in the inner sanctum, up in the restaurant. It was thankfully less smoky this year as I think the smoking ban had come in. Even though I'd given the workshop a full 2 days we were still rushed but very fortunately I had prepped boxes full of the bits we needed. I knew I needed to try to do this every time. I did find my classes liked a more complex project even if it meant I had to prep quite a lot of the materials and even some parts. I vowed to do more of this kind of work in the future.

We did the Madrid fair again in November but this time we left the car at home and tried the Socibus. It was a very long bus journey but do-able and, more importantly, cheap.

Red tape and hoops

Here in Spain you can't have a private Electricity connection until you have a piece of paper called the 'Licencia de Primer Ocupacion' (first occupation licence). You can't get that licence until you have a certificate from the architect to say the building is complete and, according to our Architect, you can't have that until everything is done. That, I was told, includes down to the last tile in the bathrooms. I resigned myself to a lot of years of our house not being a fully legal dwelling. Apparently since the building boom and subsequent bust that's a more and more common state of affairs The only option was to continue on a builders' supply. But you can't have a builders supply if you don't have a building licence. Our building licence expired in December and we were faced with being cut off just before Christmas.

It was ridiculous the red tape and hoops we had to go through. But somehow extra charming how people wanted to help us find our way through. After all, with so many rules came a proportionately large number of loopholes and wangles. There was a kind of respect earned for knowing your way through them. It is almost a local currency, like the garden produce and the wild fungi which were shared out of kindness and also to earn brownie points. Sometimes it's difficult to know the difference. One thing we always recognised was the real selflessness in some people's actions. Carlos is one of those people. As the new town technical architect (planning officer) Carlos spent two mornings a week in the Ayuntamiento. He was a clear eyed, intelligent looking man with an extremely square jaw, but for which he would be considered very good looking. I was captivated by him and mentally added him to my list of weird crushes. We were in trouble now with the stupid electricity rules and Carlos turned out to be our guardian angel. Albeit a very thorough and careful one. He wanted to dot every i and cross every t. Even the Electricity board said there were easier, if a bit more 'wangled' ways. But I appreciated his professionalism and honesty. The biggest problem I had was that it seemed every time I ended up in his office I also ended up crying. His friendly but penetrating questions didn't help. Why had we been unable to complete the project?

This year though with none of the finishing touches done we tried to get what the architect suggested which was a minor building licence. Eventually, with a lot of help and advice the local council granted us a major works licence based on the original licence. There was a bit of ritual humiliation where we had to make a declaration explaining exactly why we hadn't got finished in spite of our previous licence having had an extension. Fortunately the words 'financial crisis' seemed to work for them. Christmas was saved. I put up the Christmas tree for the first time in Spain to celebrate.

Future requests had to be for minor building licenses though. My capacity for patiently explaining the ongoing effects of the financial crisis, never an easy task wore so thin especially as our very home was threatened. Throwing myself on the kind architect's undoubted mercy was enough to open the floodgates. So I took to sending Frank each time the electricity company demanded a renewal of our building licence. Each time we had to pick out a new building project such as a few metres of tiling or a bathroom project. Each time we had to pay a small percentage of the cost of the task to the council even though we'd paid for the whole project upfront once already. and each time the council had to take the minor project to be voted on. One day, I fear, some councillor will get uppity and put a block on it. Until then we've relied on approval for the scheme and to have it presented favourably to the council.

12

Fairs And Furballs

In February I thought I would brave the cold and take a trip to the Milan fair. It was the first time I'd been for a few years and the last time it was a bit 'nippy' in Milan. So I packed my warmest togs only to find that it was in the high teens.

I love being a trader at Milan because the organiser Sabrina makes everyone really welcome and her little extra is to appeal to all the girls in the room by adding little presents to the welcome pack.

The Milan fair is conveniently located right alongside the imposing central station, at the Hotel Michaelangelo. Personally I'm not fond of big hotel 'mood lighting'. It irritates and depresses me. Besides we were on a much tighter budget these days. We decided to get a different, cheaper Hotel called the Berna. The weird thing about the Berna is that they had obviously bought up another hotel at the opposite side of the road and they were selling the idea that they'd put us in this outpost as an upgrade. It was a bit strange being on the opposite side of the road to reception and the entry system was inscrutable at first. I did quite like the hotel though because they had a coffee machine where I could also get hot water for my English cup of tea. One thing I have learned in all my years of travelling is to take a travel kettle. And as finances got tighter my collapsible (every travelling miniaturist needs one of these) travel kettle now doubles as an egg hard-boiler when pushed. This sometimes involves propping my kettle on my suitcase under some stupidly placed socket, and hoping my higher use of electricity won't somehow end in some kind of catastrophic failure of the hotel's entire electrical system. It's very rare in Europe you'll ever get offered a little tea making station. Actually it's rare you can get a good cup of tea anywhere. In Dusseldorf Ibis, near Dusseldorf station, I once had the temerity to suggest to the bar girl that English people take milk with their tea and not cream. "Nonsense" she snapped at me. "English people always take caffe sahne (cream) and never milk!" Nobody had ever complained in all her six months at the job. I tried to explain that finding an English person who complains could take you six months but maybe nevertheless they were not happy. The Fraulein was having none of it!

The Milan fair had grown a little since my last visit and we did well enough to want to return. There were also quite a few traders I've never seen at any other European fair. One guy was selling Doll hair in pieces and I saw 'my own hair' in miniature in the pile of little pieces of mohair. The only thing that stopped me paying 6 euros for it was that I realised I'd just sold a cushion made of the same wavy mohair at a car boot sale for next to nothing. I really kicked myself! Since then I've seen it used on fairy dolls and it really does look good and comes in all different colours. There was half a room of fairy doll makers which is a part of the hobby that seemed to be restricted to Milan fair at the time. They have their own tools and I found a nice silicone ended tool which I now use all the time for fine detailing.

Lovely and statuesque as a Botticelli painting, Marcella Perodo, whose business name is Minicaretti showed me, among other beautiful work, her lovely little tray of baked cabbage. Apparently a common Italian dish. Marcella's little tip, which I was certainly going to try was to use the texture from a sage leaf for a finer cabbage texture. Nice discovery. Marcella's cabbage made my original veiner look positively clumsy. In the end, for me, the sage leaf was too fine. After that I went looking for something half way between the two. A plant I found in the countryside looked just perfect for cabbage leaves. I 'stole' the texture from nature and added a new Savoy cabbage to my veiner list. I think Marcella's little suggestion set my mind on the trail of other plants to steal textures from, so Marcella's idea became one of my inspirations.

There was another food maker called Le Molecole who I'd never seen before and whose stand I passed rather more quickly than I wanted. She made really beautiful grapes and wild mushrooms and chestnuts which reminded me of home. Another stand was selling perfect miniature moulds for croissants and pastries and all sorts of other miniature foods that I don't make. All this beautiful miniature food made me hungry.

Frank found a pizza shop selling great big chunks of lovely fresh baked pizza. We also found a little supermarket round the corner from the fair which was really useful because in the present financial situation we have had to cut costs on travel and meals. Gone are the days when we used to swan into a local restaurant and pay whatever they asked us, including an extra 'cover' for breadsticks and chunks of often rather dry bread. One problem is, to my mind, Milan itself is boring. It took us years even to find the main shopping area. Since we tend to like doing fairs in areas that were worth visiting and we weren't rich enough for shoes and handbags the only added value to Milan was the best Parmesan and Felino Salami and we took home a kilo of each.

While we were chatting about this behind the stand I promised Frank that one day we'd see more of Italy, especially Rome where I had been on my trip when I was eighteen. And Florence which on that trip happened to be closed due to general strike. At that point a clearly wealthy Florencian who had heard our conversation invited us to go and stay with her for a holiday. She offered food in the best Italian tradition and luxury accommodation. I knew before I said it that explaining that I couldn't afford to travel just for a holiday would meet with total incomprehension, and so it did. For a moment there I could just imagine myself wafting around internal courtyards full of renaissance art and sculpture, just being 'artsy' and inscrutable. Nope. Back to reality.

Several years later I had a more down to earth and warmer Italian family experience staying with Miniaturist and Italian Mama, Roberta Solari and her family near Rome. Eating proper Italian peasant food and crashing in a normal bedroom after a hard day's teaching. That's much more me, much more real and if anything a way more valuable life experience.

In March we went to the second International Portugal miniatures fair. This fair was an absolute disaster for us. It was stuck out of the way in a school building and it was empty. No passing customers equals no sales opportunities at all. We decided that Portugal was a waste of time for us. Even the delicious Portugese custard tarts failed to lift our spirits ... but I did have two of them, just to make sure.

At the end of April it was time to give Farum another chance, with the new organisers, who had been doing it for several years by then. We asked if they would give us a good bright spot out in the hallway and they did. They gave us what to my mind was the best spot in the building. It was on the edge of the hall in a little porch which was flooded in natural light. It could be bit too hot when the sun was up, but it was right next to an exit door where all the smokers went out for a cigarette; so we had passing trade plus a captive audience.

We also had the great fortune to be asked by one of the other visitors if we would like to stay with her and her husband. Well, these days we couldn't afford to turn down an offer like that in spite of Frank's reticence at staying with other people and we got very lucky. This casual offer was the start of our long standing friendship with Mus and Yellow. Mus' real name is Sanne. She is a collector of mini mice and is also a motor bike fan. She, along with her partner Yellow live in a lovely red, typically Danish, wooden house down by the side of a little stream. We spent a lovely few days going backwards and forwards with them to Farum for the fair and then just relaxing and enjoying some of Denmark's countryside. After the fair I also did a class with her Miniatures group. We enjoyed ourselves so much and found their place so relaxing that it became a regular thing to stay with them at least a couple of days whenever we visited Denmark.

In May we had a visit from my brother. It was going to be his birthday while he was with us so I thought we'd treat him and his girlfriend Geraldine to a night in a hotel down at Punta Umbria. I would take any old excuse to go back and visit 'Punta'. We could only afford the enormous Barcelo hotel out of season. Actually I don't think they accept one night bookings in season. In season it's full of wealthy Spaniards. Out of season they'll take half of England and its kids on all you can eat package holidays. Like myself, Howie is a big fan of seafood so, I couldn't think of a better birthday present than to take him to the home of some of the freshest seafood in Spain. My favourites are the coquinas which are tiny baby clams with purple tinged inner shells. Simply flash cooked in olive oil and garlic parsley and salt they are the most delicious starter I've ever tasted. Whenever possible I'd also take down a good portion of Huelva's white prawns They aren't actually white but very pale pink and utterly fresh and sweet.

After the Madrid fair that spring we drove from Madrid to Noelia's place Con A De Arte in Rippolet near Barcelona to give two days of classes the following weekend. We took a couple of days to travel and enjoyed a night in Zaragoza and a couple of little stops off on the journey including one to a place called Medinacelli; a really pretty little medieval town which was unfortunately closed due to it being Tuesday!

We had problems on that journey with the air valve on my Fiesta getting stuck again causing the heat from the engine to vent into the car. We were worried we were going to get a total overheat like we did a couple of years before on a trip from Portugal to Campofrío when we had to stop on the side of a busy motorway slip road because we had steam blasting out from under our bonnet. At that time I realised the value of the red triangles and also of a very helpful pair of Guardia Civil Trafico cops who escorted us to safety just a hundred metres away. All was well this time. Just a few sticky and worrying traffic hold ups. We did realise that this was probably the last time my little old Fiesta would be trusted to make such a long journey. It being by now a ten year old car. We still have her another six years on though.

I loved teaching with Noelia and Alex. They are a really lovely young couple who were just taking their first steps in the new business which was a polymer clay supplies and teaching business. Noelia and Alex are now married and have a little daughter. Noelia is now an accomplished teacher in her own right. My classes were full and there was a waiting list. We did leaves for cabbage, cauliflower and lettuce a plate of prawns and smoked salmon, bunches and peeled bananas and a little oval basket of coconuts, rosy apples and autumn leaves.

At the beginning of June I did my last Rheda-Wiedenbruck fair. All the pleasure had gone out of it since the move from Soest. Paris became my favourite fair and that was coming up at the end of the month. We looked forward to trotting round the Villieres area chomping summer fruit from little punnets and big bags of cherries and taking my regular Batobus trip to the Sennelier shop on Quai Voltaire … The first year we'd been we took one of those open topped bus tours which was great just to give us a feel for the shape of the city but the Batobus was the best for pleasure and the metro for speed.

… and scares.

Since our first Tokyo was successful, but our visit to the city very much shortened by our delays and exhaustion, we decided to give it a second try. This year we were taking the risk ourselves. Taking all the money but paying our own hotel room. This became a problem straight away as the hotel couldn't take any of our cards, and none of the staff at the Soetsu Fresa spoke English. Eventually they put us on to a translation service who helped us to negotiate that we would take out the maximum daily amount from the ATM and pay cash on a daily basis. This left us just a little bit each day to get by on. We certainly weren't going on any Tokyo spending fests.

If we thought it was humid the first year in June it was even worse on the new dates in July. It felt like being boiled in a bag. I have always been what Frank calls a 'water dodger' because I love my tea and juice etc but water is just not appetising to me. And I certainly couldn't bring myself to actually drink a bottle of something called 'Sweat' but this avoidance of re-hydration is something later events in my life have taught me to reverse.

We spent a relaxed, if a little damp, day re-orientating ourselves and getting a few 'bits' that we still needed. We went into the centre of Tokyo to a shop called Tokyo Hands and bought the bits and pieces we needed to make up a functioning stand.

This time we had all the next day to get ready for my evening class so we were going to sleep in and get some much needed rest.

During that night something really scary happened to me, and not for the first time. About ten years before I'd had two of what can only be described as 'funny turns' where my memory became distinctly hazy and I was trawling about in a foggy soup of connections to try and make sense of the thoughts that were passing through my mind. After refreshment and sleep each time I'd got better but they were scary at the time. In the middle of the night I suddenly said to Frank "I'm not right. I'm having one of those turns again". I was very scared. I was only partially aware where I was and not fully aware why. All my memories of the previous couple of years were all mixed up and mostly lost. Fortunately I could make the connection with the previous time and thought maybe I could get out of it this time too.

I knew I had to piece everything together and so I had Frank awake most of the night helping me. I kept asking where each of my kids lived and what they were doing. I thought even then it might have something to do with dehydration and now, years later I'm absolutely sure that it did. It was extremely scary and I didn't know whether it was time to go to hospital and I was really pleased at least that I'd got health insurance for the trip.

I didn't want to be taken into hospital because, as usual, we were down to our last few pounds and we wouldn't have made the third night's hotel fee without doing the classes and fair.

So I drank cup after cup of water while I chatted to Frank who patiently helped me reconstruct my psychological state. By morning I was pretty much back to "me" and I even managed a couple of hours sleep, but I was still a bit panicky and was very, very glad we had Chris to help out again that year. I had to tell Chris what had happened but I still went through the whole day in a state of high anxiety. It wasn't until I started the class that I forgot my problems and let my natural teacher take over. I still wasn't 100% but I managed. I found out later that what had happened was probably what's called Transient Global Amnesia and it could often be triggered by vigorous exercise like swimming … or sex. There was no swimming pool at our hotel. I definitely thought dehydration had some bearing on it too because one of the other times was in hot Seville and the other on a hot summer day in England. I always had problems with water. This time there seemed to be just too little of it going in while rather a lot was coming out on my skin. Since then, whenever I have heard of someone or a relative becoming disorientated in hospital or even at home, I've suggest that first they check if they are getting enough water.

The rest of the weekend however was very much like the year before, except this time I got to meet Ichiyoh Haga. He reminded me a little of Dave Whatt, so I took to Ichyo instantly.

I didn't know who he was or how famous his work in Japan. Apparently he was also a fan of my work and bought several pieces. I hadn't had time for more than a passing glimpse of his stand. I found out later that I ought to have been in awe of him and by the time I'd gone home and seen his work on the internet I was! He creates beautiful tiny scenes of decay with real atmosphere. In the hotel that night I was woken by a rumble; more a slight shiver really. Ooh we were experiencing a Tokyo earthquake. It was a tiny one but it was enough to count towards my bank of life experiences. In fact we'd had a bigger earthquake in Hull during my last year there. But let's not let the facts spoil a good story.

Scrumping.

One of the things that became a vital supplement along with the generous neighbour's huerta-glut deliveries during our own 'crisis' (pronounced 'creesees') years here in Spain, was the 'scrumping' opportunity. When I say scrumping I mean picking wild and roadside rather than hopping across farmer's fields and over neighbour's fences. We hadn't gone that feral! Actually I'm a little shy when it comes to being seen to be free food greedy even though I was brought up in a family that was so keen on home produce and frugal living that our freezer often had a bag or two of brown shrimp and we always had jars of pickled samphire and bottles of bramble juice as well as jars of bramble jelly in the pantry alongside the garden produce.

I have to admit it was my brother who reminded me how delightful and damned useful free food was when he and his wife came over and borrowed our rental in the year before we moved over. When I got back to Spain there was a little note telling me there were some bags of chestnuts in the freezer. Oh dear what were we to do with frozen chestnuts? A short internet search and Frank came up with chestnut bread and chestnut cakes. My brother Derek had an allotment, a walnut tree and a love of foraged mushrooms and his wife made a mean lemon curd and delicious preserves which she would share generously whenever we visited. Anyway my own love for a jar of pickled freebees was re-awakened.

There were apples on a tree on the side of the little side road to Fuenteheridos. The first year I came across them they were a little past their best. A bit wormy actually. We picked them anyway Frank still too shy at that point to be seen out of the car. From then on I realised we had to get to the apples a bit earlier. In August or September whereas the chestnuts weren't ready until mid-October and done by mid-November. Eventually Frank was hooked and decided to venture out of the car too as he's a big fan of a nice hot stove top chestnut. At first we were a bit bothered by the occasional honking of truck horns as they passed and saw us picking. We thought "are we breaking some law here?" Maybe we were, or maybe they were honking to show they also would love to stop and pick a few. Certainly almost everyone I knew did, or would have no qualms about picking the road side ones.

We took to taking a long pole with a specially designed hook and basket attachment made for apple picking. I'd happened to pick it up as part of a set of Wolfcraft gardening tools with interchangeable ends at a clear-out sale at Homebase back in England. Well, I'm sure it's not the last time I'll mention that I'm a sucker for a tool bargain. Any kind of bargain actually. I've got the fatal shopping triad. I'm from Yorkshire, I'm a woman and I'm a craftswoman. My Yorkshire thrift combines with my love of shopping and the "I know it'll come in handy someday" so that if it's got that red double sticker of second discount and it's a tool or a material … it's in my bag. It was ripped on first outing so it often threw out its contents back on to my head. On the plus side that saved me continually pulling the pole back down to empty the contents.

Our favourite scrumped items we hardly ever got to find ourselves though. The Sierra de Aracena is famous for its 'setas' (wild mushrooms). Although we have found 'niscalos' which are bright orange mushrooms with verdigris stains which Frank loves but I find a bit 'meh' in the pines above the village we've never known how to find the other famous local fungi, boletus, tanas (amanita caesarea) and the very popular "gurumelos" (amanita ponderosa). Tanas which are my favourite are impossible to confuse with anything else having bright orange caps and egg yellow flesh and stems. The rest could all be confused with deadly species. This makes me a little nervous when a well meaning friend brings round a basketful of wild mushrooms. I'm always really careful and anything that isn't absolutely exactly what I would expect goes in the bin.

The cats

We didn't think we wanted any pets. After the many failed attempts I'd had at being a competent pet owner in the past I felt sure I didn't have the patience, the energy or the money for it. Nope, pets were not on our list of desires any more. One day in the laundry room, in a mostly empty laundry basket we found next door's cat and her litter of new kittens. The laundry room still didn't possess a door and so it was easy for the cat to sneak in and bed down on some very conveniently placed old curtains. I called round at Pepa's and explained what we'd found. "Oh just hand them over to me" said Pepa. "My cousin will get rid of them". "Get rid of them?" Well, when Pepa explained that most unwanted kittens were simply dispatched and buried in the garden I just couldn't accept it and told Pepa that no way was I handing over the poor defenceless things to that fate. I knew it was useless to reprimand a Spaniard for this kind of thinking but I did anyway. I was very rude in fact I told her they should be ashamed as Catholics that they valued human life so highly but had no feeling for the defenceless.

Unfortunately Pepa's cat was not an indoor cat. To be honest it wasn't really her cat at all. Just a wild cat that she fed, so when we touched her babies she felt very threatened and started to move them around the garden. We tried to keep bringing them back to their original spot but we were fighting a losing battle. All but one of the poor little things died which was extra sad as we'd called them after my daughter and her friends so it felt terrible losing them one by one. Obviously when I lost little Kitty Kira I was devastated.

Somewhere in those losses there was the seed of a new maternal instinct for me and for Frank too. So when I suggested that maybe we should get a healthy domesticated cat Frank didn't protest too loudly. We had just the kind of cat in mind. Our friend Sanne In Denmark has a long haired Ginger cat called Poushke who we really fell for even though she did give me a nasty bite one day. That was it. I wanted a long haired Ginger cat.

What we ended up with were a pair of sisters from a 'mad cat lady' in Aracena whose house stank of cats but who clearly handled them lovingly all the time. In the litter was a white long-haired cat and a short haired ginger cat, but which one? … and so it was that Marmalade and Smudge both became our 'children'. Their names were changed a little, or a lot in the case of Marmalade whose behaviour led her to be renamed Squirrel. Smudge did have a smudge on her head when she was tiny and it quickly disappeared. That wasn't the reason her name was changed. We changed it after visiting the vet for her injections. The vet just couldn't get his Andalucían tongue around the pronunciation of 'dge' and so Smoosh it was from then on.

There's nothing funnier than seeing someone who takes themselves too seriously getting a severe dent to their egos. And so it is with cats. Cats do the funniest things just because they're 'snooty' looking. We love it when our cats perch on the back of the sofa only to misjudge the width and overbalance to fall backwards. Their shame only being hidden by the chair back. They take their time re-emerging as if they know it will be to hoots of derision. It's just as if they can't take the embarrassment. Like most cats, ours love to stalk, and our ginger cat has a habit of stalking Frank's legs, occasionally causing a yelp from him. She loves to hide behind the curtains and leap out as he passes but hasn't quite worked out how much curtain is too much and sometimes misjudges it, hurling herself as a ball of curtain across the room only to be stopped and returned to her original spot by the fabric. She pretends she hasn't noticed or that she intended to swing in the curtains ... but we know ... and she knows that we know. Oh the shame!

A fully domesticated cat is a rare thing here in the campo and all our visitors are amazed to see how friendly and approachable ours are. I put this down to their 'Mad cat lady' origins. Not just because particularly the white one was handled from birth but also because when we got them they had terrible ear mite infections. We were given an oil to put in their ears daily. Well, I say given. We were charged a fortune for two rounds of a totally useless application which didn't work at all. The kittens hated it but we dutifully wrapped them in towels and gave them a squirt and a rub of each ear on a daily basis. Eventually they gave up struggling and accepted their fate. The mites refused to abandon themselves to theirs however and kept producing their black sticky waste product by which we knew they were happily living breeding digesting and excreting. Eventually I googled the problem and saw someone suggested a weak vinegar solution. Well, there wasn't too much to lose and so I mixed up a batch. Cost, pennies. Effectiveness 100% and sharpish! After that I decided I would trust my own research and intuition a bit more and when they had weepy eyes I used another effective alternative remedy. Chamomile tea eye drops! And when it turned out that Squirrel had somewhat congested lungs on a regular basis, we told the Vet there was no way we could afford regular cortisone injections etc. So he relented and sent us off to the chemist for a human drug, of which, it turns out, an eighth of a tablet every now and again was sufficient to clear her lungs and have her back fighting fit. Another thing which is still going six years later for the cost of just a few what we were by now calling 'euroquid'.

One thing we couldn't skimp on was having them sterilised. Of course our two male cats turned out to be female and were therefore very expensive to spay. We really were short of money and we'd certainly not got the sort of money they were asking for sterilisation of female cats. Fortunately we managed to contact a cat rescue organisation and had them registered as rescue cats, allowing us to access a cheaper price from a vet in Huelva who would charge 100 euros each as opposed to over 150 each. Also Smoosh wasn't coming up as perfectly healthy when we took them so they only did Squirrel first. This also made it easier to come up with the second 100 Euros for Smoosh. Squirrel hated the cone shaped collar and kept smacking the edge on the stairs and furniture. She couldn't eat or drink properly because the edge of the collar would trap her away from the water fountain and get stuck in the food dish. I felt so sorry for her I came up with the idea of cutting holes in a sock to make her a sort of baby 'body' for cats to cover her wound. It worked amazingly and Squirrel hardly even bothered to try to remove it! A couple of weeks later we did the same for Smoosh. When we showed the photograph on Facebook several friends used the same idea for their own pets. The cats hated the travelling and cried all the way to Huelva, but fortunately both came back in a rather more more peaceful state than they had left!

13

Homilies And Honesty

I've suffered from a problem all my life. It's a bit like Tourettes but it's not Tourettes. It still causes people to gape at me shocked when I open my mouth and tell the truth! No, it's not that I never tell a lie or a little fib. It's not that everything I do is completely whiter than white. It's just that when I was little I was taught "Oh what a tangled web we weave when first we practise to deceive" and "your sins will always find you out" and other such 'wisdom'. These formed part of my childhood and are very difficult to remove, being as deeply inculcated as some people's religion …

As if to prove the veracity of these homilies whenever I did pull a childish stunt I was always the first one to get caught. Maybe I should have learned something from the fact that my more devious sibling would always wriggle out and leave me in the spotlight. Be it the hiding behind the door to sneak a look at the Christmas presents or the first one to try sex out (not me) or the ones who smoked in secret or experimented most with drugs (not me either). It was me who got caught behind the door. It was me who got pregnant, in spite of the several years longer it took me to lose my virginity. It was me who got caught with my first husband's neat row of cannabis plants on the back windowsill. When asked about these pretty plants, why couldn't I come out with a snappy and believable answer? Not me. I cringed and admitted it, and when advised by my dad to burn them why couldn't I stop myself from admitting that we would be doing that … and very slowly?

I was honest with my kids. Which wasn't a problem until there were other parental figures on the scene who were less candid. I was honest with the tax man. Maybe not 100%, I won't deny on the way back from an event I might buy myself a new pair of shoes before the money hit the accounts. See, there I go telling the truth again! But really, we were more honest than anyone I knew even in England. Most miniaturists are hobbyists and don't declare and if they do it's usually a balance between outlay and income. I believed, and still do in spite of all attempts to change, that if I tell a lie, I'll be the first one to be found out. Maybe that's because I'm just not practised enough at it.

So, all my life I've worked a bit harder, for a bit less than most people I know. I've felt reasonably virtuous. I didn't mind paying tax because I'd been on benefits myself for a few years. Why should that matter … nobody else seems to worry about it!

A couple of times in my life it has helped me to know that a lie told about me could easily be proved to be a lie. If people heard a lie they would know me well enough to know where the truth most likely lay. (I still kept dates of all my inventions and publications from the first time I heard someone say I'd copied them rather than the other way around!) Maybe that's the full extent to which honesty has helped me. It seems these days nobody respects it anyway. It leaves you with a heavier tax burden, even in England, than the small business person deserves. In Spain it's beyond unjust and, it seems, beyond fixing.

Anyway, when I moved to Spain I believed we could continue the way we always had, declaring my income from all sources and paying a reasonable amount of tax. Feeling virtuous and earning my pension if and when the time came. At that time it was expected to be at age 60. Boy was I in for a shock! People had warned me this was not the case. Everybody warned me from every sector of society. Everybody said Spain doesn't work like that. And guess what? I thought I knew better. I believed honesty was the best policy and at least I believed that if I wasn't honest, I would get caught. I thought my attitude was laudable, but it was more laughable. I found out they were right and actually I was stupid!

Things started to get difficult right from the start. I struggled every month to pay the debts we'd left behind in England due to the crash. Worse than that I struggled month after month to pay my National Insurance (Seguridad Social) which was then nominally 280 Euros a month but always rose to 320 or 350 depending on how late we paid. Month by month we had to pay later and later. This has to be paid month in month out regardless of income.

Tax and IVA, (VAT) had to be paid by even the smallest business from the first Euro, good month or bad, at the end of every quarter whether your income comes over the tax threshold or not. If you're late yes, more charges. If you ask for a delay, they tell you you haven't proved that you haven't enough income … although clearly you haven't, or you'd avoid the extra charges, the worry and finally the embargoes which can cripple your business altogether. Stopping your bank accounts and taking your car and later … your home. There is no way out.

Yes there is! You can learn from your mistakes, or from mine!

So, because some people reading this book will be thinking about a possible change of life I need to say this to help stop people falling into the Expat honesty trap the way we did.

You can be more Spanish about things. It hurts if you're naturally 100% candid and have to change your ways but it's the simple truth. There is a double bind here in Spain. Spanish small businesses are taxed extra heavily because they expect there to be undeclared grey/black income. If there isn't you can theoretically, if you include social security as a tax, be paying more tax than you earn in very lean months! This has actually happened to me.

Here is how the autonomo tax system works for us. Every month, income or no income (and there's little to no income December and half of January or July and August) you have to pay nearly 300 euros each in National Insurance. Just imagine what a burden that is on a business which may not even take a regular thousand in a month.

Even before you pay the Seguridad Social, otherwise known as Autonomo, you have to pay IVA (sales tax). Then, if you make any, you have to pay around 20% of your profits including those that fall within your basic minimum income. You'll get that bit back a year or so later, but it won't cover the fines. There is no discounted rate on the Seguridad Social for low earners.

How many small craft businesses, how many couples can pay their bills and eat and run a car etc. on that level of income? So we fell behind on this major expense. If you can't pay it the fines are exorbitant. So, if you are unsure whether to become Autonomo in Spain think very carefully.

Imagine 12 months of low turnover and high National insurance payments.

Check whether your car can be considered a business vehicle or not (If it's a 'turismo' because you can't afford a swanky new business vehicle it doesn't matter if your use is 90% business. You'll only be allowed 50% offset against tax).

Think who are your customers. If they are outside Spain, look at the high postal costs and the IVA and ask yourself whether you can really compete. (I can't even compete with people who resell my goods!) If a very large percentage of your customers are outside of Spain, ask yourself if you wouldn't be better off keeping your business abroad and just declaring your worldwide income here.

Finally, ask your Gestor for advice and take it!

I didn't even take my Gestor's advice. Although I can't tell you here what it was, I'm sure you can guess.

Starting to teach

I realised that our fairs diary was too packed and with too little return. I really never did get the hang of pricing my work correctly, especially the most popular repeat items. Every fair we did became more and more difficult in terms of finding the funds to pay for the trip and became more uncertain as to whether we covered our costs at all. More and more often we started finding ourselves going to events without enough money in our pockets to pay the hotel bill let alone find our way home if everything went wrong. Those were scary trips. Selling enough to get even to the stage of paying hotels and eating out ate into our stock, squeezing the online business and the next fair, so it began to feel like we were running just to keep still.

Around that time Frank had been chatting with a young guy called Francis who was taking his exams in an attempt to get his oposiciones (competitive civil service exams) in order to follow his dad Paqui into the Policia local or, as he eventually did, to join the Guardia civil. The Junta de Andalucía exams seemed to Frank to be very tricky and I had to admit when I saw exam papers at that level they were. The exams seemed to have nothing to do with actually speaking and handling the English language and more to do with sentence transformations. A sort of grammar check that, to my mind, does nothing to either interest or educate in the actual speaking of a language. Lots of professions in Spain required this stuff to be learned by rote and precious few of the students who ever learned it and passed the exam ever used a word of English again. In addition to that, many of the papers had such glaring mistakes in them that I started to believe they really had been composed by people who had paid for their qualifications rather than handed in their own work, as was the rumour at the time. A few years later one of our friends, someone I think of as a trustworthy sort, told us he was actually writing someone else's exam thesis for money. Proving that this kind of deception really was that rife.

It was some years before I came upon the much better Cambridge and Oxford exam teaching methods for English. Frank taught "little" Francis for a few months and then also a group of about 5 teenage guys and a girl. To be honest I'm not sure Frank's heart was in it and his pricing structure was wrong so he found it a chore for just a few Euros. I listened in on a class once and was appalled at the amount of time Frank spent talking about his political beliefs in a strong Hull accent. I said "You'll lose these students" and he did. They never came back after that class. It was clear Frank had to find his English teaching methods which would clearly have to be quite different from the ones he'd been used to using when teaching Cisco Networking back in England. It didn't help that Frank could barely speak Spanish and in common with most Brits didn't know how to describe grammatical forms. To be fair, neither did I.

Shortly after this our geologist neighbour Enrique,

who at that age, looked just like John Lennon and wore the same kind of glasses and often the same slightly dazed and bemused look, got a job with a mining company with British connections. He needed to brush up on his English, and pronto. Initially I thought he'd prefer to chat with Frank but as I listened to their classes I realised he probably needed a slightly different accent as well, and someone who was going to make the effort to correct him more often, so Frank did conversation with him once a week and I gave him more of a formal 'class' once a week too. Those were my first English lessons and I had a lot to learn. I started to prepare lessons where I found myself only one step ahead of Enrique. He was easy to teach and intelligent and I probably learned as much about the geology and the social history of the area as he learned English. I met Enrique's wife at Pilates a few times but didn't really get to know her at that time. At first I thought her a little standoffish; but the truth was she was just the kind of person who took her time to get to know people. Much more an English trait than a Spanish one, and one I learned to appreciate as we slowly became good friends.

Pretty soon Enrique and Inma decided it would be a good idea to have their kids take English classes with us as well. A few of their friends wanted the same. So they asked me if I would and, penniless as I was, I reluctantly agreed. We still had fairs in Italy, Denmark Spain, Germany and Paris and this year I had a workshop trip to Swizerland so I had to rule out Fridays and some Mondays but I agreed to twice a week lessons with a small group of local kids.

Travels on a budget

I'd been talking to my friend Cilla Halbert and she told me she was doing Milan that year. Alone? Yes alone. Well I'm a bit social-phobic and I value my space and privacy so there are very few people I'd feel totally comfortable sharing a room with but Cilla is one of that handful. When I first met Cilla I used to confuse her with the Danish miniaturist Ursula, probably because they were both slim and blonde and Nordic and pretty. No, I'm not saying all Nordic girls look the same but that my memory for faces and names is sketchy to say the least. Maybe also because at one time Ursula used to make miniature birdcages and Cilla, chandeliers. Ursula had studied under the well respected woodworker Barry Hipwell. In fact Barry clearly had the biggest crush on her. I'm not saying that just to be a gossip. I met Barry once in a failed attempt to produce a video we were going to call "Best of British Miniaturists". A project we shelved when I stopped going to America (our target market). Barry spent the entire filming talking about Ursula. Clearly he was smitten. Although it's very possible that actually he was rightly smitten with her potential as an artist. Ursula has gone on to be an extremely talented woodworker and of course had learned from one of the best. Cilla is one of those artists I would say has a real eye for composition and for the cool and unusual which matches her personality perfectly. I feel a little nervous around her because our two cultural backgrounds couldn't be further from each other and our behaviour is totally different. Plus when I was overweight it always felt like I might snap Cilla if I spoke too loudly. But each time I was in her company long enough to get over what was probably a manifestation of my mild social-phobia, we spent some very happy amiable time together mooching around bead shops and flea markets when she lived in Barcelona.

I don't like going to Milan alone because outside the Stazione Centrale is one of the few places I feel really nervous. As you climb off the bus there are people waiting to offer to take your luggage to the hotel and around the front of the station you really know you have to look after yourself. I had to brave the bus station alone twice and I didn't much like it. I hadn't booked a workshop in for myself that year so I tagged along to Cilla's. She was teaching how to make pretty little handbags out of tiny book shaped lockets. Cilla trawled the flea markets and found old miniature tapestry fabrics and jewellery findings etc. for pennies, which worked for this kind of object.

That year Milan was freezing at around four below zero and we'd heard there were homeless people in real trouble. In fact we saw fewer homeless people there than usual that year so we hoped that they'd been given at least temporary shelter. Cilla and I went for a long walk around Milan. Stomping through the snow and throwing snowballs like children. It was good giggly girl-time, something I never seem to do enough of. We found the area on the other side of the tracks which Frank and I had never explored. This was going to be useful in the future because we found the 'Chinatown' area really cheap compared with the other side of the tracks and it actually felt safer. We bought a big fat plasticky lcather handbag each and for some reason we called them "bible bashers" although I'm not sure why. I think we just happened to pass someone preaching rather loudly on the street and these bags looked like quite useful defensive weapons. More so I imagine if they'd actually contained a large Bible (other weapons-grade books are available).

In April the Geneva trip was a highlight of this year. It was successful but rather surreal. The lady who invited us was meeting us at the airport which was a very good thing, as I didn't have any money at all until we got paid, which of course, was getting to be the nerve-wracking norm for us. We couldn't see her at the airport and our phone didn't seem to be working in Switzerland. I was just counting our few pennies to see if we could get a room for the night when she arrived. We'd been looking for her as she'd been looking for us. Both of us were about to give up but of course she didn't know how close we were to disaster. She really did look after us well having organised a reasonably priced accommodation (for Switzerland) and making sure we knew where we were and what we were doing at all times. She also took us for a lovely drive out into the hills and we in turn took her for a meal after the first day's class. Unfortunately there were some strange undercurrents going on in the group which I didn't understand. The second day these seemed to be bubbling up into something serious. There were whispers and factions seemed to be forming and suddenly at the end of the class when it was time for the thanks and goodbye our host chose to make us part of some political point and threw in her membership of the group in spectacular style. This was a shame because it was a very uncomfortable situation for us and we packed up with our backs to the argument. I didn't know the ins and outs of it and wasn't going to take sides, however I decided if we were going to return we had to return with the first people who invited us. This, in retrospect was quite a mistake as he second trip to Switzerland a couple of years later was a nightmare and seemed still to be part of this ongoing feud.

In September we decided to do the Barcelona fair by AVE (Alta Velocidad - which is the fast Bullet Train). We got really lucky and managed to get tickets for around 57 euros each, each way. This year I had a workshop organised off site with some of the friends of the organisers. So we tried to find a hotel which was close enough to both Barcelona Sants station, and the basement flat where the workshop was going to be held. We got lucky! The place was literally just around the corner from both. The hostess was a really sweet lady and her and her husband just looked after us like family and drove us and our luggage round to our hotel after the class. Barcelona fair this year was another one half of a group split from the previous year. It was really good fun though and the thing that tickled me was the formation of the MOMA group. MOMA stands for Maridos Oprimidos de las Miniaturistas. The oppressed husbands club. It wasn't really a club. Just a fun notion. I love how miniaturists are so in touch with their inner children, that they and even their husbands never take themselves too seriously. It seems that even through illness, hardships and losses, Miniaturists just keep on laughing.

The autumn edition of the Dutch fair had changed from the Rijnhalle in Arnhem, to Appeldoorn. Appeldoorn is a pretty town and the building was pretty similar to the Rijnhalle. We did this fair twice but it was another one where there was no appropriate public transport for stand holders at the beginning and end of each day. Once again we were conflicted. We had to consider giving up on yet another fair which became expensive with all the little transport additions where the takings just didn't merit the extra hassle and expense. Het Loo where we were staying in Appeldoorn was a really pretty area though and I found out later I'd missed seeing some of the most magnificent formal gardens in Europe which surrounded the royal palace just a walk away from where we were staying at a hotel called the Bastion.

We found the Madrid fair do-able largely because our friend Panty helped us out again by offering the use of her extra flat whenever it wasn't already rented out. Although we found the AVE was a really good way of getting there if you booked at just the right time, this year we didn't. Not having the right money at the right time. So we did it by the Socibus coach from Seville which was really very cheap but was a gruellingly long journey. The coach did have a loo but more often than not it was out of order and with just one wee stop on the journey it was a leg crossing exercise for me. Travelling gave me headaches at the best of times but trying to keep my fluids down to avoid needing the loo could make it even worse.

Gathering the orange blossom (recording the girls) 2013

In the village there is a women's choir called the Azahares (the orange blossoms). I love to hear them practising on balmy evenings and I know parts of some of the songs off by heart. Frank had offered a few years ago to record them but although they sounded keen we just never seemed to get it organised. One day however, completely out of the blue, Angeles came round and said yes they were ready and could we do it that week? Well no, we couldn't. We needed to make sure we had enough leads and microphones and that the hall was suitable. We arranged a date a fortnight or so later and told them to get a few songs practised and ready for the recording. On the appointed day we turned up early at the Casa de Cultura, a small village concert hall and we set up a microphone each for the Alto section, the treble section and the best and most directional one for the sopranos and the soloist. We also stuck a microphone in front of the guitarist. I went round and sound checked them all and the girls started to drift in.

Little did we know that our recording session was

about to open up rifts in the group that would take nearly two years to heal! The first day was absolute chaos. Nobody seemed to get the idea that this wasn't a rehearsal and when the tape was running you couldn't just stop in the middle of a song and start arguing with your neighbour. Several times we had to remonstrate with Angeles' sister for doing just that. A couple of the singers had brought along their kids who insisted on running round the hall but the most difficult person to discipline was the guitarist and leader of the group. He didn't get the concept of letting us know when the song was about to start and because both his hands were around the guitar, and the girls were uncontrollable anyway there were never any hand signals to bring people in on time.

The singers were coming in all at different times, not stressing the correct parts of the songs and worst of all was the soprano end. I had to try to teach the soloists basic microphone technique. Something which they never got. The result was that at the end of a several hour recording session we'd recorded 3 songs, only one of which was usable. Frank and I were tearing our hair out. We had also explained the difficulties to Angeles who we didn't realise, although she's a very kind and caring person who means very well, had a problem not talking down to people because she felt she was responsible for the success of the project. Angeles was for ever after labelled in our house "Angeles who can start an argument in an empty room". If truth be told that's a bit unfair as we also had difficulties not talking down to them too. And Angeles was merely trying to sort the problems out for everyones benefit. As far as discipline went though, they really were an unruly rabble! On the other hand some of them, especially one mature lady in the alto section, had the voices of angels and the rest were enthusiastic and reasonably competent in the vocal department. Not so in the rhythm and timekeeping department. We realised what they were badly in need of were rules and instructions for the second day. So, that night I typed up a list of recording studio dos and don't s and made sure the next day everyone had a copy. I also appointed myself unofficial conductor for some of the songs which had the worst discipline problems. I still couldn't get them to come in on time for my favourite Sevillana.

The guitarist certainly didn't like being told what to do one bit and made his position of power felt on the second day by turning up deliberately late. Then handing us a list of around twenty songs he told us we must record that day. Neither did he like it much when we laughed at him. That wasn't possible even if they behaved really well and if he'd behaved like that in a recording studio, they may have let him but he'd have paid extra for the privilege. We pretty much knew from that moment that he was going to be uncooperative and seriously doubted if we were going to get anything worth spending our time on from that moment. We decided to make the best of a bad job and pushed through the day actually recording a dozen passable songs by dint of determination and just a little bullying.

The worst problem we found on playback was that the main soloist had completely ignored our instructions on facing the mic (which was directional) and continued her usual trick of singing to the ceiling, which was neither good for her throat and the sounds that came out of it, nor for the quality of the recording. Of course when finished and played back to her, even though Frank had spent most of his time trying to rescue her track, she didn't like the recording and neither did the guitarist. In her mind of course it was our fault! So the recording never was released for sale which is a shame. In the end each of the girls paid costs for two or three copies each and came and printed them off for themselves using our disc copier and label printer. They were happy but the two Divas were not. A shame really because obvious failings apart it was really rather a nice CD. We'd even designed it a sweet little cover!

The young, old doctor and the old, new doctor.

We're lucky in our village of less than 800 people to be served by our very own doctor's surgery 4 times a week. It used to be the old system which was a heart sinking experience. You had to arrive well ahead of the half past 8 opening hour. An ungodly hour for the Spanish, and add yourself to a very large group of people who were already sitting gossiping but who all stopped and stared when the English arrived. Fortunately for my mild social-phobia, they always nod, greet and turn back to their chatter; after first asking you if you're ill. Spanish people are masters of asking rhetorical and obvious questions. "Are you going for a walk?"(You're walking) "Have you been to the pool?" (you're dripping wet and wrapped in a towel) "Are you ill?" which is actually a more reasonable question in the doctor's surgery, leaving room for the possibility that you aren't. Normally we're not and it's just a routine trip for a blood test, but if I was, I definitely wouldn't want to get into a conversation about it. They already call us "pareja del pueblo". (The village couple). I'm not sure whether that's a compliment and suspect they think we aren't really married and this is our secret hideaway. Obviously we're strange folk, we appear to still like each other!

Then there was the minefield of trying to remember every face in the place so we could work out when we could slot ourselves between those that came before us and those who turned up later. Further complicated by people arriving and then leaving for an hour only to arrive later and jump into the door just as we thought we'd arrived at our turn. Sometimes you could wait three hours for an appointment. I hated this and preferred not to bother. So I guess you'd think this system weeds out malingerers, except when you realise the old folk of the village like to malinger. They love nothing better. This was a more important meeting place for the retired of the village even than Loli's shop. Eventually we noticed that each new arrival asked "quien es el/la ultimo/a" (Who's the last?) It sounds as if we were a little stupid not to notice this system until you realise that the campo accent is so thick that no two people speak the same and that contractions of words to grunts are very common. It was only when someone else arrived a bit late one day and half a dozen pairs of eyes and half a dozen bony fingers pointed in our direction that we realised. By which time we already knew that we were in for a three hour wait.

It took us several earlier and earlier visits to notice a pile of scraps of paper in the centre of the table. Ahh! Then we thought we'd got it. As long as you arrive to get one of the bits of paper you can wander off and come back later. Got it! …Just in time for the change to an internet booking system. Fabulous for us. You now only have to wait a few minutes or half an hour after your appointment time. Yep, great for us, but for the poor oldies, and for Loli, not so great. They'll all have to crush into the aisles of Loli's shop for their four times a week dose of local gossip.

We got used to having Doctor Carmen, so that when one day Frank went on his own to pick up some blood test results he came home with a face like thunder. "Well

I hope that B* doesn't stay here long". "Wassup? Did you get Doctor D"? I asked him "Nope" he said "even worse!" Well how anyone could be worse than Doctor D I don't know. Doctor D could understand every word we said in our faltering Spanish and spoke more clearly than most locals, the fact was that he didn't want to listen. No, what Doctor D liked, was to prescribe. Not necessarily (in my opinion) appropriately. I was not fond of Doctor D. Fortunately he wasn't our normal Doc. Carmen was.

I've suffered from a certain amount of anxiety all my life but in the last 10 years I've been almost completely free of it. Really just the normal level that most people have with occasional bouts of stress. I got to this point by hard work on myself and an absolute refusal to take antidepressants or tranquillisers and I certainly wasn't going to start now. One thing that I have always suffered from is a very acid stomach. This is obviously partly genetic but is worsened when there's a particularly stressful period of work or too many bills to pay or if there's a family crisis so of course at that time it had been a been a bit 'off'. There's an easy answer though. Just up the level of my stomach acid reducing drug and, as they say here 'ya esta' (that's that). Oh, of course a little recognition that I maybe should cut the overwork down a little might help. Nothing new there. Local gossip had it at the time, that most doctors augment their income by prescribing particular brands. Recently this has been severely restricted by the government's new sensible cheapest drug regulations. While we were waiting Doctor D was deep in conversation smoking like a chimney outside with the 'pusher' from one of the companies. The locals were tut tutting about it, more because their appointment times were getting later and later and I was pissed off because I have a bee in my bonnet about such things. I was not surprised then, when I explained to this doctor that I was on long term acid suppressing tablets and that I needed the stronger dose for a few days because I was overworked and that affects me by raising my stomach acid. "It doesn't work that way," says Doctor D, I tell you what medication you need and you clearly need something for your stress, oh and how about some statins while you're at it?

It's hard to be patient with such, well let's call it ignorance rather than desire to over prescribe. After all I was always taught "never attribute to malice that which can be adequately explained by stupidity" but I'm afraid I had to tell him it absolutely did work that way and that this little old lady hadn't avoided the dreaded tranx well into my fifties only to roll over and become a zombie to increase his prescribing levels. Yes, one thing I can do is lay my agenda on the line when roused!

The upshot was that I got my prescription. The doctor got an extra buzzing in his ear and we've avoided that doctor ever since. Fortunately the new system gives you the name of the Doc you're going to see. So Frank knew that that he was going to see another locum. "So what was wrong with him?" I asked. Frank proceeded to describe the scene. Apparently you could hear Doctor L (loud doctor) outside the building, the volume increasing with every step towards the waiting room. Frank said it sounded as if they had a Spanish version of Brian Blessed in the room but with a somewhat more barking tone. When Frank's turn came he'd barely opened the door when the doctor, rapidly scanning his notes, started to bark guesses as to why Frank was there.

All he'd gone for were the results of a blood test but he couldn't get a word in. It seems all doctors around here have a different understanding of their job. This guy was here to diagnose dire ailments and didn't really want to bother with anything routine. It took Frank ten minutes into a six minute appointment to get the result that his blood levels of whatever the body chemical is that means you need extra iodine, had dropped. Another doctor off the acceptable list.

Well the lovely Carmen came back and we appreciated her even more. Unfortunately a few months later she'd gone again. This time for an extended move to another surgery nearer to her ageing mother, and we really missed her.

Then it was time to go for my smear and mammogram results. No, I don't understand why they don't post them either. Frank needed his six monthly blood test appointment. We hoped it wasn't Doctor L or Doctor D again as we'd forgotten the names by now, and this appointment had a double barrelled impressive forename which sounded like it might just belong to Brian Blessed's Spanish cousin. So we waited, expecting to be shouted at.

The new doctor was in fact a very old doctor who seemed highly intelligent but probably really well past his pension date. He was delighted to see us and he said so, leaning over his desk and proffering us his hand each in turn and, giving us a hearty handshake, started to talk to us in rusty English about his time in the United States. He told us about his several 'licenciaturas' (degrees) and then asked us what we did for a living. When he heard that I wrote craft books, he only heard the word books, as most people do, and assumed I was an author of some standing, at which point he hushed conspiratorially, asking me if I might be interested in translating his memoir from his time in the militar during the coup in the 1980s. He said he wanted it published as an ebook in English and made scary slashing movements with the side of his hand at his neck. Now being an educated man his accent was understandable, but I couldn't make out who might want to do him in for his role in this era, the left or the right. In this country it still matters on a fundamental genetic level. Mostly people are still concerned enough, if they're over thirty, to fudge their allegiances, which is why the south only seems to have young mayors if they're left wing, as among the older people, only the right wingers feel secure enough to stand up and be counted. The great grandfather (I think that's correct) of the present young and lovely lady mayoress was 'put up against a wall' in the civil war and her parents "Loli the shop" and her husband, are still nervous about their daughters' political life. Mayoress Merche also has a sister Inma who dabbles in environmental issues too which could lead her to come up against some even more powerful foes.

We finally got to the here and now and the medical profession and tried to get my results, the test having been done more than three months previously. 'Old doctor' didn't seem able to find them and insisted they would therefore be coming by post. It was August and the tests had been February and March respectively. Well, I knew it was hopeless, he clearly didn't understand the newfangled computerised thingamabob.

I left without my test results, but with Franks appointment, hard fought for because even that required him to call the nurse in to work the system. But hey, I respected the guy and had a sneaking hope that he would both contact me to do the translation, and that he would turn out to be excitingly, radically left wing which would be much more fun than wet on either side, or radically right wing.

I didn't hold out much hope on either count.

Farmacia

As I get older, like most people, more and more of my rants are on the subject of health. It's an undeniable fact that most of us start to get very wise about certain things just before we sink into terminal decline. One of those things that we notice with fifty years of hindsight is that both medicine and nutrition and especially the crossover, are subject to fads and fashions as well as heavy marketing.

I also had a little argument a few years ago with the lad who I rightly supposed at the time to be the son of our local pharmacist Ignacio. What a wonderful name. When was someone last called Ignacious in England? Well Ignacious' son is also called Ignacio. Young Ignacio had clearly recently qualified and, though I didn't know it then, was taking over his dad's business. Like most educated people of his age he was initially very opinionated and I'm sure he was much more used to the quiet acceptance or grumpy silence of the little old ladies and little old men he usually has to deal with here, who leave the pharmacy with armfuls of drugs most of which are clearly there to counteract the effects of other drugs in the pile. A sort of Escheresque mobius strip of drug effects.

Well I arrived at the pharmacy with my prescription for Glucosamine without knowing the brand and when the lad brought out the box I had the temerity to ask why he'd given me the version with aspartame in it. No, not his fault of course. That was what was on the prescription. "But aspartame isn't dangerous!" he assured me. He knew that because of all his training, he carried on, and besides it was a subject of special interest to him. I'm equally opinionated on the subject however, partly down to my obvious and uncomfortable adverse reaction to the stuff. It alters my hormones I think. In any case it gives me swollen breasts with a feeling like mastitis. So I refused it and said I couldn't understand why they chose to put such rubbish in so many of the drugs here in Spain. To make it more palatable he replied. I feel Spanish people are being somewhat patronised here. We're not all babies and the amount of sweetener in the pack is enough to stun a horse on a daily basis.

We continued our 'discussion' where I included the new findings that using sweeteners can actually make you crave carbohydrates more, with the young man hopping about all over the place clearly rather angry at having his scientific 'facts' concerning the absolute safety of this favourite product, for such he insisted they were, questioned. Eventually I left having made a little effort to placate him since he would most probably be my pharmacist into my declining years.

I think young Ignacio must have looked up these side effects because since this encounter he has been very sweet to me and extremely helpful. Over the next few years he's settled into his job and I can now say that he seems to be a very thorough and careful dispenser and generally I trust his judgement and would certainly be prepared to ask his advice. Even though I still catch him talking down to old ladies in the village and it still irritates me on their behalf. It has to be admitted that not all of them are knowledgeable on the subject nor as feisty as I am. You'll never convince me that medical opinion on any drug or nutrition isn't going to change from one year to the next. There's something about being older that I really rather enjoy and it's the ability to say, with absolute certainty, that a large proportion of those scientific facts which he now holds so dear will succumb to the 'half life of facts' and will be disproved within five or ten years. After all I had this same argument with a much more experienced doctor nearly thirty years ago about the "absolutely non-addictive" Ativan which is now recognised to be highly addictive. They wanted to prescribe Ativan to me then and it was my somewhat fortunate knee-jerk resistance to that 'easy way out' that has informed my relationship with drugs ever since.

Now the Pharmacist and I have long chats in English, which he speaks very well. He has a great sense of humour and I always try to make him laugh when he's having a bad day which seems to be more and more frequently. I think it may not be easy being a pharmacist in a small village these days, with smaller incomes leading to longer hours for lower profits and I sometimes sense that this is a downward spiral for what was once a highly respected profession. Our early disagreement behind us I've really become quite fond of young Ignacio, I'm not sure he's quite learned not to talk down to the other old ladies in the village; but this is still Spain.

Karon's place

One of the really wonderful things about being a miniaturist is the kind of people other miniaturists are. There's something about creating, buying and selling very small things that keeps you in touch with your inner child. I'd say some of the makers are so in touch with their inner child that their inner adult may need a little work. Not so Karon, who is a dealer, with a keen eye for all of the miniature arts, rather than a maker. She seems to combine the best of both. The sense of humour of the miniaturist with the business brain some of us lack. But it's not just about business, Karon likes to encourage the makers too and she decided to organise a workshop for me in September in her and her partner John's home. We'd spent some enjoyable evenings together after fairs and so we knew each other well enough for them to invite us to stay at their home. Staying with friends with similar interests is a step out of my normal hermit-like existence. I've learned to enjoy it immensely. Originally we insisted on staying at local hotels, but our financial situation made us change that rule and to be honest I've enjoyed it more, Once we get over the "don't try to feed the vegetarian" rule.

Karon and "Trouble" as Frank called her husband were really wonderful hosts and they put us up in their lovely old Gloucestershire farmhouse which they were just building an extension to. John told us that he was one of those people who'd had a payout from the banks for mis-sold PPI and because he'd funded all his previous business exploits on credit cards, it was a substantial sum. For him it turned out to be kind of like a savings scheme. It was paying for their extension! John is a very likeable chap and kept us entertained with his tall stories and jokes all weekend.

We spent a full day making the squashes and pumpkin board, another making leafy and graduated colour vegetables such as leeks, cabbage, radicchio etc.

I repeated the squashes and pumpkins class at the Dutch fair at its new venue the Americahal. This was another fair we'd just had enough of due to being out in the middle of nowhere. I know this irritates the organisers when I say things like this but there is a plain bald formula:- income, minus cost plus or minus pleasure.

Let me explain this better. If you're a craftswoman/man you either have time or you have money or sometimes you have neither because getting to fairs means you have to sell a lot of stock to make an income. That stock can't be sold again. It has to be replaced which is very time consuming. A good fair has three benefits. Income, exposure and travel pleasure (otherwise known as days off at your destination). So if you've been to a place before a few times, you really aren't getting any new exposure because there are very few new potential customers from year to year. For me as a teaching miniaturist, new customers mean a flurry of sales of books and craft materials which are the only things that are really profitable since miniatures themselves are so time consuming. Travel to fairs is time consuming too. Since my nasty experience in Tokyo I certainly wasn't thinking of doing any more trips alone, so trips for two of us were costing a lot of time … and a lot of money. So it wasn't easy to get income or exposure out of an old fair unless it happened to be a really good year and I had a lot of new ideas, tools, books and miniature stock and time to turn these around. No that's right, I never had that much time. That leaves the benefit of travel. At this point you ask yourself; is there anything I actually enjoy about (whichever place)? If the answer is no, its not worth the risk of a loss. Its that simple. Some fairs just don't do it for me on a business level and so they'd have to be really pleasurable for me to take the risk these days.

Building

Even though finding any money or time for building was very difficult, we tried to do a building project every summer and Xmas and any other holiday that gave us enough time. And whenever we had enough money for materials. Sometimes we bought materials piecemeal and then completed the projects during the holidays. During Xmas 2013 Frank boxed in the pipes and we tiled the downstairs bathroom and part of the little laundry room/guest kitchen. I had some guests coming the following March and I wanted the place to look just a little more reasonable by then. I always warned my students they were coming to a building site but I don't know how many actually believed me until they arrived. Frank was finding that far from being a klutz with a drill, he was much better at it than me. I always beat him on the tiling though but little by little I stopped being the 'mujer albañil' and Frank started to be more and more 'el constructor'.

14

Darkest Hours

Sometimes I thought back to the first day we'd slept in the house. It had felt weird and not a little scary. Here we were setting up camp in a brick box like a cross between a third world shack and a palace. To the outside world looking for all the world like a small, nearly completed house that just needed a few Euros and a touch of loving care to fix. In the pre-crisis years, that's not only what it looked like. That's what it would have been, but these weren't pre-crisis years and the enormity of what we had done weighed heavily on me. This time, I had said to myself, we really have taken on too much. This time, sooner or later the job would swamp us, buckle, break or even kill me. I'd been sure of that in those early days. Now, six years later the job was still a long way from completed but although successive summer and Xmas projects had made a significant change and I began to think, on good days, that maybe it didn't matter that it wasn't finished. Maybe it would never be finished. I even began to think I could live with that. That was on the good days, and the previous year the good days were outweighing the bad.

Sometimes as I passed through the light well on the way to the bathroom and looked up and mused about the future (this had become my habit) I smiled at the memory of the hard building work that, at the time had broken us both many times over, and I thanked my lucky stars that I'd been blessed with a 'can do' attitude that made the redoubling of efforts possible. Although in February 2014 in anticipation of a guest visit we added electric underfloor heating to the guest room with tiles and tile adhesive left over from last year, there was precious little extra to spend on projects, and we were living on air. How many more times could we redouble our efforts? It turned out that this was the year I didn't have any more to give.

Social security (not what it means in England).

Seguridad Social (National insurance) is supposed to help those on a low or no income. It's not supposed to be a stick to beat them with. However that's what it seems to be for the autonomo (self employed) here. The very people who could help Spain to survive, even grow, the small businesses, are being destroyed by present government policy.

~Come and have a drink with us Mr Minister (The minister, whoever he is that thinks all small businesses have money hidden away) ... only you'll have to pay because we can't afford to go to the bar. Come and take a ride in our car. You'll have to squeeze up because it's not very big, and it's full of bottles of water because our well pump has broken down and we can't afford to fix it. Oh and you may have to push because if it breaks down we can't fix that either. Still, come and search under our beds for the money you're sure must be there. It isn't, and you will get dirty knees from the cement floors. No floor tiles in our budget. Oh and if you want to wash your hands after your exertion please feel free to use the bucket of well water in the bathroom. Fortunately we still have clean towels because we've only been ten days without water so far and we have lots of towels from the time we were in England and used to earning a living wage and paying the correct amount of tax. We're not the worst off either. Oh no. We still have food in the cupboards and in the garden. There are those who don't even have that.~

That year we reached rock bottom, our debts to the government heavily outweighing our possible income. We couldn't afford even to pay our accountant. My courage had reached breaking point and I was starting to get very anxious. I decided to lose myself in typing up some of my dad's writings for several hours a day, or night especially late at night and the early hours of the morning when I couldn't sleep otherwise, for worrying.

On my birthday though, I had some incredible news to lift my spirits. I was going to be a Grandma for the first time. The baby was due just before Xmas I was told, but that I shouldn't tell anyone for another couple of months. I'd only been told the news because it was my birthday. What a great birthday present, I only wished I could flood my kids with baby stuff as expectant grandmothers usually do. Of course I could still window shop and dream, especially in the continental baby shops where clothes seemed just that bit more fashionable and quite a lot more expensive.

Sharing the creativity

While I was deep in thought about a title for my dad's memoirs, I got an email through from Tove, the organiser of the Tune Miniatures week, asking if I'd consider doing the talk on the second evening. This was a long tradition of the Tune retreat and all the other tutors had done it before me. I jumped at the chance. I don't know quite why because I suffer rather badly from stage fright and I thought I'd given up my performing days. Maybe it was because at the time I was transcribing my dad's writings from scraps of paper. I needed a break. Although his writing could be somewhat long winded and rather turgid, there were bits, as I went through the stories that I started rather to enjoy. "Oh that's why" moments where I realised that my dad actually had a life beyond being my dad.

Parts of his memoirs made me realise he sometimes struggled to be the great parent he was and there were times when his need to be creative overwhelmed him. He always wanted to publish a book and dreamed of having the time to be a writer. Somewhat sadly he committed himself to being a good father to four kids whatever else he had to give up on. I thought how I'd got a double dose of it because my mother also came from a creative family and her mind and her hands were always at problem solving. I started thinking of the Tune talk in terms of writing my own short autobiography and sat down in front of the computer and got started ... but then got so totally bogged down in it. I went miles off the road of a short interesting story for a group of friends, tired after a long day of concentrating on miniatures. So I left it.

I finished typing up my dad's memoirs, finished my Colour Book, started the next in the series and in between all this and making a few (too few for a good income) miniatures found some time to be very very lazy. Because that's what creative people do isn't it? We vacillate like manic depressives between periods of excessive hard work and dedication to the minutiae of a task ... and equally excessive idleness.

When Tove reminded me of my upcoming monologue I didn't know where or how to start again, so I gave her the suitably wide title of 'Sharing the Creativity' so I could think about it again. I did ... and then I didn't ... I stared a bit at Facebook and I answered a few emails and then I shared a few more videos of cats doing humorous things.

It just happened that during a few days of that incredibly lazy behaviour my daughter sent me a copy of the article she had just had published in The Dolls House Magazine. It was a lovely little story about what it was like to live in a home full of miniatures with a slightly nutty miniaturist mother … Yes, me! The end of the tale was so moving. Just a few words which basically said, when you're surrounded by creativity all your life it rubs off.

So I settled down to write a piece for Tune with the title I'd given Tove about how creative people just can't help certain things that they do, and celebrating these foibles:-

The Tune talk

"Creative people seem to be motivated to do things other people wouldn't think of doing. Or is it just me? Do you recognise any of these?

Interrupting … No I don't mean to interrupt you but there's this idea I just have to get out before I forget it. You've triggered such a wave of inspiration in me I don't need you to finish your sentence and I just HAVE to share this thought with you … Yes it's very rude and here's my apology and my confession. I do it … because I just can't help it.

Telling the truth … Yes I'm creative. I really ought to be able to think up the most convoluted and believable lies … but I can't. I'm too expressive. I'll give myself away. Nope, I'm not even very good at those little white lies. And as for too much information to authorities, on forms or just when it's inappropriate, yes, I do it all. Like a Tourettes sufferer I say it … whether it needs saying, or not.

My husband calls me 'head of the department of too much information' and I just can't help it.

"Giz od" is an east Yorkshire expression meaning

"give it to me". Whatever you're doing I always know a quicker way or a more effective way. It runs in my creative family. We just can't stand to see someone making a mess of something, so we take over the task. Nope we're certainly not cut out to be managers. I wonder if I'd be cut out to work in a team at all. Clearly not … and that's why I don't do it. I'd want to do every job. I can't help it.

Everyone knows about the state of most of our workrooms. I once did a mini tour of Great Britain interviewing some of the best of British Miniaturists, with the intention of making a DVD. I visited Jamie whose workroom at the time was a shed and very comfortingly like mine. Except a bit tidier … which I was convinced meant it was even more like mine before he'd given it a tickle before we came to film.

No such effort had been made by the late Barrie Hipwell. At my very worst I can and do attain that kind of chaos. It was a wonderful spider's lair of bits and scraps and many layered leaning towers of half made work, of tools and materials of paints and stains and smells of all kinds. There are some tidy workshops but I believe that, like Barry, most creatives are messy. We just can't help it.

Waking up at silly 'o'clock with yet another crazy idea we haven't got time for unless we leave something else unfinished which we always do, even though it means that our lives are full of unfinished projects. We just can't help it.

Here are a few other things from my life which seem to be common to a certain type of creative person.

Seeing an old house and wanting to buy it and do it up.

Wanting to live everywhere all at once.

Believing you'll write a novel one day, or return successfully to poetry or painting. Or that you know how to solve the political problems with your philosophical ideas. All these things may just be me and many of them are the negative side of the creative coin. They sound like megalomania or egotism and whatever they all are. I suffer from them all. I just can't help it.

But there's another side to being creative, and that's the sharing. When you have an idea that fires you up you can't help sharing. It's the artists version of 'religious fervour'. Here I know I'm in good company. We teach … because we just can't help it.

Maybe we'd be richer or more famous if we kept our ideas to ourselves shrouded in secrecy for all time, and became mysterious and very rich 'artists' who cynically exploit their gifts or in some cases the gift of being able to manipulate others, but we don't, and we aren't because we're so excited by the ideas we just can't help sharing.

Because your butterfly wings beat faster than many and your creativity, though not necessarily on display in the big galleries, affects the person next to you … and next … and next … and in this way you will affect the world in a million small ways. From the smile of a child seeing your work to the passing on of a technique which is taken and amplified by someone who otherwise may never have done it, to the recovery from anxiety of a person for whom your teaching was a necessary therapy and who may then go on to affect the world themselves. Sometimes just the small pleasure of seeing your work, of sharing your teaching opens eyes to possibilities. As creative people you will affect your children's attitude to creativity. Your students' and your family's. You can't help it and they won't be able to help it either; because it's an addiction.

-I'm Angie and I'm a Creative"

When I finished the short talk I saw, to my surprise

that several mouths were open. Some of my friends and other people I didn't yet know congratulated me. Jamie Carrington was in tears and gave me a big hug and told me he'd seen a side of me he'd never seen before. Most moving of all a lady came up to me, waited patiently for everyone else to move away and took me to one side. She told me her son had been giving her some sleepless nights because he wanted to give up university to do something creative. She thanked me profoundly for my insight and said she was going home to tell her son he could do whatever he wanted. Even if it didn't bring him wealth. What's more she wanted to bring him to the next Tune.

So anyway after that outpouring I decided on a title for my dad's memoirs. He used to say "Scarrs can make anything ... but money" So that's dad's books title. "Can make anything but money".

Oh deer

One of our major and most enjoyable fairs of the season was normally Paris. 2014 was not a fair to want to remember though. Marie Paule Hostyn my good friend and translator of my Challenges book into French, had died just a day or two before the fair. It was a very sad weekend, especially so as another miniaturist from Spain who I knew very well from Madrid, also died suddenly just the day before the fair actually in the city of Paris. It was to have been her first fair in France and she had been very excited.

This year Paris was followed in short order by the Tune retreat, in Denmark. This was our first visit to this miniaturist week and we were very excited, but as usual absolutely penniless having had to pay out for all the flights in advance. Those flights to Denmark were not cheap. We reduced the cost slightly by combining the two trips and fitted in one to England between Paris and Denmark to try and minimise the number of flights for the maximum effect. I wanted to visit my son and his pregnant wife. This was an exciting time for them and I wanted to be part of it. I also wanted to pay my middle son back for a loan he had made us to help us print some books.

We booked one of the cheapest flights to Paris, but that meant it left horrendously early and we had to set off at an ungodly hour in the middle of the night. So we got up, or rather Frank got up at around three am. I hadn't really been to bed and just had an hour's snooze on the living room sofa. We rushed to pack up and set off. As we closed the door on the house I said to Frank "Watch out for deer at this time of day". "Deer don't come out at this time of day" said Frank but then saw my face and followed it with "do they?" Oh yes they do … and they did. When she, for it was a big female, stood stock still in the middle of the road I shouted "DEER" at Frank. It didn't seem like he took any notice or braked at all and we smacked hard into her rump, at which point Bambi's mum skittered and leapt off over to the other side of the road and down an embankment. Frank was dazed but insisted he had braked. Weirdly a few seconds after starting the car again he said "I've just hit a deer" like it was news to him. From then on I worried about whether our cars brakes were up to the job until recently in the re-telling of the story he insisted the deer had leaped out from the verge. No she hadn't. She was stock still in the road when I cried out to warn him. He hadn't seen her until the very last moment and no there was nothing wrong with our brakes. To be fair Frank had always warned me that he found it extremely difficult to wake up in the dark.

After the episode around 15 years before, where my

mum's car had been written off, I think Frank began to see my mentioning of potential dangers as bad luck and from now on I'm forbidden to say anything about animals in the road or any possible dangers. I only have to remember back to my hazard perception video test to realise why. I'd found it difficult to master on the home practise runs until I realised I saw potential dangers way too early and had to learn to delay my pressing of the panic button. It's just that this time, more by bad luck than good judgement, I was right. Animals on the road are a frequent occurrence in the Sierra though and you start hardly to notice the multiple road signs warning you of cows and deer every few hundred metres. And the rubber tyre marks on the road. Sometimes with the reassuring dotted format of the ABS reaction. You really do have a very good chance of meeting a deer any time you drive at dawn and dusk in this region where they pop out from the cork oaks to graze on the long grass at the side of the roads and get startled by the headlamps. You could even, if you're really unlucky, run into a wild boar. Although they seem to stay away from the roads and you're much more likely to see one or two strapped to the top of a hunter's 4x4.

The car of course looked pretty bad. The front right wing was dinged. The lamp was broken and the bonnet was trashed. Miraculously though she moved, so we cautiously set off looking like dubious stock car racers and made it to the Airport. On our way back with some money in our pockets I suggested we nip into one of the many auto-wreckers (desguace) which was just off our route out of Seville. The first one we came to said they had a bonnet to match but in silver and they had wing mirrors which we needed to change as they'd been taped up for ages. That was OK I said and we took both. We shelled out about fifty or sixty Euros for the lot. They didn't have the correct headlamp though, so off we went to another larger auto-wreckers who told us we'd bought the wrong wing mirrors and by the way on the same car as the headlamps they had a blue bonnet which matched ours exactly although with some flaking to the paintwork.

It looked like a better idea to have the colour match and, since we had to go back to the first company anyway, we raced back and asked them to take both the erroneous wing mirrors, and the wrong coloured bonnet back. They agreed providing we paid them 10 euros for the time they took stripping the bonnet off the silver car. We were happy to do that. It seemed fair. In the end we had a total cost of about sixty Euros for the lot. We stashed the bonnet over the luggage and went home with the sense that things could have been a lot worse. Laddio pushed and pulled at the chassis using the car's own power against itself and Enrique's still unfixed digger (he'd only been waiting about five years so far) as a stable mount to attach the ropes to, and straightened everything out. He attached all the new bits and took only another 30 Euros from us. Disaster averted. The rest of the money from the trip was already owed and much much more, for our Gestor's bills and for the late Seguridad social payments.

Bomba de Pozo (well pump)

Things were getting to be a very tight squeeze again as there were no classes during summer, and therefore no cash income. Paypal was slow to transfer what little money we had. We just managed to squeeze enough out for a little bit of shopping including paper as we were doing a lot of printing working on books while there were no classes to get in the way of a full day's concentration. Of course if something can go wrong it will and so it was as our water pump broke down, leaving us with no water to the house for washing, toilets, showers etc. and none for our veggie plot and it was in the 30s outside.

To be fair the pump was at least 6 years old and we don't know if it was old already when we paid the builders an extra 300 "euroquid" as we called Euros, to leave it and all the hosepipe and wires in. We didn't know if it was a small problem or a big one, but we thought we'd made a smart couple of moves a few years earlier.

Whenever a reasonable chunk of money coincided with a good Lidl offer we took it. Sometimes we've had to leave bargains in the shop but once we shelled out about 60 quid for a spare pump to put in the cupboard against a day like today. Our friend Enrique knows how to fit a pump. So we were hoping our replacement, though it's a different type, would do, as in our current financial state no petrol money meant no trips to the 'fuente' for drinking water. Still, always looking on the bright side I thought we'd at least have enough drinking water for the weekend and we certainly have good neighbours for emergency washing/flushing water. Except that by a strange quirk of coincidence we couldn't even go to get water or shower at Mama's because her sewers were up in the road to her house. Even if we got enough drinking water our garden was going to get parched in the 32 degree heat.

The pump had conked just before the washing was finished and before I'd put the dishwasher on. That morning I had to de-stack and wash up in Fuente water. I was planning on finishing the tiling in the laundry room that weekend too and everything was in our light well just waiting to be used. I wondered, could I still mix the cement glue? I soon realised that the clean up afterwards would be too expensive in water. Ho hum. Another job that would have to wait. One bright idea I had was that I'd heard urea is great for compost heaps so I suggested that we only used the toilet when absolutely necessary. Frank wasn't so keen on that idea.

On Saturday we played the usual game of 'waiting all day for Spaniards'. Eventually our friend Enrique who knows a lot about fitting pumps but nothing at all about fixing them came to take a look at ours. Bless him he spent 3 hours or more helping us dismantle and test our pump … nothing. So we tried to fit a garden pump after frantic searches for parts … still nothing. We tried by various crazy methods to backfill the tube with water in case that was the problem … nothing. At sundown we gave up, realizing that the summer water levels were just below the 7 metre max head height of the new pump, and gratefully accepted the shower back at his place.

On Sunday we were waiting again. This time for rain. The first rains in about 3 months were promised but failed to appear. Later we had a sprinkle. I was gutted. That weekend there was a 2 day Romeria to the church at Alajar from Campofrío and I was torn between being desperate for rain and not wanting to see the poor girls in their flouncy dresses getting soaked to the skin.

We took our well pump into the repair shop of our local builders/electrical merchants for repair but asked them to please let us know before they repaired it, what it would cost. We had to pay 15 Euros upfront for it to be looked at by the repair man. Now I have some experience of garages and mechanics and felt pretty sure repairmen were in a similar league. When they called back a few days later and said the pump was burned out and beyond economic repair I simply said OK, we'll pick it up. Our type of pump costs 250 new and the second hand market for pumps here is quite healthy and the price isn't much lower than new. I was beginning to get very cynical in my old age.

I wasn't so surprised when an hour later I got another call from the company to say that they'd made a mistake. They had a few pumps in and ours wasn't the burned out one. They would take another look at it and tell us whether it would be the 'condensador' which they suspected I asked how much that would cost and was told around 28 pounds. So that left me waiting to see if they find any other problems or if they were going to let me have my old pump back repaired at a reasonable price … or un-repaired. Well it turned out that the pump was actually beyond reasonable repair. My cynicism was unfounded. In the end Wamma lent us a pump which worked perfectly for a year. We originally thought at the time that it was coincidence that it gave up in the August of the next year.

There were certain items we often didn't have to pay for during these years because we were not connected or only temporarily connected. The truth is that we really should have been connected but the paperwork is way too complicated, requiring your house to be signed off or for you to have a builders licence and a licence to build (two different licences). The former requires you to be registered as an autonomo and under that title as a builder, which we often were but not always. Without these three items it's simply impossible to be connected as a home. The problem is that the wheels of local government grind very slowly and it's damn near impossible to get every piece of paperwork in at the right time. So we did without.

We had water from the well and we also had a generator and various other methods of producing electricity. We had gas bottles for cooking and if needed for hot water. You don't need a lot of hot water in summer but in winter you really do.

There are laws in Spain that say you have to pay a tax on self generated electricity. This effectively stops people using it. What an utterly ridiculous law; Spain ought to be one of the richest countries in Europe, bathed as it is in free electricity. With huge areas of barely occupied windy plains and mountains but, it seems, there are vested interests keeping the alternative energy industry down. This is a real shame because manufacture of solar and wind power collecting equipment could take many thousands off the unemployment register.

Social security?

I must explain again to all Brits that paying Seguridad Social even though it translates directly to the words social security is not the receiving of a benefit. Neither does it give a self employed person any rights to receive unemployment or sickness benefits. It's a National insurance payment. It's just a huge monthly chunk towards a piddling and disappearing pension I may never receive, and a national health care. At the time of writing this I didn't realise how important that healthcare access was to become.

We were late paying. We'd almost always been late paying because we couldn't pay. Every month we got later and later and every month it cost more and more in late charges until this year, instead of costing an already wicked 280 Euros a month, that's more than the cost of a 2 bed rental here, it shot up to 350 with penalties, for which incidentally you could rent a veritable mansion.

So this year soon turned into our darkest hour so far. The darkest hour among many dark hours.

The money from Paris and Tune covered only part of our arrears to Seguridad Social and our gestor, and there were no classes for the 10 weeks of the holidays. I was reeling from so many demands from Hacienda so many 'Multas' (fines) adding hundreds of Euros to the thousand Euros we already owed for 3 months of late payments. Firstly Hacienda dipped their hands into my bank account and took what was there and then we received a letter telling us there was an embargo on the car and if we didn't pay up in very short order it would be picked up by a tow truck and we knew if that happened we would never get it back.

This was so near to the edge I could feel my finger nails breaking. I thought about what it would have felt like to hand over the deer-battered car to Hacienda. I fantasised about adding a few more hammer blows myself for good measure. Yes that's getting close to the edge mentally and that was the month or two I allowed myself a tiny, semi-controlled breakdown. At least I liked to think of it as partly controlled. Basically I said "Can't cope. Won't cope". And that was that. That was when I'd finally had to beg my middle son to give me back the money I had just repaid him, as an open ended loan that we both knew was really going to have to be a gift. That was when there really was no money and nowhere to go and when we were days away from losing the car and therefore the business. I'd already sold the only thing I had of any value which was my Dobro guitar. That was when I decided the time to give up and hand over responsibility was now. So that is what I did. Not before shedding many tears for my pride and my independent nature. That was the time I handed the baton back, for the second time in our relationship, to Frank. That was when I vowed from then on to be decidedly more Spanish.

I love my new country. I mean I want to love it but it's like an abusive partner. At times it treats you like shit. At least its government does. I'm fairly convinced it's in the government's interests to keep most of the country dishonest, as a way of keeping them under the thumb. That way if at any time they step out of line they have something to slap them with. They also seem randomly to slap fines on people when they're just a bit short of money. Another night awake most of the night after another day when I received yet another demand with menaces from the government for some "infraccion" I knew I hadn't committed, because with our system it's impossible to make the mistake they had accused us of. The fine was 300 euros not because it was (had we commited it) a serious misdemeanour, but because there was a minimum fine which equated to six such infractions. I felt equally sure they'd make me pay anyway because that's how they operate. Like a protection racket. Pay up or we'll pressure you harder. Because most people in Spain don't want their books looking at too closely. In the end we went back to the accountant and challenged the fine because we knew we definitely hadn't made a mistake. The accountants paid up. Presumably because they didn't want looking too closely at either. Nobody does in Spain.

I'd had it up to my eyeballs. Every part of me was shrieking "don't let them kill you" I wasn't sure what next for me. We decided if Frank could make it work for a while we'd take that option. At least we could try it while there was a new rule in allowing people to start new businesses with a reduced Seguridad Social payment. I'd finally learned my lesson. It now sounds ridiculous that my Gestor even had to make up facturas (paper bills) for any cash income to keep it within the normal forms. Because declaring cash was not the Spanish way. Spanish people just balance that against the bills they can't put through because of other rules which make you have every single receipt stamped and with your name address and NIE number. Most people don't want to wait 15 minutes to have someone go through the hassle of making them an official 'factura'.

From now on we had a plan. Frank was to take over the business and I was to become technically unemployed. Still making a few miniatures, still writing a few books. Fate had other ideas for me. More and more parents were asking me to teach their children. I was getting a bit of a reputation and even the local schoolteachers were recommending me. It looked like my forced partial retirement was going to be a short one.

The long school summer holidays ended and just before it was time to start teaching the local kids, there was the first fair of the second season of the year. It was time to go and see Cilla again. She and her husband Par rented a little attic in the Barcelonetta area and it was a really cool place to hang out when doing the Barcelona fair. Par liked to socialise and, being a Swede, quite liked the cheap accessibility of a bottle of strong liquor to share with friends in Spain. We always drank much more than usual when we were with Par because he wouldn't let us stop until the bottle was empty. Lovely evenings on their attic Patio were, unfortunately, invariably followed by a mosquito fiesta as we slept on their living room floor. The second and subsequent times we took our own mosquito net as Barcelona mosquitos were much more go-getting than our Andalucían variety.

MOTs and Angels

Being short of money is no fun. Being extremely short of money is hard work because you have to care for and prepare everything. You also have to ask for or call in favours and that's my least favourite thing. I have a friend here in the village who has said, and I believe she means it, "Call me if you need anything". Our car was due for its ITV and we'd got an appointment a little over the due date. Frank doesn't mind this one bit because, he says, it pushes our ITV back by a month each year so we get 13 months (and an irritating driving free couple of days) a year. True it's probably worth it, especially if you have no money for the test anyway and certainly nothing for any emergency fixes. If it failed that year that would be us off the road for as long as it took. Given we were already threatened with a collection of our car for late payments of Seguridad Social the car was becoming a bit of an issue.

Around this time (the end of summer 2014), the car was off the road for a minor repair and a new ITV certificate. Being without the Spanish equivalent to an MOT meant it was un-driveable. The Guardia Civil Traffico were under pressure to hand out 'multas' at least that's what everybody believes. That and the fact that there was an embargo on it made me doubly cautious.

So, at that time the car was threatened on all sides and so were we, but this day it was having a day off. Well, three actually until the IVA test date. It also happened to be Frank's birthday and so we were having time off too. Frank having been generously given a few nice notes from mummy and stepson for his birthday. I'd had to beg for, and just received a chunky loan from my other boy to try to clear the debt. We were on a mission. To pay a big chunk of the social security and to get some shopping in. I made Frank call Angeles to ask to borrow her car. Poor Angeles, as far as we knew was still bed-bound with a very bad back. But no, it seemed Angeles was feeling better and needed to get some shopping in herself, so she offered to take us to town.

It's nice to find an excuse to spend time with Angeles as I'm not that sociable a person so I need an excuse. Angeles is a recent divorcee and her story is not so dissimilar to my story with my first husband, without the alcohol. She generously drove us in to the centre of Aracena and waited for us for the usual round of waiting in queues at one bank, gathering money together and then paying it into another. All that done we went off to the supermarkets together. Angeles clearly didn't shop in town as often as we did so she was like a kid in a sweet shop and clearly loved to amble around taking her time. Fortunately Frank really does have the patience of a saint and must have waited 20 minutes for her to finish, with me accompanying her.

We stopped off at the fish stall and I was just chattering about the difference in taste between a northern British mackerel and a softy southerner of the same breed. It's my contention that Brixham mackerel taste of prawns whereas north sea mackerel taste, albeit mildly, of cod liver oil. I spied our local language school teacher hovering and told Angeles that this guy was English. It seems Angeles had seen him around town before and suspected or knew that. Of course I said hello and re-introduced myself to Danny. He bumps into all sorts of English people because Aracena is not short of an 'Angle' or two so I reminded him I was the 'Campo' Englishwoman and apologised that I'd been teaching English there but said those students that I had wouldn't travel anyway. Oh by the way I said, If you need someone to fill in in emergency you know where I am.

We had a fairly long chat, in the scheme of things about English teaching ... not so long that his turn to be served had come up yet. We left with a cheery wave. It's always nice to chat to a cheerful Englishman. The kind who live around our area are usually pleasant types. As we drove off Angeles, looked up at her mirror and said "He's good looking" and she blushed just a little. "Aww Angeles" I said, "Your heart is not completely turned to stone" "Not completely" she said and blushed some more. Then Angeles lent us her car so we could go down to the seaside for Frank's birthday. Three days later the car sailed through its MOT "good little motor" we said patting it. Very pleased that its recent fight with a deer had not put anything irrevocably 'out'. Unfortunately we did get a multa … on Angeles' car.

Our decision to make me a teacher and Frank the owner of Angie Scarr Miniatures, helped a little.

Of course later when Frank's costs started to rise we realised he has no real product of his own and I had even less time for miniatures it would begin to get more difficult again. It was breathing space for us and the only thing I could think to do was try to design product that he could make longer term and of course write as much as I could, for as long as I could. I certainly had no shortage of book ideas. Towards the end of the year we planned that, as soon as we could, we'd get a laser machine for Frank to turn out stock for 'Frank's craft shop'. Sod's law had a go at us again though because our major investment turned out to be absolutely useless and our using Paypal offered no protection at all. The fact we'd bought it from Germany neither. Nobody accepted responsibility for the fact that although it was described as new it was actually not only 'drop shipped' but also pre-broken. We had no chance of fixing it and no way of getting our investment back. We finally understood why people said "Ebay doesn't work in Spain".

Henry and Dominic

The phone rang at 10 pm on the 4th of December. "Oh no, really?" grumbled Frank as he usually did when the phone rang or someone knocked at the door of our 'hermitage'. "Do I have to remind you?" I tutted, expecting to hear some early happy but nervy news of labour pains. Expecting to go to bed with nothing more than the slight thrill of apprehension in my own belly. “We have a stillbirth”. The words registering as blank and cold, and later as an unusual choice.

I took it that the drama and the tragedy had already unfolded as I was idly going about some unimportant household task. All I could utter was “Oh baby. I don't know what to say” … I knew these words were empty and I knew there was supposed to be something more. I was supposed to feel more. Wasn't I? The call was short. It was strangely unmoving. I sat down, my mild irritation with Frank dissipating. He knew of course. He put his arm around me and I started to talk about how I was not feeling. How I wanted to feel for the baby but all I could feel was the beginnings of a tiny black dot of pain in the middle of my heart for my own son and his wife. I thought about the fragility of life in the womb and the stupidity of the design of the placenta and umbilical cord.

I thought of my own three births and how all had been a little oxygen deprived at one point before or during birth. I wanted to go back and lift my own fragile first born out of the incubator I knew now that he needed less than the touch of my own skin and the beat of my own heart close to his ears. I was angry that I let the nurses bully the barely 20 year old single parent I then was into leaving him alone for hours on end to lift and drop his own head rhythmically to make up for the loss of the movement of his mothers womb inside my often over-active body. Somewhere in the middle of these thoughts the desire to undo those few days of unintentional neglect wound around the feeling of wanting to comfort the adult he now was in his own parental loss. Then the hot silent tears started to flow. Slowly at first and then in great torrents. The now and the then barely separated in my mind. The guilt of being one ward and a screen of plastic away merging with the fifteen hundred miles now between my hand and his back, now broad and shouldering all that undeserved guilt of his own.

I didn't realise that for my daughter in law the worst was yet to come. The baby was still, but not yet a birth and she would have to experience the pain of labour just to endure that loss all over again, when the faint hope that there must have been some mistake became hollow and hopeless as the beautiful and perfect but lifeless child was put into her arms.

There was nothing I could do. No way I could make any of my child's pain go away, and certainly nothing I could do for his wife. Fortunately she had a supportive and close family of her own. Sometimes I felt just a little envious of this close bond and my, on the surface at least, more exciting life, suddenly felt hollow and selfish. So I busied myself finding out about how cruelly or otherwise the system might treat the couple. I also knew from other people's stories that they would have chance to hold their baby for as long as they wanted and that, by all accounts they should. That they should take imprints of the baby's hands and feet. These footprints walked across the fitful sleep I took that and many more nights as did many other strange thoughts. Why had I cruelly dropped the caterpillars I'd picked off the broccoli plants that morning, into a tub of ash? I felt keenly now, the bad karma in that action. I wondered if a self-confessed witch I had had not completely friendly dealings with recently had also sent bad karma our way. These crazy thoughts piled up, one on top of another but were nothing, I had to remind myself compared with the equally undeserved guilt my son and daughter in law would be putting themselves through in their darkest hours.

The truth was more shocking still. The truth, I found out pretty quickly, was that one in 300 births is a stillbirth. Added to the number of spontaneous abortions and neonatal deaths and birth defects the odds look pretty scary of not having the perfect healthy little person gifted to your family. This made me feel triple blessed. Triple guilty and also defensive for not having been the perfect mother and triple sad for the young couple, who weren't actually so young that they could afford to take their time about deciding on another roll of those so cruel dice.

This year had truly gone from bad to unbelievably worse. Of course we were in no position financially to visit my grieving children more than once. The funeral was planned just a couple of weeks later immediately before new year and of course we chose to be there at that time rather than immediately. The sight of my boy carrying his own tiny son in his little white box was possibly the saddest thing I have ever seen or will ever see in my life.

We saw 2015 in as a family and through the tears we began to see a spark of hope for the future.

That hope was seeded just four months later. Ten days after what would have been Henry's first birthday little Ada was born. The parents understandably nervous commented that she didn't cry a lot. "Don't worry" I said. "She'll soon make up for that". And so she did.

15

Digging Ourselves Out Of ... And Into The Mess

In order to try to pull ourselves out of the financial hole, Frank was now running a craft business incorporating Angie Scarr Miniatures and I was an English teacher. This should have given me more time for the garden and the house, but of course it didn't. I was still doing everything I did before but I wasn't in charge of the business and nor was I paying Autonomo. To be fair, the stress of accounts and answering to the government were the thing I found most onerous and that was what I had managed to pass on to Frank to my great relief. My chat the previous year with Danny had resulted in me working part time for the local Academia and I still had my few students at home. I felt like this was the right balance because being on regimen general meant I was paying some and Seguridad Social, and that felt right.

Garden produce

I looked out on the garden the last week in March to see that the rains had boosted the weeds which never really slept except in the parched days of midsummer. The first bramble flower had appeared. The first raspberry flowers too, tightly budded and furry. The artichokes would be producing shortly and just a handful of broad bean plants were in flower. The rest had been eaten by rodents and birds. It was also the season for spring onions and garlic greens. The garden was a mess as usual.

Although it was Frank who had insisted that we have a fairly generous garden to be honest he never did his share of the maintenance and this irked me. When he did get the urge to do something he had the strange idea that you could plant late and hang on to retarded plants and so the garden was sprinkled with out of place stunted plants which would never come to anything but which he hadn't the heart to root out.

In spring the garlic and the onions I'd managed to harvest and plait up into strings had dwindled and the remaining few had started to sprout. The freezer was still full and there were bunches of herbs everywhere. The new harvest of chard had started to come in and there was so much 'bounty' to pack into the freezer or leave to rot. I decided it was time to make a big investment. I can be, as my husband says 'a bit spendy' at times but this was something I'd been thinking about for a good while, so from our next trip I'd taken some money out of the fund I'd been trying to build up to prevent the horrors of the penury of the previous year and went for it. A bright white shiny new vacuum sealer.

Not the bigger fridge Frank had longed for, but a temporary solution to our food rotation problems. I spent a happy morning chopping up and packing chard and garlic greens and when I'd run out of things to bag, I re-bagged some cabbage that had been thrown into the freezer just before a trip abroad, into smaller portions. Satisfied I scribbled the new items on the glass door of my kitchen cupboard, determined, as I always was, that this time we would use the produce or rotate it more strictly. Who am I kidding? I muttered under my breath. Frank, who was the chef, after all wasn't keen on frozen foods and would always take fresh over frozen.

The process was really cathartic though and I began to think about buying the bags in bigger and smaller sizes. I could certainly see the application for small quantities of items such as herbs and frozen fruit portioned off for summer smoothies. I also thought that maybe vacuum packing could help with preparation for fairs and even stock control. In fact I did use up all of the garlic greens which would have been lost, and all of the chard. The red cabbage never got used though and I realise that's a vegetable that I find more attractive than tasty.

Recently we have got to grips with this concept and we know what and how to rotate our foodstuffs. Now we do get the best out of our freezer. The biggest surprise is how nice pre-frozen bread is. If it's thawed out correctly. Now we pack our bread a slice at a time and even re-use the vacuum sealing bags several times. I'm even scribbling down our little tips and Frank's vegetarian recipes for a possible frugal-living book.

The garden did produce and of course it produced seasonally. Whenever something was in the garden it was also on the shelves as cheap as chips, and more often than not brought over by friends in the village who didn't know what to do with their own gluts. I was always pleased to receive these gifts though as we largely avoided planting the most popular crops, going for more expensive and rarer items or varieties.

The generosity of friends and neighbours did make a difference to our ability to get by. Especially appreciated were the eggs my Mama gave me whenever the hens were laying.

Neighbours generosity

I have never been as impressed by great philanthropy as some people think I should be. Whereas I'm mightily impressed by random acts of kindness and 'paying it forward'.

100 billion dollars given away to good causes? Wow this person must be a saint giving away 90% of their income! Not to me they aren't. To me the saints are those who can only give 1%

If you give 1% of your income and those earnings are already not enough to buy you a new pair of much needed shoes and have your teeth fixed or to give you a working vehicle, its really a massive gift. It is in fact a sacrifice. While most of us face these dilemmas every day of our lives, the great philanthropists of our time are considered to be saintly, although they have covered all of these expenses BEFORE they decided to act charitably and therefore their percentage, no matter how large doesn't hurt at all.

My Spanish 'Mama' (not really any relation) handing me a bag of eggs even when her hens are not laying particularly well, is a much greater act of charity than most of the super-rich will ever understand. She has maybe given me 1% of her total wealth for that week. However it's probably 100% of her excess. Maybe more even than that. It wouldn't surprise me if, at the end of that week her generosity has left her short of eggs. Bless her, she certainly doesn't have "Hollywood teeth" and neither do I.

I'd like to see some of the mega-rich get anywhere close to that. Until then I won't gape in awe. Even if they decide their 'needs' are ten or even a hundred or a thousand times what normal people's are, including as they do all the above expenses which your normal struggling neighbour can't afford. If they have more than that, and they give it all away they might edge a little closer to the heart-warming generosity shown by neighbour to neighbour in poor society.

While I'm on a rant about the wealth gap especially for us artists, it does seem to be that you only get rich if you're already rich. More often than not this is true? Why? Well, look at the percentages. The top 1% own fifty percent of the world's wealth and the top ten percent own nearly 90 percent. Leaving precious little to be divided between the rest of us. To get into that exclusive club you have to be given a hand up from the one side and be able to climb over the other side of the wealth divide. We many of us think it's wrong but we almost all want to do it.

An artist in Andalucía

Because money rules, people look down on artists and creative people because they don't have 'proper jobs'. To add insult to injury the contribution that they do make is often scorned even when it forms a part of the very objects we most treasure, or changes the lives of others through education and therapy or beauty to be appreciated by all, or perceptive social commentary which changes the future, or scientific invention. Lateral thinkers are worth more than society has ever given them credit for.

How many of the most famous artists, designers and scientists of history ended their lives as paupers, or at least poorly off often scorned until the day they die. A disproportionate percentage of contribution to society as a whole, meriting only a meagre income and little respect - " Twas ever thus".

So we, as good parents, should educate our children to get jobs with good prospects shouldn't we? It seems there are no 'good prospects' for the creative child. Our school system is there to help them out of having any "big ideas." That's why really creative children simply don't fit in, and why sausages get to be Prime Ministers or Presidents.

If you want it and you're not born into it you have to

spend your whole life dedicated to getting it. This leaves very little time for artistry and invention. Never mind. If your goal is money you can buy ideas in. Creatives are cheap because they are never rich and are always in need … because they don't have time to be both creative and dedicate the time it takes to get rich. So you have to be rich already. Or dedicate yourself to getting rich or you have to be very lucky to hit the right concept at the right time and roll with it.

One of these very few very smart ladies is the wife of a friend of mine who recognised a gap in the market at just the right time in the market and used her creative skills to fill it. Still, she had to work very hard, almost against her own creativity, and certainly against any idea if she had one of raising a family or indeed much family life at all, to make sure she was there first and stayed up there. Somehow she succeeded. She had 2 of the three. She was smart and lucky. Now she's moderately well off. Not in the top 1 percent nor even in the top 10 but she got herself to the top of the bottom half. That's no mean feat these days.

Mostly however, artists can be bought for pennies because the real money is to be made by putting the money behind the art and that's why most of us would have to bow to the smug 'Dragons' in the Den if we wanted to take an idea all the way.

As an artist I am lucky to live in Andalucía though. Lucky for many, many reasons, the greatest of all these being the quality of the light. Even more luckily and almost by accident, because of our position in an east-west facing terrace and the architectural rules which mandated that in a long thin house a light well should be incorporated for efficiency of both ventilation in summer and solar gain in winter. This has turned out to be a beautiful place where I can take photographs of my miniatures in almost perfect diffused daylight. For this and many other reasons I love my light well! .

However, there are a couple of things which spoil this photographic heaven. One of those is Andalucían dust which rains down summer and winter on all of my furniture including my photography table, and on all of my work. This has recently been augmented by mining dust which, for some reason, they roll up a belt to a spout only to pour back down onto a hill, losing a seemingly huge percentage of it to the wind. Then onwards it blows several kilometres directly, it seems, to my light well. Add to this the fact that we are in constant building works ourselves and this increases the depth of the dust by a significant sandy cement-y factor.

Then, in winter there was always the dust from our ancient stove. Fortunately that year we replaced this with a long awaited, half price, 'stove of my dreams'. It's much cleaner-burning but, although this lowers the total dust, it does produce an even lighter airborne gossamer which falls onto everything and has to be removed almost daily. Then, very occasionally there's a strange Saharan dust fall which happens stealthily and you wake up to a 'brown out' which drapes itself all over the sierra, most annoyingly on our car and the glass roof of our light-well.

I never understood dusting in England. I was a fan of the 'dust if you must' poem. I didn't see dust as a problem. Now my life is governed by it and it's becoming an obsession. Every speck of dust raised upstairs, in our living and my sometimes working area, If it doesn't fall on my un-cured clay upstairs, seems to find its way downstairs to my photography table. I do cover my work, but it's not always covered I have to admit. Sometimes I'm working on it. Sometimes I simply forget when my mind is distracted and then I go off and do something else, quite forgetting the silent but deadly dropping of particles building up like overnight snow.

Then there are the two demon fluff monsters Squirrel and Smoosh who roam the house doing nothing useful. Simply shedding. Just exchanging the food we feed them and the care we lavish on them for the unasked for and unwelcome gift of 'fluff'. One gifts straight ginger hairs and one long white wiggly strands. These are totally invisible to my ageing eyes but like great ropes of sisal on my 12th scale miniatures, at least according to my sensitive macro lens. I sometimes wonder whether my work would look better under less perfect light conditions and taken with a dodgy old camera.

And there's another problem I discovered only when I was writing my colour book. I'd always been known for my realistic colours and yet, when I got my perfect dual aspect workshop, overlooking both the back garden and side walkway bringing in loads of Spanish sunlight, I found my colour choices turning out more wrong than they'd ever been before. Then I discovered the demon metamerism and polymer clay pigments suffer very badly from it.

Of course I didn't know what it was called and I only finally hit upon the problem and the term when I commented to my husband that "that flannel" was doing its thing again. We'd bought some flannels which were brown in the shop and in our bathroom and green on the clothes line. I'd been looking at this and marvelling at it a couple of years before I twigged while I was writing the book. Different pigments show up differently in different lights. I'd been mixing perfect greens in the sunlight only to have them look really dodgy and dull under a different spectrum of light. No wonder Van Gogh went mad! From then on I had to check my colour mixes under several different lights and choose a mix which works reasonably well under them all. remembering that most people see miniatures in various different spectra of artificial light. Always keeping in mind that my students aren't interested in being asked, instead of a straight answer to a colour mixing question, "What light are you showing your work under?"

Local mining industry

A couple of years before the mines re-opened the parent company was obviously sending their staff to take a look. One day a tough looking Australian appeared in our local bar. Of course speaking very nearly the same language we couldn't resist chatting with him. Although it was difficult as he was obviously the worse for a pint or several. It turned out he'd recently been given an ultimatum by his bosses that he had to join the AA if he wanted to keep his job. This was the result of having had a drunk-driving accident on the way back from the local 'club'. (A Club here is the name for a roadside brothel). Well this chap had decided on a really good answer to the problem of there being no local AA groups. He'd joined an online group. It transpired he was in a meeting at that moment, pint in one hand, telephone in the other.

It's really weird watching life come so quickly back to an industry that's been dead for so long. We drove past the mines one way and had to avoid a rock that had fallen into the middle of the road, reminding us that the enormous trucks must actually be carrying mineral ore from the site, and on the way back a little later I was surprised to see the long arm conveyor belt thing which had recently been patched up with shiny new corrugated sheets, spewing out something black and dusty-looking. I wondered, not for the first time, whether new life in the mines would bring worse air conditions. Just a little further on, on the other side of the twin beautiful but toxic lakes of Gossan and Cobre, some new work was being done to the access roads. Later we were to see new toxic waste being pumped into one which over the next couple of years grew fat rust coloured crystalline deposits on the dead tree skeletons which still stick out of it maybe many decades after it was first built and give it a weird Martian landscape look.

Last year the Gossan lake fell so low I even wondered if someone was sneakily removing some of the waste. Yes it was a drought year but the other of the twin toxic lakes, Cobre, stayed pretty full. In full sun Gossan and Cobre are about as different in colour as it's possible to be. Cobre is a deep turquoise and Gossan is a murky dark purple brown. The pair are really quite beautiful when viewed from above. Running down the centre is a roadway with a dangerous little wiggle. I wouldn't like to come off the road into either of them but if it were Gossan I'd probably come out quite dead and encrusted with scary looking crystals of something lethal. There used to be a skull and crossbones sign at the top end of the lake. But it disappeared as the mines came back to life.

Cobre is the Spanish word for copper and, according to my geologist friend, the word gossan meaning gold-producing ore, comes from the Spanish inability to keep the two words gold and sands separate. In my 'Palabrario' of the region however, it states that the word 'gossan' means an abbreviation for gold and silver colours in the same rock produced by the oxidation of pyrites. In Wikipedia its claimed to be a Cornish word "The name gossan appears to come from Cornish miner's slang. The terms "iron cap" and "iron hat", common in America, are direct translations from the German "eisenhut", which term was also used in America. All sounds like rubbish to me. I like Enrique's history better ... and it sounds so much more likely. Also gold has been mined here for as long if not longer than it has in Cornwall and its perfectly possible that miners travelled from here to there carrying terminology back and forth.

It's not only the mines that are coming back to life either. Just beyond Gossan and Cobre, nestled half hidden by trees, three new enormous animal sheds which I was convinced were destined to be chicken houses were looking newly complete. They were sporting three tall silos to add extra proof to my guess. It was a good sign that the area was coming back to life, but it's all dirty and polluting.

What's app?

I bowed to peer pressure in 2015. Well, I say I bowed. I nodded in its general direction. Friends who I enjoy keeping in touch with had been asking me why I don't have Whatsapp as if I'm in the dark ages being only on Facebook. Well, I admit I have my gripes with Facebook but I have to say on balance I like it ... no I really like it. Why do I like Facebook chat when I can have Whatsapp? everyone asks me. They say it's easier. I always replied that I like it because as a communication tool. It puts me in charge of the when where and how I choose to communicate. More importantly, as a parent, I can keep in touch with my kids who are in a different country without the pressure of 'the weekly duty call to mum'. No more making up an excuse when you just want to say hello, I love you and nothing much else. It takes the pressure off answering if you're busy, or they are. It makes the relationship more relaxed and natural.

Only one of my kids actually likes using the phone and yes, I love that when we get to yap on about stuff for nearly an hour because he wants to as much as me. Even then sometimes he may not want to call or I may be too busy to answer … or vice versa. The icing on the cake of course, once you have an internet connection, which, let's face it most of us have now, is that it's free. Oh and the cherry, on the icing, on the cake is that my screen is large and so is my keyboard. I have never liked texting, nor squinting at keyboards. The sad truth is probably that smartphones appeared just as my eyes started to fail, as did my finances. Putting glasses on to text, grr - no thanks. In Spain the sun makes it impossible to read your screen, outdoors at least. So I got used to not having a smartphone until one of my sons started to pass his old ones down to me … for which I'm very grateful but which at first gave me a love of playing Word Jong and taking good quality photos rather than making me any more likely to connect to the rest of 'smartphone behaviour'.

I was visiting a workmate for his birthday and he had a couple of young mates visiting too. His girlfriend and the two mates sat, each fiddling with their own phones for a couple of hours. Eventually we had twenty minutes of good fun conversation with them. What a shame. Underneath their phones they seemed really nice.

This all makes me sound like a Luddite. Actually I was computer literate ten or fifteen years before the majority of my peers. I had a website when only one in a thousand knew what a website was and when websites themselves numbered only in the thousands or tens of thousands in the UK. Yes, admittedly I haven't kept up the computer skills because having my own 'computer geek' for a husband, I don't need to, and can get on with other things, occasionally learning what I need to for both of us to collaborate on a project which requires me to handle the technology myself.

Well my friends and my students, my new boss and

workmate all use Whatsapp. It's really common here in Spain and they seem to think my use of Facebook strange. So, when I went to an English teaching seminar, and the lecturer was also banging on about the use of Whatsapp as a teaching tool, I eventually decided to see what all the fuss was about and dip my toe into the water.

So, the next problem I had was Frank who was wholly against connecting to it. I never really knew why. When it comes to technology Frank usually sounds like a grumpy old man about certain programmes and apps but almost invariably he has it right. So I twisted his arm and eventually got him to do the connecting, but only on my Pay As You Go phone and only through wifi because contracts could lead us into using more than our free download limit. Our limit is very low and when we go abroad particularly, that could mean a catastrophic bill. So Frank just turns off cell data and my phone normally is just a phone.

So. I got started. I did the rounds of the "Hi. I'm using Whatsapp". To my closest friends and gave my phone number to my students. Telling everyone I wasn't always on but would pick up messages a couple of times a day. "Great," they all said. "Finally!" they all said.

Unfortunately, after that, the few hours a day that I did leave wifi on to collect any messages I had constant irritating bonging and pinging from whatsapp, mail from the phone company and other advertisers and in 4 days, two messages from friends I talk to on Facebook anyway. You can't ignore it can you? It might be important.

I had wondered why my friends who are Whatsapp users look 'wrung out' half the time. I thought maybe they worked harder than I did. They thought maybe I had the secret to a Zen life. On Whatsapp you are constantly at the beck and call of anyone who cares to interrupt your train of thought. And the people you really want to talk to, that you used to chat to on Facebook are too busy answering other boings and pssts to answer you, and you wonder why. At least Facebook only sucks my brain out when I invite it in. I only talk to people because I really want to. I only expect them to answer me when they really want to. So I went back to being Zen about communications and turned Watsapp off. Forever.

I learned a lot about stress when I used to have panic attacks. You get what you ask for.

Housebuilding and repairs

Nowhere near as much had been done to the house as we would have liked because 2014 had seen us crushed by the 'honesty trap' that is working as an Autonomo in Spain. By this time we were down to a project however small each Xmas and summer. The only time when there was enough time due to an almost total lack of sales during August and December and, of course, no English classes. We intended to get the downstairs under stairs toilet done last Xmas but the tragedy of Henry's loss had put paid to any interest in or ability to work, so that project was shelved for another year.

After each of our fairs that year we bought a few more boxes of tiles and Frank insisted that we bought electric underfloor heating pads for the training room but it was going to cost way more than we could afford with the insulation and the extra layers of extra flexible adhesive. In the end I opted to tile the light well because we had had to clear it out anyway so that my friend Montse could paint it. Montse wanted English lessons but she too was always short of money so she and I had ability-swap sessions. She would do things I couldn't or didn't want to do and I would teach her and her daughter

English. This suited us just fine and it wasn't the first or last time I'd swapped lessons for favours.

It took me just two days to tile and grout the light well floor and I was really glad I had done it. It made the house look so much more like a house and so just a few weeks later I decided to tackle the teaching room. That really was a horrible job because not only did I have to chip away some of the raised sections of the cement, as we couldn't afford to lay a layer of self-levelling compound but I had to add two layers of adhesive to get the job done. One was to stick the insulation to the floor. It did turn out to be the wrong type of insulation although Frank had insisted it would be fine. - Notes were made to self never to go against gut feeling.

I then had to add another generous layer of adhesive on top to stick the tiles down. I was finding the whole thing very difficult and exhausting and I now think that I was already unwell. I wasn't too happy with the result either. The over-thick, over-flexible felting meant that sometimes the tiles moved and I had to take a whole section out again the next year to re-lay them and this will probably have to be repeated in the future. Still, the end result was much nicer than the horrible lino with the mould patches underneath. I also discovered the sheer joy of mopping floors that summer. I decided that Spanish Mamas were pretty damn clever though they didn't realise it. Every morning and evening they would open their windows and doors and mop their floors "to refresh the house" I was told. The light went on in my mind and I amused Mama by telling her "You're a scientist Mama". They had many a clever trick up their sleeves, the Spanish. The sheer thermal mass of the old houses evened out the hot and the cooler days in summer and the cool and the cold days in winter. As for the brazier under the table, what at first seemed simply weird, was genius when you thought about it. In the old days the dining table stood over a pan of hot charcoal made from rock rose stems and roots. In modern days the idea is the same but the 'braziers' are electric or gas powered. This stands in a hole in the middle of a support under the table. On top of the table is a thick, warm, blanket-like table cloth and on top of that, a glass sheet to form the table surface. On cold winter days you simply pull the blanket up around your knees or even your shoulders and you are toasty warm while eating, chatting or watching TV. When you move away from the table you are doing something active so you simply don't need it. For the couple of months of the year that it's really cold this saves having to have a centrally heated house.

Well well (not again)

If water is my nemesis it seems it has now become Frank's 'Moriarty'. Well of course we would expect water to be a problem for us living in Andalucía. Even though we are in the centre of the pueblo we are still 'off grid'. An unusual state of affairs these days since the well water is not considered potable because of possible contamination from animals.

We use it for everything except drinking and our friend Enrique and his family who according to his geological surveys lives on a slightly different water table, use it for everything. So that's good enough for us. Since Spanish paperwork means that connection to any grid is more trouble than it's worth, we get this lovely free water from our wide deep well which has served us faithfully for the 10 years we've had this house, only running out, and then only temporarily, when we've been foolish enough to stick the watering system on and walk away in the middle of August. A very expensive mistake the first time because it cost us our good quality but very old pump. A good quality pump is a very expensive thing.

In the end it turned out that Wamma's on-loan pump also failed during August in similar circumstances. So we dug very deep and squeezed enough money together to buy a new good quality pump of our very own. We realised that low water was causing the problem only after sending the borrowed pump back to Wamma who told us there was absolutely nothing wrong with it. Apparently the little cut off float not only has to be floating in water but it has to be vertical and not horizontal otherwise it switches the pump off. From then on we've been much more careful how we water the garden, Well, at least we will be as summer comes along. We also turn our water off at night, for reasons that will become clear.

Just after installing the new higher pressure pump, inevitably the pressure head failed causing a strong flow of water back down into the well, but nothing in the house. No surprise there as that had also been sitting in the Andalucían sun for a decade and we were lucky it had lasted that long. Back to the Ferreteria, (DIY shop) or the "ferret shop" as we, and apparently many ex-pats, call it, to buy the big red bomb that was rccommended to us in place of the pressure switch version that we had. Frank, like most men, likes a gadget and was prepared to put his new-found budding DIY abilities to the test to own such an impressive beast. It needed some method of support and he built it its own 'cradle' on the top of the well wall. From here on the failures have turned from the irritating week-long buckets for the loo and trips to neighbours for showers to much more dramatic high-pressure events. At every opportunity our new 'extra fuerte' water chooses to find its way out of the pipe in noisy and impressive fountains. The first time was when I foolishly tried to bend the old pipe connector out of the walkway where Frank had left it as a trip hazard. The extra pressure on the joint meant I got an unexpected (to be honest it should have been expected) shower full in the face. Unfortunately to nobody's amusement, as it would have made a brilliant youtube. Sodden, I went back to the house, woke Frank out of a late morning oversleep and shamefacedly admitted my wrongdoing.

Somehow I managed to 'bodge' that one with a very deep wrapping of a special clear stretchy tape, but a couple of weeks later Squirrel the cat used the new grey pipe connection as a springboard. Just piercing it enough to allow the water to make its own bigger hole; which resulted in a spectacular fountain right across the garden. Pure comedy to turn off when I discovered it, as it was mid winter and the fountain was directly above the stop cock. Once again there was no audience to witness my humiliation. At least this time we had a blame-cat.

A new pipe was bought and glued to the correct connectors by me. Frank says I'm the only one trusted with glue and grey pipe, having been well taught by my 'Polish Al'. All this was then re-connected by long-suffering Frank, who was also by now getting to be quite the expert water-bodger himself, and we waited for an opportunity to divert the old white pipe round the other side of the well where it would be safer from gardening wives and climbing cats. Eventually Wamma came and lent us his pipe crimper and Frank manfully reconnected the white mains pipe round the back of the well. A few mornings later I woke to the now familiar fountain sound. Once again the grey pipe had developed a leak and Mr and Mrs Bodgitt now realised for sure that you can't use fat grey outlet pipe for high pressure water. Ah well. Another trip to the ferret shop, another new bodge to find. We'd only be away three days. Maybe, we thought, it would rain on our poor garden. Probably, because this time we were only going the short hop to Portugal for a little break with family. And wouldn't you just know it, when we most needed and most looked forward to a short sunny break we were likely to get more water, this time from the sky. Fortunate for our plants. Sod's law for us though …

The rains had started

Our house was very well designed and very well built except for one little thing. The design of the internal channel round the inside of the roof. A foot wide channel of lead which took the run off from the front, side and back of the roof and the glass light well roof and carried it to two internal downpipes. When it rained hard the falling water is audible and not unpleasant to listen to. Our 'El Mere' had put some mesh over the tubes to make sure we didn't have anything falling down them both for the safety of our cats and because if anybody else's cat had fallen down it would have been a hell of a job to un-stick the inspection hatch and to get them to come out. While he was doing that he cleaned the gutters and warned us they would need checking and cleaning every couple of years to make sure the tubes weren't blocked.

Well we hadn't found anyone and to be honest couldn't really afford anyone to do the sealing job the glass roof really was in dire need of. So it hadn't been done since.

That winter when the rains came down very heavily after a long, dry and dusty summer we were going to regret that. Over the previous few days we'd noticed the odd drip coming through the light well roof walls and I'd been a bit concerned at first but then the rains got heavier and heavier and more and more water was leaking in and running down the walls. In the end it got to the stage where we had to put a couple of umbrellas upside down to catch and channel the water into a couple of roasting pans and I had to empty these every couple of hours. This meant that my sleep was being interrupted several times a night.

One night it just got beyond a joke when suddenly there was a crack of lightning followed instantly by a roll of thunder. I had jumped out of bed, and hurriedly shuffled the bag of tile cement (because there were always bags of cement around in the light well at this time) out of the way of the possible drips from the still not fully sealed light well glass roof. I wondered whether I could force myself into the courage it would take to drag my now less than agile 14 stones, at now nearly 58 years old, on to the roof to have another go at sealing it. There are some times, I thought to myself, you should just say no. I was irritated that my son had pointed out, last time the discussion had arisen, that some women remain slim and active well into their seventies. Another stick to beat myself up with.

I shook my head. I wasn't accepting these unfavourable comparisons. I'd worked as hard as anyone could over the last few years and I was worn out. Well, maybe I could … would have to have just one more look at it, but only if we had the heavy duty scaffolding and a proper safety harness. So we erected the scaffolding which I found scary enough. For some reason I couldn't move the way I used to. The following year, during tests for other health problems I found out that I had degenerative bone disease and that my muscles were much less flexible from holding myself free of back and neck pain. My 50 year old self had found scaling the roof a breeze physically, but I did remember that it was a bit frightening especially the descent backwards and finding my footing onto the ladder. That was why I insisted on the big scaffold largely to break my fall in case I slipped backwards. I clipped on my harness and put the coil of rope on my shoulder, With real fear I went up the scaffolding and on to the roof one more time.

On a previous roof mission I'd had the foresight to put a very solid loop into the wall to thread a safety rope through, so I only had this one trip to do without the safety rope. I scrambled over the admittedly tiny rear section of roof and with great relief threaded the rope through the loop on the wall and attached my harness through knots in the rope with a carabiner. Frank passed me up a bucket, a brush and some gloves to clean out the channel but actually the channel wasn't too dirty. I cleaned it out anyway and set about trying to discover the cause of the leak. Was it a crack in the leading or a badly made side gutter? No. The answer turned out to be much more simple, and as far as the builders were concerned slightly stupid.

Unfortunately the connection between that channel and the tube into the downpipe was slightly raised meaning that in heavy rain there was always water in the gutter. In very heavy rain at the end of a dusty year that ridge could be augmented by dust and debris. This in itself wouldn't be too much of a problem but, it turned out, there wasn't a high enough layer of lead up the raised section of the light-well to stop a filtering of the water through the bricks and down into the house whenever the rain was very heavy. So, back over the ridge I went and gave Frank detailed instructions about where he would find the bitumen bands that we fortunately had leftover from trying to seal the connection between the glass roof and Pepa's wall. A job I left unfinished because I was way too afraid to lie full length on a glass roof 30 feet above the ground.

To this day that job still needs doing and it's definitely not one for either of us. Frank brought the bitumen bands and the scissors and a paintbrush and a small seam roller, all of which he surprisingly found from my instructions. I lowered the bucket on a rope for him to put them in so I could pull them back up. As the sun was going down I raced to get enough strip well enough sealed on to the joint and just as it got dark the job was complete. I was so proud of myself and also rather sad at being so positive that this was one of those never again moments in my life I made sure to take a photo of my own shadow against the roof to capture the moment.

The next heavy rains proved my hypothesis was correct and so far we haven't had to find someone to effect a more lasting repair.

Switzerland

A couple of years before, we had been asked by friends of the organiser of the previous trip, whether we would go to a fair they were organising. I said maybe we would, and left it at that.

The organisers approached me again at the Milan fair in 2015 and gave me the details of the fair. Of course I was coming … Wasn't I? No, actually I wasn't. I hadn't heard anything about it since. Hadn't planned to go and frankly couldn't afford it. The organiser's wife was in tears hearing this. She said she was sure I was coming, I'd said I was and she'd told everybody I would be, and unfortunately I softened. I really shouldn't have because the fair was a disaster for us. We really couldn't afford to and shouldn't have even considered taking such a risky step. Especially as the fair seemed to have been organised mainly as a competitive challenge to the other half of the Lausanne group and I still wasn't comfortable with that. I should have just said no. Frank warned me against my decision, but I said OK. And we went. Once again, as was becoming normal, with barely the cost of a couple of nights accommodation in our pockets and no safety net. In those days there was no credit card to save us if things went wrong. We were biting our finger-nails when we arrived in Lausanne for an overnight stay in the cheapest available hotel which cost around 100 euros a night in CHF which we called "chuffs". We'd had difficulty finding the hotel which was on a street behind the station. There didn't seem to be any access. Eventually we found out that there was a subway under the station which led up to a car park and then from the car park we could descend again to the low street behind. At The Hotel Alagare we were given our room key to the tightest room I have ever stayed in, where just passing the end of the bed meant risking knocking the TV off the wall. The toilet and shower could only be accessed by squeezing yourself down the edge of the toilet while you shut the door. As if to celebrate the smallness of the room it was wallpapered in deep red vinyl. Very cosy. We nipped straight back out to the little supermarket handily situated in the train station where you could buy a box of four eggs for the price of a dozen free range, gold plated eggs in Spain and that was going to be my most affordable option for supper and breakfast. We were shocked by the price of everything. I'd only seen more expensive fruit in Japan. I knew the fair organiser was an importer of fruit and vegetables from Spain. Now I knew why they were apparently so prosperous. The mark up was extraordinary. Frank settled on a packet of crisps and a bar of chocolate. In the morning we hopped on a train to the town nearest to where the fair was to be held. We were picked up by a friend of the organiser. After we'd set up our table we were taken to our guest house. Once again the cheapest in the area and out in the wilds of nowhere and, to be honest, a bit odd. Like a bed in an empty wood panelled conservatory. Really basic and a bit chilly, although the owner was friendly enough. We hoped she wouldn't be asking us to pay the whole weekend upfront as we simply didn't have the funds. We were also picked up the next morning which was good because I wouldn't like to imagine the cost of a taxi from Nowhereville to the tiny town where the fair was. The doors opened for the fair. A few flakes of snow blew in and little else. I was very uneasy and that feeling grew through the longest day of my miniature fair history. It had finally happened. The thing we feared most. We were stuck in a strange and expensive country and we weren't going to be able to pay our guest house bill and eat and get the train home. Something had to give. Fortunately my mini friend Sabine could see how distressed I was and when I explained the situation we were in she offered to take us home with her that night. Wow. What a relief. There then just remained the question of how to tell the guest house owner. It was simple really. We couldn't pay the three days so she was going to have to take the one night and put up with it. Actually she was really nice about it according to Frank who went to pick up our things. We didn't attend the Stallholders meal because Frank is Vegetarian, but neither could we afford to go out to eat, so we disappeared behind our stall. Actually for part of the time I disappeared to the ladies' loo to have a good cry.

I will draw a veil over the rest of the fair. The second day was slightly better in that we did have a couple of customers and a small trade order but it still ranks as the worst fair we have ever attended for visitor numbers, although since then there's been another Portugal fair which came close.

The greatest pleasure of the trip was getting to know Sabine and her husband Martino, and their home city of Bern which otherwise we would never have seen. Fortunately they had a second flat that we could stay in because they had a couple of big dogs who were very friendly but rather too interested in sniffing in inappropriate places. Inappropriate to us, obviously a source of wonder to them. The second flat appeared to be Martino's haven and it was really lovely because it was filled with his drawing boards and his illustrations and the bathroom was filled with paintbrushes in between the tooth brushes. Though way tidier than any space of mine, still I felt right at home. That evening Frank and I went out for a walk and we viewed Bern at night which was spectacular as it's divided by a deep ravine and was all twinkly in the dark. The day after the fair Sabine took us into Bern again for a look around, and we visited the bears which fascinated us. I've never been heavily into captive animals but the bears seemed happy in their pit and on their enclosed hillside. We were so happy to get home after that trip we forgot as much of it as we could. Except our vow to avoid fracturing miniaturist groups like the plague. Unfortunately it seems to happen way too often. What is it about human nature? Even miniaturists are susceptible to playing games of one-upmanship.

At Tune that year my offering for the three day class was going to be a hefty chunk, though not all, of a Miniature vegetable garden. As soon as it went up the class was sold out and Tove called me up to apologise that she'd oversold my class by two places. That was OK by me to be honest, and in the end two people couldn't come, so I was back down to my maximum. Obviously we were pretty much in need of the money and also Birthe and Tina offered an extension weekend at their place near Mariager on the other island. So this was going to be a good trip for us. The only unfortunate thing is that when my classes were popular James Carrington lost some of his potential students and when Jamie's were popular I lost some of mine. It was always swings and roundabouts. This was my swing year and it couldn't have come at a better time. Towards the end of the week a little of Jamie's good humour slipped, showing that he wasn't really quite as relaxed about it as he said he was. He needn't have worried though. The swing went his way the following year and his classes were first to sell out and mine were much smaller. That was always the problem of having two polymer clay artists in the one week. The same students would swing from the one to the other to pick up new skills.

October in Finland.

I was still feeling bruised from the Switzerland experience when we were asked if we would go to a Finnish fair. Suuri Snadi means something along the lines of "The Big Little". We were invited by Leea Lehelma and she'd made sure her invitation was one I couldn't refuse. I had told her that finances were tight and that we couldn't really afford just to pay out for airfares, so Leea did all the organisation, collected the fees for classes for me and sent me half in advance to buy our tickets. I was to give 4 classes over the whole weekend during the Big Little Show which comprised miniaturists, miniature railway modelling with a side order of war gaming figures. We were also offered a free stand which Frank was going to look after.

You would imagine that Finland in October would

be very cold and snow covered, but it wasn't. It was overcast but certainly not cold. Finland was another place I'd never been so I was nervous but excited. Leeah was a little bundle of Finnish energy. She picked us up at the airport and drove us to the exhibition hall where we met up with Suzanna who was going to let us stay in her house. The miniatures section of the show was quite small and, to be honest a little underwhelming. I think the hobby is quite new there and there are few really expert artists. Sadly one girl called Jana who went by the business name of Wooper, and who had become a seriously good ceramic maker had recently died of cancer. Her friends had made a beautiful pottery workshop in 12th scale in her memory using a lot of her work including some broken pieces. I was lucky enough to have the opportunity to buy some of her lovely fine slipware while I was in Finland and I hoped to do it justice by filling it with my own work. My classes were short but sweet and I met lots of miniaturists including a talented deaf girl who had her own interpreter. This was my first experience of tag teaching and I have to say I really enjoyed it.

We didn't really see much of Finland itself apart from the centre of Helsinki. We enjoyed trying the local berries and fungus, bought from a little market and taken back to Susanna's house to cook and I had some deep fried fish down at the harbour area. Helsinki was massively expensive. Everything cost an eye-watering amount of money and I suddenly was not surprised that people were so eager and happy to pay my fairly high fees and to buy my miniatures in large quantities. The expense came back to bite us though when we offered to take Susanna and her husband out for a meal to thank them for their hospitality. They also brought their daughter with them. I have no idea whether the restaurant they took us to really was one of the most expensive ones in the city. Probably not, but to us it certainly felt like it. It was a relief to get back to Spain where we could half tile a room for the cost of a Helsinki sandwich. And so we did. Just before Xmas I finished tiling the kitchen floor. I say finished, but part of me doubts it will be finished in my lifetime because I've had to leave a generous gap around all the edges for water pipes which we may never be able to afford.

.

16

One Off The Dreaded Six-O

I was just beginning to get comfortable in my older body but it really isn't easy for women. No, I know it should be, and we shouldn't bow to pressure blah blah blah.

I teach English to young kids. Very nice young kids who are quite socially aware and kind to and respectful of their elders. And I live in Spain where kids adore their grandparents, who adore them even more. Cambridge English Starters book however tells it the way it really is. There's an adjective exercise to identify opposites using tall and short, big and small, old and new, young and old (again) and beautiful and ugly. You're supposed to match the beautiful frog and an ugly frog but without exception the children choose the picture of the old lady as "ugly" instead of for the opposite of young. Sigh!

We started the year feeling positive and over the previous Xmas we'd laid down the floors for my teaching room over an electric underfloor system. Unfortunately the draw from that was way too great for our builders electricity and it overstressed our major fuse and that had to be replaced. The underfloor heating wasn't used again. It did however cause problems on the adhesion of some of the tiles.

In February we took our usual trip to Milan and we took a trip back via England as an excuse to see my new granddaughter again.

April 2016 I marked my last birthday in my 50s. Next

year would be the big six 'O'. Frank had not bought me a birthday present and I'm not one to say "oh never mind." It was now 10 years since our hoped-for completion date on the house. Back then I had been hoping for a big 50th birthday in my new house ... which was never going to happen. I put my foot down. I'd not had an 18th nor a 21st party nor anything since. No hen nights, no baby shower; nothing. I'd organised a couple of surprise parties for other people or surprises at parties, but nobody had ever done that for me and I knew if I didn't ask for it they never would. The last couple of missed birthday and Xmas presents from Frank were absolutely the icing on the cake ... or rather lack of. So I told Frank that next year I was having a surprise party so he'd damn well better get on and organise it!

I got a great birthday present from my daughter though. She sent me a 3d pen. Funnily enough I'd been trying to buy one the year before through Dominic but it had got a bit complicated trying to work out what I was getting for my money so we dropped the idea and forgot about it. I wasted no time having a play with it. The very first thing I made was a long pink adornment for my husband's head. "That'll teach you not to miss my birthday!" Ideas were flooding in and I was having a seriously creative spurt. I was in the middle of writing my gardens book and this pen had so many applications for building trees and plants, but first I had to have a go at making faux wrought ironwork. This was great fun if a little clumsy-looking. At a distance it looked great for iron gates and balconies though, so I quickly added the Sevillano patio to the list of gardens I wanted to make. Best of all it was quick and free flowing allowing me to have real fun playing again. I made several short Youtubes about my first experiences with the pen. I quickly realised that the branded pens wanted to sell consumables and didn't encourage the use of spools so, although I initially thought of working with one of those companies, it would hold me back eventually. I wasn't the sort who could pass work off as using a material that I wasn't using. I could have had a mountain of free stuff if I hadn't had principles though. Damn, those principles got me again!

Ooh you've lost weight!

I finally snapped and unfortunately I probably snapped within earshot and in the language of the person who least deserved my tirade. You see I'm overweight. Like a lot of my family, relatives I suspect, of the once 'fattest man in Britain'. There's no proof of it, but he was called Lambert, as was my overweight great granddad and my overweight grandma who died before I was born, My overweight mother and my sister and I. All of us more than a little bit 'cuddly'.

However, In spite of being fairly normally rather than abnormally large, almost every time I engage with a local they seem to feel the need to pass comment on my weight whenever they see me. Most of them mildly and, they think kindly, like to say "Ooh you've lost a little weight!" In Spanish of course "No" I say firmly, "I haven't". This used to be less firmly and with a lot more amusement. I'd laugh it off and say "que va" (not at all). More recently a little irritation has started to creep in. You see, if they were right, and from day to day, one or two of them might be, but if they were always right, the cumulative effect of all that weight loss would be devastating and dangerous. But they aren't right. Those who say it every time aren't right but are kindly. Those who are right on the day they say it, presumably have days when they think I've put it back on … which I probably have. And the thing is, one of my friends even sees fit to tell me those times when I've put it on. She used to give me dietary advice, between puffs of cigarette, often in my face. I did try telling her in the old days that if she cared to stop passing judgement on my weight I would stop myself giving her advice about her smoking. This seemed to work. Until she gave up smoking that is.

Yesterday, In front of a full bar she thought it appropriate, since she has now given up smoking, to resume her 'kindly' comments about my weight. "Ooh I can see you've put a little weight on!" she said. "really" she said "I can see it!". Yes she was right, but there was a clear intent in my voice when I said loudly and firmly, "how kind you are to point this out!" The assembled crowd laughed with me and I felt I'd made my point.

What did push me over the edge into a tirade about villagers and their narrow and cyclic conversations then? Well, it was the poor woman at the bar who, later that same day, (being back then on the generous side herself) very sweetly said "Ooh you've lost a little weight haven't you?"

Sold a lemon

When I was first planting trees in my garden back in the days after the demolition but before the house build, I decided to get an orange and a lemon tree. These trees were very slow to take hold because the soil in my garden was so shallow and so poor. Three years later we'd had plenty of strong smelling flowers every winter, but not one fruit. The orange tree was particularly sickly-looking so we rooted it out, threw it on the compost and then bought another orange tree to plant in a more fertile spot. The lemon tree was a bit further over and may have had a little more depth of soil; so we kept it to give it another year to prove itself.

I decided I wanted a citrus tree for my internal patio too. I loved the idea of having a tree inside my house and I was sure there was enough light. I thought since we'd already planted oranges and lemons outside I'd like to buy a lime tree for the internal patio (which we call the light well).

So off we went to the local 'agricultural supplies to the public' warehouse to ask about buying lime trees and were told that limes were the same as lemons … just younger. Well we were sure that wasn't true and so we opted to buy another orange tree for our courtyard instead. After all, I'd always fancied having my very own orangery. The tree in the courtyard grew quite quickly although its trunk always remained very spindly it had huge citrus-smelling leaves and when the orange flowers came out we were really excited. Maybe, just maybe we'd get fruit from this one. The next winter came and there were the flowers. We waited for the baby fruits to appear but then thought that since there were no bees to pollinate the tree, there wouldn't be any fruit. Suddenly, in spite of that I noticed a few very small green fruit forming. They were the wrong shape though. Instead of being oranges as we expected, they were very clearly lemon shaped. We thought maybe we'd made a mistake when we bought the tree. They were young but as they grew … well were they maybe what we'd asked for in the first place? Were they limes? One by one the fruit turned brown and dropped off and in the end we were left with just one small but swelling lime. We waited and waited and it grew and grew. I kept wanting to take it and test it but I'd read somewhere that the fruit would be ready the next Xmas. I could believe that, as that's when the village fruit trees put on their best display. Around October there was a sudden cold snap. A cold which crept its fingers deep into the light well of our house and clearly affected my citrus tree's little fruity brain (wherever that might be located). Slowly but surely our lime turned into a lemon; and delicious it was too the next time we got a winter cold and needed a honey and lemon. "OK" we said, "we were sold a lemon". Oh ha ha!

The next warm day that I ventured out into the garden I was surprised by the sight of some colour on my lemon tree. There, nestled between a bunch of sickly yellow leaves, was a tiny but perfectly formed (and, it turned out perfectly delicious) Clementine! Of course my 'song-Tourettes' forced me to sing "Oh my darling" to what until then had been our lemon tree! I should have taken a photograph of the fruit before picking it but it only crossed my mind later that it was quite amusing to have a second little fruit tree and that really I should have been singing the song about the nut tree which only produced one tiny fruit and not the one we expected.

That year as the flowers arrived in quantity on both my more mature trees and I told Frank I was going to "sex them up". I became quite adept with a soft paint brush making sure as many of the male flowers met as many of the female flowers as possible. With a great deal of success. The next and subsequent years we really got a pile of fruit on the indoor tree and for just one year a good crop of Clementines though that tree has regressed a bit since then.

We then decided that fruit was so rewarding to grow and that we could do with a little cover over our walkway, to keep out the prying eyes of the next door neighbour and to keep the sun off our offices in summer. We decided to buy two or three grape plants of different varieties and planted them down the dark side of our walkway hoping they would grow into the sun. We waited and we waited as we had done several times in the past, for various and expensive 'dead sticks' that we were assured were fruit bearing bushes and trees, but which resolutely refused to sprout. These too it seemed were going to defy us. Irritated I pulled them out of the ground. Well, to be honest, I pulled two of them out and left the third because even though it was a dead stick, it was a fat and healthy looking dead stick and I wasn't absolutely sure, but was that maybe a tiny red leaf sheath there on the side?

Within a month the dead stick came to life and spread up and up and up until it reached the roof of my neighbour's house. Pretty cool I thought. "Not cool" said the neighbour, worried that it might creep around her failing roof tiles. "Cut them off" she demanded. What I actually did was tie them over onto lengths of nylon and steel clothes wire zig-zagged across from her wall to our house. After all, that was my intention all along. It wasn't the grapes I expected to enjoy so much as the screening from the gaze of a bored and nosy neighbour who, more than anything else enjoyed telling me what I really should be doing instead of what I was doing. I don't think we got any grapes that year but the second year it produced several fat bunches of honey-sweet big red grapes. They were the most delicious grapes I had ever tasted so the next season we decided to try again with another plant and we did. This stick proved its worth about a month later than the red grape and so I realised I'd most probably thrown away two perfectly viable plants!

Scandinavia

We had been invited back to Finland. This time summer in Finland sounded like a very good idea. Our second trip was quite different in that this time we really got to appreciate the country without the pressure. We had extra time and we had the offer of staying in Leea's summer house. I think Finns seem fundamentally different and on the surface even more standoffish than Brits. I say "seem" because I don't think that's the full story. It was a real delight to get to know Leea better. She has a wonderful dry sense of humour and her summer house was full of all the "kooky" things her husband clearly wouldn't really appreciate in her house which was very minimalist Scandi in comparison. To be honest it's what some people would call 'clutter' but it was warm and friendly and cozy. What made Frank most happy though was the on-site sauna in Leea's garden. Every evening he lit the stove under the coals and twenty minutes later we stripped off and baked ourselves. It was heaven. Frank has always harboured a desire to have our own sauna. One day Frank … one day!

I wasn't on top form at all though. Something didn't feel right at all. I was feeling as if I'd aged ten years in the last year or so. It wasn't just because I was overweight. I was overtired to the point of exhaustion and I couldn't understand why. I usually had more energy than this! We went out for a walk the day before the fair and I was very breathless. I found it really difficult to climb the hills and it made me a bit panicky. I felt out of control and afraid. I actually ended up crying. This wasn't the first time I'd felt I might not be able to give my classes when everything relied on me being able to do so. The saunas did seem to help my asthma though and by the day of the fair and the main classes I managed to force myself to get going. I have to say I was happy when the day was over. It was a one day fair so the next day I gave a class to some of the stallholders who weren't able to come during the fair. I was certainly feeling a bit more human by then. Just before the class I saw a guy wild camping in the grounds of the school building and stopped to say hello. I told him I'd been reading some travelogues recently and so it was nice to meet someone who was actually living that life. He was called Rob and came from Canada. He told me he normally travelled (by bicycle) with his wife, but she was at home for this leg of the journey. I pointed him in the direction of the town and the lake where two days before we had enjoyed the best sandwiches and quiche I've ever tasted and wished him well with his travels. I have a little seed of a desire to travel like that and write about it. At my age and health I'd probably be happier in a mobile home though!

We had to go back via Madrid because there wasn't an affordable option to Seville. Even including the AVE (Alta Velocidad or Bullet train) back to Seville it was still cheaper to go that way. Plus the AVE is so comfortable. I needed to get home quickly this time because Paris SIMP fair was just days away. As was becoming fairly usual when I visited Paris I met up with my cousin Claire and we went up to Montmartre and Claire and I ate Moules Marinieres in a little shop facing the square where the street artists were working, or hassling passers-by to let them work. There was nothing special about that day's artistic offerings, though there was something a bit special about that hot, salty meal. I remember it was an old favourite of both of our fathers. The Scarr brothers, Geoff and Roland. Roland had married a French girl and so all my cousins were vrais Parisiennes.

We had just a few days of relative rest at home and then we flew back out to Denmark for one of the favourite trips of the year, if a bit full-on from a teaching point of view. We were going to the Tune Miniatures retreat of course. This year was a bit different. It was Tove's and her team's last year as organiser and I felt like Tune might never be quite the same again. We had a really lovely meal on the Thursday, which was usual of course, but this time there was an added extra event. A presentation from each and every student and teacher of one miniature flower each to Tove and Lisa until they both had a box full of flowers of all different kinds. I had made some greenery instead of a flower as I felt that's what they might be short of. I know the girls were moved and I can't think of a better way to thank them for all their efforts. For Tove nothing seemed too much trouble and though she seemed a very composed and elegant lady, Tove has a wicked sense of humour which often had us hooting with laughter at the end of the day. Fortunately although leaving her role as organiser Tove isn't going anywhere because she will be able to join the week as a relaxed student in future.

Even though there seemed to be quite a lot of interest in my offerings for classes in 2017, during the teacher's meeting at the end of the session for some reason I found myself offering to step down as a tutor the next year so that we didn't have too many tutors, as we'd recently got 2 new tutors. I felt there shouldn't be a greater ratio of students to teachers than 1:10. The organisers later accepted my offer. I was just a teeny bit miffed at how easily that offer was taken up! On the other hand my health wasn't looking good by this time; there were clear signs that something was not right and I did feel by that time it might just be a good thing that I wasn't going to be taking on too much the following year.

Campo life

That summer suddenly it seemed everyone in Campofrío was building. At least on our plaza they were.

Not building so much as re-roofing. I think May had been such a wet month, all the problems with the old roofs that were going to show, were showing. Just before we went away to Denmark the neighbours to the left of us started. Then after we got back we were immediately into fiesta and building and banging about. A week or so later another site started up just opposite us and our friend Mari-lou was also having her roof raised.

I was very pleased that we had the siesta. I needed it. My nights were broken by the fiesta the middle of the night I awoke regularly with a need to pee and other health worries. I'd found blood in my urine and initially thought it was from my uterus. By the time I got back from Denmark the blood was getting more and more noticeable every day. I'd already been to the doctor and was on the list for a small op to biopsy a polyp that they thought might be lurking in my womb. I had a feeling it was something more serious as I realised the blood was definitely from my bladder. I'd been to the emergency room one day. I'd decided deliberately to misunderstand the locum doctor, who maybe expected me to do just that. Apparently the protein in my urine was very much on the high side and I'd be quicker getting an appointment if I went in to the hospital myself. So I went to the emergency room instead and got my urine checked by a doctor who told me that they would send me to an urologist to see why I was having so many UTIs. I was hoping that now something would be done.

I was stressed. We were woken each morning at 7 by banging from the builders. Plus the highest temperatures that August were over 40. It was noisy, dirty and swelteringly hot. Somehow we managed to keep our cool I got up with the builders to air out the building before the sun came up to mop the floors and let the evaporation from the water remove the worst of the heat. We had the ceiling fan which Frank had fitted the year before and then re-fitted over my recently-fixed patchwork of plasterboard. When we tried it on fast though, its wobbling gave us the heebie-jeebies, so we hardly ever used it on more than number one setting.

We'd also moved one of the sofas downstairs into the training room while we laid the living room tiles in preparation for the guests we expected that summer. This turned out to be a very good idea and the extra sofa stayed there for summer cool-downs and later it became a favourite of the kids at English class. So we went off to Ikea to buy a couple of their bouncy little Poang chairs which made the balcony doors much more accessible. Looking around the house it was starting to look like we'd crossed the threshold into looking more and more like a "normal" house. We'd finally added a proper woodburning stove and tiled the wall behind it with some 'rusty' looking tiles which I really wanted. Although they were relatively expensive (compared with our minimalist white bathroom tiles) at over 10 euros a metre, they fitted just perfectly with the decor and somehow looked "in place", reminding me of colours in the Riotinto mines. This work all remained unfinished as my health concerns became more and more of an issue. One morning I woke too early as usual with bladder discomfort and I looked round the house and started to cry. What was upsetting me was the idea that if I died with all these jobs incomplete, I would forever be seen as a bodger rather than a successful housebuilder! As an idiot rather than an artist perhaps.

It was around that time I started to make myself a cocktail of foods I was recommended by a UTI infection group. I had been taking this home made medicine which consisted of raw olives, cayenne pepper and raw garlic for 2 weeks when one day I had the most awful pain trying to wee. The details of what happened next aren't something I want to share here. I went back to the hospital the next day and asked the status of my wait for an appointment. I was horrified to hear that I wasn't on any list! I explained that I'd been waiting since my emergency room visit and why wasn't I on a list? It turns out that the protocol here is to go through your GP but nobody had told me that. I had simply assumed from the Emergency doctor's words, that she would pass my name on to Urology. Fortunately I was lucky enough to bump into a hospital administrator who heard my story and saw a picture that I'd taken, and put me straight on the emergency list. Next would be a scan of my tummy. Just like you have in pregnancy. What really foxed me was my first Urologist's dire warning to me about my homemade medicinal cocktail. Olives, he said, were very fattening! I was not to worry about infection. He had another theory. I looked at the scans and I could definitely see a mass, and it looked quite knobbly. Was I going to turn out to have a rather unusual form of bladder stones called jackstones? I wondered. It did look a bit like it. That would be a better result than my worst fears. So I cheered up a bit and waited for my next appointment.

Visitors

We carried on building in spite of my health not being optimal and it was time to lay the living room floor. Frank offered to do the tile cutting which really helped since I was feeling like a very old lady and getting up and down from the floor seemed like a task of herculean proportions. Whenever we had visitors it did seem a very good excuse to get something else done before their arrival even though it was hotter than hell and I had to do a bit in the early morning and a bit more late at night.

That year Mus and Yellow, our Miniaturist and biker friends finally decided to visit us from Denmark. Just in time the temperature dropped to a median 32 degrees. Much more comfortable for us, but unfortunately hotter than hell for poor Yellow. At least we had the garden and the patio to minimise their stresses. And they loved the food. Unfortunately the heat was just way too much for Yellow and I know we won't have a visit in midsummer again!

We also welcomed our lovely granddaughter for her first visit to Spain. Dominic had been worried about Katy's health. She'd been a bit off and there was a whispered question hanging over whether there was a possible serious illness underlying a rash that she'd had. I could tell Dominic was seriously concerned and I was too. All of a sudden everyone around me either had cancer or was in fear of it. Mama had been diagnosed and was being treated for bowel cancer. Her friend the one of the lovely group I called "the golden girls" was worried that she might have the same diagnosis, and underlying all that was Dominic's worry about Katy's health. I certainly couldn't tell him about my own problems. I made a silent wish for Katy's diagnosis. How unfair it would be if Katy got a life-threatening illness too.

They had only a few days before they headed off for a free holiday in Singapore given to them by Dom's good friend (and best man) Rob, who had tickets he couldn't use. What a well-travelled young lady Ada was already, and she hadn't yet reached her first birthday. We had planned to meet them in Barcelona after the Miniatures fair, but I'd made a terrible mistake. We'd booked cheap AVE tickets to Barcelona. I'd booked them for the Thursday but when my appointment for my long awaited bladder scan finally arrived for Friday the 16th. I was confused and thought, maybe we could still make the train in the afternoon, forgetting the tickets were actually for the day before. When we got back after the scan we realised our mistake because there was a note from Booking.com asking us to confirm whether there was an error on our booking.

We were distraught when we realised what we'd done but made a snap decision to buy a new set of full price tickets with our recently arrived credit card (our first in 6 years) and send off a message to Booking.com explaining our error but saying we'd be at the hotel later.

Barcelona was to slap us twice more. When we arrived at the hotel MybedBCN we were told that as we were a 'no-show' the night before, our rooms had been re-sold for that night and that it was hotel policy not to give any refunds. Not even on the re-sold nights! I was tired and distraught and refused to leave the place until they organised us somewhere else. I was threatened with the Guardia and I dug my heels in and told the receptionist to bring them. Eventually the woman on reception booked us a place at a hiker's hostel for 2 nights for 80 Euros which we had to pay. This took us right up to our new credit card limit.

But Barcelona had yet one more nasty trick to play on us that year. For us the fair was a complete flop. Even at the original cost we wouldn't have made our money back. Our only gain from the whole trip was the pleasure of the smile Ada gave us when we first met up with the family in a plaza in Barcelona. Although we hadn't seen her since she was a tiny baby the voice must have been familiar from the phone because she took to me completely and immediately. She also made a kissing noise after I blew her a kiss, which her dad insisted was just a noise and not a kiss, but I did manage to get her to do it on demand for ever after! I reckon her other Grandma Janet had taught her it. When we all got back to Campofrío after an AVE train ride together Dominic and Katy kept saying she was grumpier than normal. But I didn't see her as a grumpy baby at all! But then I did get to appreciate my first taste of the granny privilege of handing her back whenever she did become a bit grizzly. Then I heard the fantastic news that Katy wasn't sick at all. She was pregnant again!

Katy's favourite part of our house is the garden. She's always especially loved being able to just pick edible things from the ground and the fruit bushes. This year the cherry, the almond and the outdoor clementine all suffered badly from the very heavy April rains which stopped the insect activity for a whole month and knocked the flowers and any embryonic fruits off to boot. So there was only a handful of cherries and no almonds at all. Not a big problem as we still had a basket full from the year before, an attempt to get a redcurrant growing resulted in one single, shiny, jewel-like red fruit, which I thought I might photograph for Facebook. I'm not sure if I ever took that photograph and if I did I've no idea where it is now. It was getting to be a bit of a joke; this single fruit thing.

This year however the produce on the red grape vine weighed several kilos and kept us in lovely juicy grapes for a couple of months. And some for 'Mama' too. Whole grapes pips and all were on the recommended foods list for her. Mama was a real rock for me she took her diagnosis and treatment with real cheerfulness and hope. I was also half expecting a cancer diagnosis so grapes and a side order of cheerfulness were on my list too.

Not only the grapes and the indoor lemon did really well in the fruit department this year. The rapidly-spreading fig tree also produced a mountain of fruit although the figs mainly fell before we could harvest them and they had a lot of bugs. We decided that the following year it would either come down or be very heavily cut back.

The raspberry canes also took to producing very well and twice a year! The blackberries (just once a year) were large and delicious although we were away for the major part of the cropping time. This meant a happy family of very large and well fed rats moved into the garden and they were almost totally unafraid of us humans, just scuttling across the back wall whenever we got too close to their fruit-munching. They weren't afraid of the cats either which did eventually prove their undoing and one morning we woke to the fresh entrails of what had obviously been a very large rat plastered across the training room floor. This was only the first and obviously the daddy of a family of much smaller rats. They were still rats and I didn't want them in my house dead or alive! Fortunately either the family was wiped out in a furry tooth and claw feeding frenzy or they wisely decided to move house to avoid the very cute but exceedingly carnivorous Squirrel and Smudge. I think the fact that we left them so often on basic rations from the dispenser without any treats honed their skills.

Also this year I finally got one fruit on my orange tree, having moved it yet again! I knew by now that one fruit this year meant more fruits next year if the weather was good. I watched the orange grow and start to change colour. It looked like we were going to get one juicy fat orange and this time I was definitely going to photograph it! One day Frank came in and said "you've got an orange from that orange tree!". "I know" I said "fantastic isn't it?". "Yeah" he said … "I kept it for you"

There on the bench looking just like any old

supermarket orange was my trophy. Once again un-photographed!

Life goes on

When I first accepted the idea of teaching English, I wasn't sure I was going to get on well with it. I didn't like children. I was sure I didn't. I wouldn't have the patience. I was sure I wouldn't … and yet. I did need the money. At the time I remembered I had actually had patience with children in my time as a playscheme organiser and as an unqualified social work assistant at the Family centre where I worked for nearly a year. I had no trouble with my own kids and the kids of friends. I loved answering intelligent questions and I loved creating the right ambience for kids to have fun and learn at the same time. So, once I had decided to accept the challenge for the good of my wallet I decided to do the very best I could. After all I've always been principled enough to want to give good value for money.

The first year was a learning curve. The kids were bright but noisy and prone to scrapping whenever my back was turned. I soon found that you have to divide an hour into three twenty minute sections in order to keep the kids from having even a moment to start 'playing up'. I never liked the way kids were taught at school and always strived to adapt my teaching to the needs of individual kids while working as a team whenever possible. This was difficult at first and I didn't always get it right but after losing a couple of children whose hearts weren't really in it eventually I got down to a group of 5 really motivated kids plus another group of younger kids who I was still working on.

After about a year when my first group all came back I had the sudden realisation that I was actually enjoying it and that I cared about how much the kids were learning and, more importantly, that they were enjoying it! I even had a couple of kids who professed to hate school but to love English class. I realised that in some small way I was having an effect on these kids' future. That was ego boosting and humbling at the same time. At that point I realised that, whether I liked it or not I was an English teacher! Especially as I was starting to get a reputation in the village and the local teachers were starting to suggest to the parents that the kids who were coming to my classes were also more responsive and successful in school. I wasn't sure how much of that was down to me and how much was down to the fact that the sort of parents who were likely to encourage their kids to do my classes were also the ones who were more likely to give more parental support to their kids.

I soon realised that one class a week was not nearly as good as two since my "top" class, who came twice, were learning at more than twice the pace. The most important hump I learned to get over was the one dealing with responsiveness from the kids. So I learned that teaching them the two phrases "How do you say … in English" and "What does … mean?" Learning this even by rote meant that even the least able were able to say something even if it was often just repeating "How do you say" … (followed by a string of Spanish gibberish).

I also learned to have little back up games for times when the main work of the class was completed early, or when I'd given up on a theme that just wasn't working. The absolute favourite of these among the youngest students was a shoebox, with hand holes in both ends, full of pictures with vocabulary and containing a few pieces of paper which simply said "Bang". The goal was to collect and repeat as much vocabulary as possible without getting a "bang" paper which meant you lost your collection. The kids regularly asked to finish on this game and I often found variations on the theme and sometimes liked to make the kids squeal by putting my own hand in the other side of the box and pretending to grab theirs. Or simply banging the box on the top or bottom during their choice.

There was another "Bang" game for the older and more competent students which we called "Bang Bang. You're Dead", an idea I got from the internet where the group divided into two teams and the kids asked each other "How do you say … in English" If the member of the other team responded incorrectly they were "shot down" with cries of "bang bang, you're dead"; but if they got it correct they could shoot the asker. Tactically this resulted in the weaker members of the team being asked questions more often by the strongest student in the opposing team which was very helpful in sharing vocabulary learned. With teams of only three members no-one was left out for long. If I had to step in I was asked to translate phrases into Spanish which I didn't always find easy! In the end I had 4 separate classes. One class of older kids who were starting on their journey towards B1 level. One class of intermediate which was my original class with the top student having gone into the top class and replaced by two students who were top of a younger age group. So then I had 2 beginner level classes the second of which were a bit more advanced having been with me since the age of six, and one which had the younger ones and any newbies.

I had to start turning students away because there just wasn't enough room for them. I also started to get a really good stream of adult learners including the local primary school English teacher whose vocabulary and grammar was excellent but who needed a bit of polish on her pronunciation and on some regular errors she was stuck with. She brought several other students from her friends and family making up an adult class of four but I also had quite a few lone adult students.

These classes kept our heads above water and food on our table for many months while Franks business was only just keeping itself going with precious little actual "income", just really enough to pay the Autonomo and the phone bill and we really missed the income from the classes in the summer period and at Xmas where holidays in Spain are very extended.

It was very difficult for me managing so many hours teaching at the same time as trying to keep the stocks of miniatures up and write books and make videos as well as getting housebuilding jobs completed whenever there was enough income. At least we weren't slipping backwards any more. Not that there was a further backwards to slip! Two years running I even managed to teach at a local Academia de Ingles but there were a couple of problems with that. One was that I needed to take time off too often for trips to miniatures fairs. Plus there was a little undermining of my position from the other teacher there. I don't know if he felt threatened by me (he shouldn't have) but he kept telling the boss I wasn't teaching quite in the way he would have and that I continually used Spanish in the classes. This was only partly true but it was enough to cause a bit of friction so when I started to realise my health was failing I decided not to ask for any more classes at the Academy. Well, I did try at first to get my boss to agree to shared classes so that there wasn't a problem but he thought it was unworkable and that was that. I missed working for Danny who I had a bit of a soft spot for and who also got along well with Frank when he visited to bring my wages. At least I didn't have to worry about time off for appointments.

It's so easy to make romanticised comparisons

between the places we lived in the past and where we live now. Usually in the one direction. Where we live now is better. Incomparably so, in almost every way. Teaching my 'swap' student, that is to say the student with whom I swap English classes for help with the housework, I find other people have other dreams which have an equally strong pull. She wants to live somewhere cold and wet. I have a few ideas for her! I taught her the English saying "The grass is always greener".

Whenever we discuss our difficulties, both financial and health problems, with members of the family they always suggest that the answer might be to return to England. Of course this would never be an answer. Although big and reasonably comfortable for us, our unfinished house is totally unsaleable. Any money it did bring wouldn't cover our debts and England wouldn't help us make a living. Quite apart from that, our life in spite of all the difficulties is charmed here. We have almost everything we ever wanted. Except money.

We live in a wonderful community of happy and welcoming people, in beautiful countryside in a sunny country. We have a home and a garden and most of all we have each other and an appreciation of everything that we do have. Of course we also have arguments, usually over our different attitudes to work/life balance but even so, each of us suspects that the other may have a point! Added to that, once you get into the health system it compares very favourably with the NHS. From my experience it has a few lessons worth learning by the Brits!

My bladder cancer was finally diagnosed in mid October and on December 2nd I had my first tumour removal. Frank was with me during the operation on the day but had to dash off the next morning to Madrid for a Feria de Belenismo (Nativity scene fair) with only 50

Euros in his pocket, for the fair we'd absolutely promised to go to. Fortunately my son Alan and his girlfriend Lucy stepped in and arrived a little later on the same day that Frank left and stayed until a few hours before he came back after the weekend.

I'd already been told that this type of cancer was always malignant, so I wasn't much surprised when it was the day for my results, just a few days before Xmas. As I sat down the urologist simply shook his head and said "Jhelen Jhelen Ija". - Helen Helen, Hija ('Daughter." - A Spanish term of endearment).

"Not good then" I said. "No … not good" was the not-unexpected reply.

Epilogue

I had a serious renaissance after my cancer. A complete overhaul of the very foundations of my being. It started small just with me allowing people to look after me, because I didn't have any option at the time. I had time to ponder, to think, to rebuild myself in a different image.

To start off with I needed to give myself time. Not to ask so much of myself; not to be so down on my efforts when they fell short of perfect. Money was an incredibly difficult issue. It became emotionally draining especially as I had to cope with the discomfort of asking for even more help than we'd already received over the years. Being grilled about what Frank was doing to get us out of the mess and reminded (as if I needed reminding) that our mess was nothing new, and that it had gone on for years. Right by my side is where Frank was. Running the business with very little stock and teaching my English classes since there were no sickness benefits and no other source of income. Most of all he was looking after me, running me to chemo sessions, sitting with me for hours, bringing me sick buckets and making sure I drank enough.

But I was also stronger in many ways. I was certainly feistier. I didn't for a moment think "why me?" I thought "why not me?" Given how I'd treated myself in the couple of preceding years. It made sense. I knew I'd been physically and mentally at rock bottom and the cancer was the result.

This was my second life though, and however long or short it was going to be I was going to make the most of it. Not everybody gets a chance like this one. So when I had a bit of a downer after one of my knock backs I decided not to allow my mind to go round in circles any more. I decided I needed a bit of therapy. The help I got was really minimal but it was a turnaround for me. I had given myself permission to really look after me for the first time in my life The actual therapy appointment was largely symbolic.

After chatting it out and blubbering a bit ... well quite a lot. I went back to self therapy and told myself Its all OK I can handle that other people don't see things the same way as I do, and that they have every right to make their decisions in life even if they don't go the way I want. I returned to my old anti-anxiety mantra "Healthy Happy Loving and Kind" and I re-learned letting go of negative thoughts. I added "Smart Creative and Successful" well why not?

At one point on this journey my new strength rubbed someone up the wrong way and I received a telling off for being wrong and out of touch and 'entitled'. I was told this was something that wasn't expected from me because I'd never been like that before. And that, at least, was true.

After several days of trying to digest this and not feeling the need to go back to my old apologetic self a light suddenly dawned. I understand that this is fairly common when people change their victim behaviour. I'd had such an enormous chip on my shoulder and had been undervaluing myself for so long I'd left people in no doubt at all of my low value! This of course wasn't going to change as quickly for them as it was for me. After all I was really valuing my own life for the first time.

So after reading some really interesting posts and contributing to them too, on forums about successfully marketing yourself as an artist. I started to write down my thoughts on subjects like the impostor syndrome. About how artists always undervalue ourselves and let others do it too. How in my work life I'd invented as many tools, diagnosed as many problems and found as many solutions as an engineer, given as much therapy as a therapist, and created a damn site more human wealth than a wealth creator. The only difference is I didn't get a monthly pay check or a pension scheme.

Then, just at the right time in these musings someone shared with me Amanda Palmer's Ted talk "The art of asking". This fitted so well with my re-evaluation of myself that it made me make a somewhat pivotal decision. That I was the person responsible for telling people that my life had been of low value and that I was now responsible for telling them that it was more valuable than I'd given them to think before. I had been an artist all my life because I was good at it. But far from being 'entitled' I'd shrugged off all entitlement and I needed to get it back.

Then I looked at Patreon which is a young platform developed by creators as a way to value your work and get paid for it especially if your work was of the more nebulous sort such as music, art or indeed art teaching. This is now a bit of a crusade for me. Not just for myself but for other creators like myself who constantly suffer from self doubt. Young people are leading the way in revaluing creative endeavour and this old lady is getting on board.

Creating the page itself has been both a difficult transition and a joyous self affirmation, an exercise in the self-promotion that I couldn't do when I was a musician. I had always asked too little for my work and given everything away in terms of teaching and supporting. It's not that I think free sharing is a bad idea. I still want to share as much as I ever did. Only now I want to ask the living wage that all working artists and teachers need and deserve for the effort they put in. A little late, but the subscription economy seems to answer the what am I worth question, and that need.

It's been somewhat unusual and very much a learning curve but I've never been one who believes you can be too old to learn. I still find myself apologising for the quality of my old music, my writings and my miniatures, then I have to stop myself or someone else has to stop me. And it isn't always the people that you imagine. One of my patrons and I have had a somewhat prickly relationship, because we have quite a few differences of opinion, but because of that I know she's not soft soaping me when she tells me something is good. And so she has helped me even more than a closer friend might. So thanks for that Netta! I'm going to follow her advice and put out some of my old musical work as a sort of retrospective, along with this book.

The thing is, I don't have to care whether anyone else values my life's work as long as I value it myself.

As a teaching miniaturist my mantra is I've made all the mistakes so you don't have to". And my biggest mistake ever was having the impostor syndrome and undervaluing myself. You don't have to make that, or any of my other mistakes.

If you've read this far and enjoyed my story, please consider becoming one of my Patreon Patrons I'll see you there with more of my "daft ideas daily" whether they're miniature tutorials, tall stories and short musings or just one to one support for your own creative journey.

Also please leave an Amazon review. This will really help others to see the book and give a real boost to self publishing and to me!

Thanks and Acknowledgements

There are no words adequate to thank the work of the Urology and Oncology departments of Riotinto Hospital, including the two Doctor Manuels, Maria de la Paz and Doctora Dominguez, Oncologists Fatima and Marta and their lovely assistants, all the staff on the intensive care and urology wards and in the day hospital. They helped brighten my darkest days and gave me my second life.

Thanks to my family, and Frank's mum, my friends Rosie and Rachel and the community of Campofrío including Angeles and Montse for your care love and many sacrifices. And of course to Frank. For doing all the stuff mentioned in the epilogue.

And thanks to my new Patreon supporters who helped make it possible to finish and get this book out, you helped not only financially, but you also gave me courage:

Allan, Marshall and Jeannette Murphy who also helped me with some much needed corrections and editing respectively.

Allen &,Lyla Phillips, Anita Patterson, Barbara Taylor-Harris, Louise Win, Denise Osborne, Dominique Ceuppers, Dorte Hedegaard Pedersen, Essie Kenneway, Frank Fisher, Gillian Heckford, Gillian Thompson, Grethe Holme Jantzen, Helen Cruickshank, Hellie Durans, Jeannette Fishwick, Jessica Deacon, Karin Sørensen, Kasia Win, Kira Swales Lesley Symons, Loredana Tonetti, Lucy Rider, Macie-Kaye Hamblin, Michaela Stange, Natalie Martin-Burrows, Nicola Croad, Rachel Taylor, Roberta

Solari, Robyn Donald, Rosemary Mulley, Roslyn Hill, Sandi Smith, Sean Sullivan, Stephanie Ryan, Sue Heaser, Tara Jane Susie Langworthy, TeeBylo, Tina Knuth, Kathy Buchannan and Susan Deans. You are all now 'patrons' of these small arts, and moreover, much appreciated and loved friends.

Hugs X

Links

The link to my Patreon page
www.patreon.com/angie_scarr

and to my website with easy access to everything else
www.angiescarr.co.uk

36609076R10195

Printed in Great Britain
by Amazon